How to
Change a Rotten Attitude

*A Manual for Building
Virtue and Character
in Middle and
High School Students*

Michael C. Loehrer

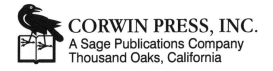

CORWIN PRESS, INC.
A Sage Publications Company
Thousand Oaks, California

For information:

 Corwin Press, Inc.
A Sage Publications Company
2455 Teller Road
Thousand Oaks, California 91320
E-mail: order@corwin.sagepub.com

SAGE Publications Ltd.
6 Bonhill Street
London EC2A 4PU
United Kingdom

SAGE Publications India Pvt. Ltd.
M-32 Market
Greater Kailash I
New Delhi 110 048 India

Printed in the United States of America

Library of Congress Cataloging-in-Publication Data

Loehrer, Michael C., 1952-
    How to change a rotten attitude: A manual for building virtue
        and character in middle and high school students / by
    Michael C. Loehrer
        p.   cm.
    Includes bibliographical references.
    ISBN 0-8039-6649-0 (cloth: acid-free paper). —
    ISBN 0-8039-6650-4 (pbk.: acid-free paper)
    1. Moral education (Middle school)—United States—Handbooks,
manuals, etc.   2. Moral education (Secondary)—United States—
Handbooks, manuals, etc.   3. Virtue—Study and teaching
(Elementary)—United States—Handbooks, manuals, etc.   4. Virtue—
Study and teaching (Secondary)—United States—Handbooks, manuals
etc.   I. Title.
LC311.L58   1997
    370.11'4—dc21   97-21059

This book is printed on acid-free paper.

98 99 00 01 02 10 9 8 7 6 5 4 3 2 1

Production Editor: Sanford Robinson
Production Assistant: Karen Wiley
Editorial Assistant: Kristen L. Gibson
Typesetter: Janelle LeMaster
Cover Designer: Marcia M. Rosenburg

Contents

Part I: Measuring Virtue

Part II: Dealing With the Data

Part III: Restoring Broken Lives

Tables and Figures

Preface

In this preface, I have asked two people whom I deeply admire to offer their comments. Why two? Well, because both have meant so much to my personal development and the existence of this manual; one at the beginning of my educational career, the other at the end.

The first, Frank N. Priester, was the vice principal of the high school from which I was graduated and who first taught me virtue. Quite truthfully, I would never have graduated were it not for him, and my life would have taken a very different turn than it has. He lived what he asked of me. I knew it, and most every other student did too.

The second, Reuben H. Brooks, served on my doctoral committee and guided the early development of this book. But more important, he continues to inspire me toward virtue in my professional career with a wonderfully winsome lifestyle. I have been fortunate to have had two such mentors, and I want you to hear from them both. After that, I'll tell you how to take this book by the horns.

What follows in this manual is commonly is called "down-to-earth" practices and procedures. Dr. Loehrer has presented a guide extremely useful for all educators functioning at the secondary level. His LVAQ (Loehrer Virtue Assessment Questionnaire) is easily read by the teenage audience it is designed for and a most reasonable instrument for staff usage (acquisition, scoring, and follow up).

By reading this manual, you will obtain some of the vital and valuable components of instilling virtue in young people. Look at the first half of page 154 in Chapter 10 for the real "nugget" of his work. It was a surprise and genuine pleasure to find myself as an inspiration to the author who has himself proven virtue can be learned and accomplished. "Virtue is its own reward."

It is not often these days that educators experience a positive closure to their professional careers. The unusual developments of Dr. Loehrer's life have brought a fine closure to mine. All during my 38 years in education, I only rarely questioned, "Was this the right career for me?" Now I know it was.

FRANK N. PRIESTER
Santa Barbara, California

Ten years ago, a new graduate student came into a doctoral course I was teaching. He was one of almost 20 students in a course that examined the integration of moral education with the cultural and scientific world. There I met Michael Loehrer for the first time. Striking in size, nice looking, and neat to a fault, this personable, gentle man with a Texas accent made a strong impression on me. As time has shown, the chemistry has been mutually rewarding.

I recall telling the class that very first evening, in essence, "Take a good look at yourself, a snapshot of your own person, because when this semester is over, you will never be the same again. You will have changed, stretched into more tolerance, openness to other options." Michael took these words to heart. Thus, I saw this bright and gifted doctoral student unfold his wings only to soar far into the rarefied air of honest intellectual rigor, to study tough questions, and enter new arenas. Dr. Loehrer probes questions most others have never cared to try. The present volume is a fine indication of his creative response to the challenge of changing the moral climate of our schools and through them, society.

Dr. Loehrer's research, including this present volume, reveals insight into the rare ability of this man, his craftsmanship, his skills of writing, and his social science research. What you will read is the product of true scholarship hitched to the plow of the human heart. You will become a better person and a much wiser teacher for taking the effort to study the entire volume and to employ it in your school setting. Even college professors can profit from this one. I know!

REUBEN H. BROOKS, Ph.D.
Tennessee State University
Nashville, Tennessee

Ways to Use This Book

There are all different kinds of people. Everyone has a different perspective on life, and everyone will probably take a different approach in using this book. Though I can't address them all, I offer the following to assist you in making the best possible use of this material.

If You Need a Quick Overview

Some people find it helpful to get an overview at the start so they can understand better while they read. To give you a better sense of direction, begin by scanning "Things to Review and Remember" at the end of each chapter. These short summaries contain information that will stimulate your mind while reading. If you wish, you can quickly review the entire book this way.

If You Are Very Busy

If you don't have a lot of time to give but you want to begin using the Manual right away, there're really only three steps necessary to get started:

1. Understand the problem.
2. Measure it and make sense of what you measured.
3. Begin living out a solution.

First, to understand the problem, work through Chapters 1 and 2; it will take about an hour. These chapters lay a conceptual foundation for the rest of the book.

Second, give the questionnaire to your students (15 minutes), and score their responses (10 minutes each). The questionnaire, scoring form, and guidelines are in the Resources section. Then learn how to make sense of the scores by reading over Chapters 3 and 4. It will take 2 hours at the most. After that, simply build a mental picture of the information your students provide. You can do this over a weekend.

Third, and this is the most difficult, begin living out the solution. The key to this is found in the Self Cycles of Chapter 8, which takes a half hour to read but a lifetime to practice. To help you get started, why not ask some of your colleagues to discuss these things with you? It will make it a lot easier and a lot more enjoyable.

If You Need Close Guidance

If you want to be systematic and get the most from this manual, closely follow these procedures:

1. Take the test yourself (takes 10 minutes).
2. Read Chapters 1 through 3 (2 hours).
3. Score your test (20 minutes).
4. Read Chapters 4 and 5 (2 hours).
5. Administer the test to your students (15 minutes).
6. Read Chapter 6 (1-2 hours).
7. Score your students (10 minutes each; with our scoring program you can do 20 students an hour with no grief).
8. Interpret their scores (time depends on your perception).
9. Read Chapters 7 through 10 (2 hours).
10. Develop an approach (takes a lifetime).

If you are concerned about following through with all of this, ask some colleagues to join you and hold each other accountable. There is a Group Discussion Guide available to assist you; you can contact me for a copy (see Resource G).

Acknowledgments

The beauty of a newborn baby is not shared equally by all who behold it. Certainly, the mother marvels and the father beams, but innocent bystanders frequently find it difficult to share their enthusiasm. This manual is my baby, but her attire has changed considerably since she was delivered, largely because others initially saw her for what she was; a rather unattractive thing. And they cared enough to help clean her and clothe her, rather fashionably, I think. For that I am grateful. Deep respect and appreciation go to Dr. Reuben Brooks, Dr. Don Brown, Dr. Fred Wilson, Dr. Boyd Luter, Dr. Kris Moore, and Barbara Johnston, MSW, for their technical assistance. Oftentimes, ideas never become reality for lack of opportunity. I would like to publicly thank those who gave me a chance when others would not: Janette Rothe, George Dupree, Jim Revill, Gordon Lockett, Charles Griste, Jack Wilson, and Earnest Pack. For keeping my feet planted firmly on the ground while my head was in the clouds, my heartfelt gratitude goes to Matt Stroder, Tim and Donna Rodgers, and my son John, the journalism major. Special thanks belong to my parents. Though I did not know it at the time, my father's sense of justice and my mother's heart of mercy somehow together molded in me a love for virtue. Furthermore, I must pay tribute to my brother Bill, my greatest supporter, without whom this work would have been impossible. Last, I owe a deep debt of gratitude to my wife Paula, who steadfastly endured it all.

MICHAEL C. LOEHRER
Frost, Texas

About the Author

Michael C. Loehrer has a bachelor's degree in history from California State University, Fresno. He has done postgraduate work in advanced statistical analysis and theory of measurement at the University of Southern California. He also has earned a doctorate in education, specializing in educational research and moral education, from Biola University. Presently, he is director of Educational Diagnostics, a group providing teacher training, student testing, and diagnostic consulting for educators facing students with attitude problems.

Virtue

Is

Wanting to Do

What You Have to Do,

Good Character

Producing

Good Conduct!

1

Restoring Virtue to Education

Thirty years ago, I was about to be expelled from school for fighting. It was the latest in a long string of offenses. The school counselor considered me incorrigible. Teachers and administrators were worn out. Even my friend, Mr. Priester, the vice principal, could not prevent my expulsion. The only question left: Would it be permanent? Most wanted me gone for good.

Mr. Priester asked if I even wanted to graduate from high school. If I did not, there was no keeping me. If I did, I would have to stop my foolishness, come to school early, stay late for the next year and a half to make up classes I had failed, and even attend summer school. If I really wanted to do it, Mr. Priester promised to do everything he could to make it happen. I was expelled for a week to consider the options. If I decided I would not change, if I was unwilling to do the work, I was finished. It was a turning point in my life. I changed. I worked hard. I graduated. Then, I graduated four more times until I had received (irony of ironies) a doctorate in education.

How on earth can teachers reach those with attitude problems?

What made the difference? Virtue! Not mine, Mr. Priester's. More about the kind of thing Frank Priester did later, but in essence, he gave me a transfusion of virtue. I caught a glimpse that I will never forget of noble character producing good conduct when I felt broken and defeated. He showed kindness to me when there was nothing in it for him. But that's only half of the reason I'm writing. The other half is guilt. I feel guilty. That's not reason enough to secure your interest, I realize, but it's reason enough for me to write. I feel guilty because I ruined a good many teachers—intentionally.

High school days were the worst days of my life, and I've had some bad ones. Nightmares from being molested marked my early years. The influence of alcohol in the home left me feeling insecure and inadequate throughout adolescence. I survived brutal war experiences during the Siege of Khe Sanh. My best friend, who was there with me, did not. I watched helplessly as two of my children died from an incurable genetic disease; Billy died 2 weeks before his first birthday; Jeremy, 2 weeks after his first birthday. I've experienced the heartache of my wife leaving me during her midlife crisis. We are restored, but I know the pain of separation, firsthand. I have known what it is like to be without work and for a short time, destitute. I'm not saying this to complain, I just want you to realize that when I say my high school days were the worst days of my life, I know what it's like to have a bad day.

After reading this, a retired teacher told me, "Nothing could be worse than losing your children." In a sense, she was right, because of the indescribable, unrelenting anguish of loss. Nevertheless, though continually consumed with grief, I never despaired of life. In high school, I did. I can still remember calmly discussing with my mother the deep and continuous desire to die—not to take my life, just to die—an unshakable discouragement and dejection. Sure, I had fleeting moments of exhilaration, but they only made the difficult times seem deeper by contrast and longer in duration.

I felt insecure, inadequate, ashamed of my appearance, utterly unacceptable to others. I was growing so fast, I was constantly tired and hungry. I gorged junk food until I couldn't sit still, then crashed and slept, wherever I was, for as long as I could. I was extremely sensitive to criticism and rejection and intensely attuned to innuendoes, nuances, and allusions about myself. I was living (?) under an incredible load of increasing expectations. My family expected me to do this. My friends expected me to do that. My teachers piled on the work. My friends wanted to play. I had to have money to do things and be cool, so I worked a little in the evenings. I slept in class and fought sleep at night. No one was really happy with me or anything I did, least of all myself. Feelings of guilt grew, for reasons unknown to me, until I wanted to scream.

Yet as hard as it was for me, it was as least as bad for my teachers. They dreaded having me in their classes. Like difficult students you face today, I made a mockery of my teachers. I was impossible to control. I dominated the classroom. I tormented my teachers until they wanted to scream. What's more, I enjoyed doing it. I had absolutely no desire to learn. That was 30 years ago, and today, I feel bad about it. So I'm writing to make restitution to them. Oddly enough, I'm fulfilling the age-old axiom that "Those who can, will; those who can't, teach; and those who can't teach, teach teachers to teach."

It's so hard for teachers to teach these days. You know how to teach. You love to teach. You have good plans and programs, and you have fantastic facilities. But a good number of your students not only do not want to learn, they hate your classroom, they hate your subject matter, and sometimes, they even hate you. They have what the old-timers called *an attitude*. How on earth can teachers reach those with attitude problems? Such students are often so sharp. They have so much potential. They hold such promise, but they are destroying your classroom. What's worse, they are destroying their own lives and taking others along with them.

What a sad day for U.S. educators! I grieve for those who teach in the public schools of America today. I feel bad because I did what I could to ruin the order of the classroom and undermine the authority of my teachers. I made many a teacher miserable. I thwarted many a lesson plan. I led other students to do foolish and destructive things. For that reason, my heart aches for you, and for years, I have longed to play some role in reversing the damage I did.

This manual is for middle school and high school teachers. It's for use in your classrooms. It's for your students, and most of all, it's for those awful attitude problems and the chance to produce noble character in them. You face incredible pressures today, and you need all the help you can get. You have to face the exacting expectations of administrators. You have to face angry parents, who don't understand you and don't appreciate what you are trying to do. You even find your country ridiculing your profession and the attempts you make to restore credibility to it. And you are tempted to think there is nothing you can really do to change all this.

Sometimes you question if it's worth it, if it wouldn't be better to try your hand at something else. Intuitively, you know that's not a good thing to do. You've given your life to teaching. You don't want to throw it all away. Not just yet, anyway. Maybe next year, but not just yet. Besides, your students need you, more now than ever. I realize it's not very exciting to consider bringing one more thing into an already crowded schedule. It's not comfortable to rearrange your classroom routine. Yes, it will mean extra effort. It's always harder to break new ground than to rework a plowed field. No, I can't make any promises, because the outcome is contingent on what you do with what I give you. However, this little manual might just breathe new life into your classroom.

The Problem You Face

Effective teachers live for the teachable moment; when students are interested, asking questions, actually thinking, dialoguing, acting like real people. When I was young, such teachable moments became my challenge to ruin my teachers. I tried to divert attention to something trivial. I tried to make other students mad or humiliate them—anything to destroy order. If teachers didn't like me, so much the better, because then, they were emotionally bound to me. And once I found out what bothered them, I could push their buttons whenever I wished.

Some of my teachers sensed that if they showed interest in me, I could not get to them. They were right. If they didn't react, I couldn't counterattack. I had to find another approach or another classroom. No matter. I could endure one teacher and at the same time, ruin another and not be bothered by it. Yet I was really torn inside, wanting love and wanting to hate at the same time. Actually, life confounded me. I didn't have answers or even really know what the questions were. I was just bouncing around, using love and hate to sort things out in a clumsy kind of selfish experiment.

Teachers could love me, and I might like them enough to let them teach, or they could allow me to run wild at their expense . . . at least until they couldn't stand it anymore and threw me out. But by then, I would have made a fool of them before the entire class. I would have wasted an incredible amount of classroom time and would have given them emotional fits. And would I care if they threw me out of their classroom? Fat chance! I would have become bored by then anyway, ready for a new challenge, and happy to be a martyr for my cause. I would literally laugh when a teacher suffered an emotional breakdown, and some did.

I have a hunch. Tell me if I'm right. Many teachers today secretly (some openly) resent having to deal with the attitude problems of someone else's children. I realize that teachers consider teaching a team effort with parents. You're right, it is. But

Attitude problems should be dealt with at home by parents. But what if they are not?

what about those parents who are clearly not doing their part. They may not want to. They may not know how. But it kind of rankles, right? I sympathize. Really. But that doesn't do you any good, and neither does seething resentment.

So what's your choice? Do you want to learn how to effectively deal with difficult students or let them ruin your life? I know it's not your fault. I know it didn't use to be this way. You're right! You shouldn't have to deal with attitude problems. They should be dealt with at home. But look, my parents couldn't do anything with me, either. They had a lot more time than my teachers did, and they really tried. Besides that, my kind don't go away, not these days. If you expel us, someone else will come along. So what are you going to do?

The Solution You Need

Ancient Greece was in many ways more secular than our society, and they knew virtue had to be taught. They just didn't know how.

You already know the problem. It is students like me. You've encountered us before, lots of times, if you've taught very long. The solution is virtue. Yes, VIRTUE: the desire to do what you know is right. Think about it. I didn't have much when my teachers encountered me—that's the problem. Teaching me virtue—that's the solution; instilling in students the inner character that produces good conduct. Yes, you can do that in the classroom. Of course, it's legal. But it takes insight. It takes courage, initiative, and sacrifice. Don't be afraid. It's not something new.

It was considered a must in ancient Greece. For Socrates (Plato, 1901), the question was not, "May we teach virtue?," but "How can virtue be taught?" He realized how imperative it was for those in a free society to police themselves. He knew that if even a small percentage of the people refused to willingly regulate their lives for the betterment of society, it would soon become impossible for a police force of any size to maintain order. And ponder this, ancient Greece was in many ways more secular than our society, and they knew virtue *had* to be taught. They just didn't know how. You probably sense, intuitively, that it must be taught too, but I'm guessing you don't know how, either. The ancients understood the value of personal virtue. In Plato's *Republic* (Plato, 1946), Socrates and Glaucon agreed that "virtue is the health, and beauty, and well-being of the soul" (p. 163).

However, the concept of virtue is shrouded in fog these days. It has been lost to time, and that's a problem. In early America, virtue was an everyday word, and the context for its usage was good government, a sound society, and the education of youth. William Penn wrote in his famous *Frame of Government* for his new colony (as quoted in Millard, 1991),

> Let men be good, and the government cannot be bad. . . . That, therefore, which makes a good constitution must keep it,—namely men of wisdom and virtue,—qualities that, because they descend not with worldly inheritance, must be carefully propagated by a virtuous education of youth. (p. 44)

Benjamin Rush, a signer of the Declaration of Independence and later called the "Father of Public Schools," said, after the adoption of the Constitution (Barton, 1993), "Without virtue there can be no liberty, and liberty is the object and life of all republican governments" (p. 3). Benjamin Franklin, (as quoted in Hall, 1976) when writing to Dr. Samuel Johnson, the first President of King's College (now Columbia University) regarding the education of youth, said,

> I think with you, that nothing is of more importance for the public weal, than to form and train up youth in wisdom and virtue. . . . I think also, general virtue is more probably to be expected and obtained from the education of youth, than from the exhortation of adult persons; bad habits and vices of the mind being, like diseases of the body, more easily prevented than cured. (p. 221)

John Adams (as quoted in McDowell, 1988), another signer of the Declaration of Independence and later, the second president of the United States, would say,

> A general dissolution of principles and manners will more surely overthrow the liberties of America than the whole force of the common enemy. While the people are virtuous they cannot be subdued; but when they lose their virtue they will be ready to surrender their liberties to the first external or internal invader. . . . If virtue and knowledge are diffused among the people, they will never be enslaved. This will be their great security. (p. 148)

When our country was founded, most everyone knew what virtue meant. Even those who didn't think about it sensed how important it was to the structure of society. But the teaching of virtue has been slowly abandoned. Today, it's lost.

There are a few trying to revive it in education, such as Allan Bloom (1987) of the University of Chicago and William Kilpatrick (1992) of Boston College and most notably, former Education Secretary William Bennett (1993). But for the most part, it's gone. That's where you come in, and the important thing now is to consider that virtue is not foreign to education, it's imperative. By abandoning it, U.S. educators have kept the structure of the classroom but lost the invigorating spirit of their teaching. Without it, students cannot properly assimilate the knowledge you give them.

Virtue takes knowledge and turns it into wisdom.

Virtue greases the bearings in education. Consider Abraham Lincoln's early education. Though Lincoln had little opportunity for formal learning, he maximized what he learned from personal study. With a strong desire to do what he knew was right (personal virtue), he studied how he could do it (practical knowledge). This continually guided him to find an appropriate way to accomplish what was good (applied wisdom). Virtue takes knowledge and turns it into wisdom. Vice takes knowledge and turns it into craftiness. Virtue is a must for education. Without it, we do little more than create crafty criminals.

Ways of Teaching Virtue

Virtue can be taught two ways: by exposure and by transfusion. It can be taught over a long period of time by exposure through example, such as with parents at home. But it can also be taught at critical moments in life through transfusion, such as those times of crisis in the classroom. Those are the only two ways I know. The first option is not available to you. You generally only have students for an hour a day. True, it's for the better part of a year, but that's usually not enough to teach by way of exposure. And if parents haven't been exposing their children to virtue as they grow up, your students' only hope is to get a transfusion at crisis time.

I want to say emphatically, from the outset, that teaching virtue conceptually does not compute, for anyone, anytime, period. Concepts don't mean anything during a transfusion unless the time is right and the donor is available and willing to sacrifice. And even then, concepts are secondary and don't really convey much. Virtue can be caught, like a Texas accent, from exposure, but the relationship must be meaningful and lasting. Most high school teachers don't have that kind of time or that meaningful a relationship with most of their students. Sacrifice at the crucial moment makes the teacher-student relationship meaningful enough for a transfusion of virtue to take place.

There is a third way of teaching virtue, really an artificial combination of the other two—the exposure and transfusion approaches. It involves three things: imaginary involvement, memory storage and retrieval, and application at the critical moment. It's the approach I use in this book. It is not nearly as effective. I would rate exposure first, transfusion second, and imagination-memory third, and each about half as effective as the one before it. I hate to say the imagination-memory approach is the weakest, because that is the approach I am using here, but that doesn't mean it's bad.

I also offer seminars to teachers who are in the middle of real-life crisis situations and who need transfusions. So I'm not confining my efforts to the weakest approach. But let me give you an example of this third way. Educators have effectively used this approach for many years. Some still do. It involves storytelling or even the simple reading of stories, but not just any stories—virtuous stories. With teenagers? Absolutely! Here is an excerpt taken from *The Eclectic Second Reader* by William H. McGuffey (1836/1982), originally published in 1836.

There was a little boy, about thirteen years old, whose name was Casablanca. His father was the commander of a ship of war called the Orient. The little boy accompanied his father to the seas. His ship was once engaged in a terrible battle on the river Nile.

In the middle of the thunders of the battle, while the shots were flying thickly around, and strewing the decks with blood, this brave boy stood by the side of his father, faithfully discharging the duties which were assigned to him.

At last his father placed him in a particular part of the ship, to perform some service, and told him to remain at his post until he should call him away. As the father went to some distant part of the ship, to notice the progress of the battle, a ball from the enemy's vessel laid him dead upon the deck.

The son, unconscious of his father's death, and faithful to the trust reposed in him, remained at his post, waiting for his father's orders. The battle raged dreadfully around him. The blood of the slain flowed at his feet. The ship took fire, and the threatening flames drew nearer and nearer.

Still this noble-hearted boy would not disobey his father. In the face of blood, and balls, and fire, he stood firm and *obedient.* The sailors began to desert the burning and sinking ship, and the boy cried out, "Father, may I go?"

No voice of permission could come from the mangled body of his lifeless father, and the boy, not knowing that he was dead, would rather die than disobey. There that boy stood, at his post, until every man had deserted the ship, and he stood and perished in the flames.

Oh, what a boy was that! Everybody who ever heard of him thinks that he was one of the noblest boys that ever was born. Rather than disobey his father, he would die in the flames! (pp. 205-207)

Reading this aloud thoughtfully, contemplatively, takes less than 3 minutes. Add a few searching questions, such as, "What made the young man remain at his post in the face of such danger?" "What character traits made him so much admired?" "How do you feel after having heard this story?". Allow for some interaction, such as, "What a waste of such a good life!" "His father should have been more careful in giving instructions." "I don't think it would have been wrong for him to abandon the ship under such conditions." Probe the hearts of difficult students with penetrating questions, such as, "What kind of father would this boy have made?" "What effect did his short life have on others?" "What do you admire about him?" Having done this in class, what have you accomplished? Five minutes of preventive maintenance, greasing the bearings of education, that will yield hours of effective teaching.

This kind of teaching does three things: (a) it actively involves the imagination, (b) it fuels the memory with positive input for future events, and (c) it prepares the heart for a transfusion of virtue when the critical moment comes along, even if you're not around. The story by itself is not nearly as meaningful as when a virtuous person tells it or reads it and then interacts with those listening. If a virtuous person has done this and then is available at the moment of crisis to give a transfusion, and if that person is a parent or close friend with a long and meaningful relationship behind them, the result is transforming. Teenagers yearn for such people to take an interest in them.

Having said that, you must recognize crisis situations for what they are: not as distractions from your routines but crucial opportunities to give a transfusion to someone who is bleeding internally and who will die without it. To be able to do that, you will first need to get a grip on the concept of virtue. You can't play with it if it's fuzzy in your mind; you'll end up chasing it all over the place. Second, the concept will have to become functional, or workable for you to use, so you can evaluate your students' attitudes in the classroom. Third, you will need to measure that invisible something called virtue so you can tell where your students are, discern how to help them, and explain what you are doing to administrators and parents. But before we head down that path, look behind the scenes for a moment, and suppose with me that certain things are true.

Suppose These Things Are True

People operate at different levels of virtue and, consequently, some virtues do not seem virtuous to all people.

Suppose that virtue *is* something. Imagine it's real. You can poke it with a stick and watch it jump. You can dissect it, look at the parts, and play with them. You can turn them this way and that, see how they fit, and put them back together. Having done that, you would understand what virtue is. Understanding virtue through such investigation would make it measurable. If it weren't measurable, you would be wasting your time. Educators have to give account in measurable terms. In order to measure something, it has to exist in reality. Let's suppose that virtue does and see if it can be measured.

In addition, let's presume that virtue is common to all cultures and subcultures, that it's part of what it means to be human. People within a culture or subculture could disagree over this virtue or that, but assume that within all peoples, there is a desire to do what they know is right. And surmise that children, very early, can throw that away, but let's suppose it is there in every human being. At the same time, imagine that nonsense fills the heart of children and that they need to be trained in the way that is right. Let's assume these things are true and see whether our results hold up.

People are ready to reconsider virtue in education.

Furthermore, suppose that educational researchers are beginning to realize that virtue needs to be taught but aren't making progress integrating it into education. Why not? Because the current dialog is breaking down. They can't agree which virtues should be taught (Sproule, 1987). Trying to teach only those virtues which most people accept won't work, because some students will always get upset with that approach. Guess which ones? Right, those who are the least virtuous. Their parents will likely be in your face about it too, for the same reason. You might get a measure of agreement from virtuous people, but they aren't the ones you really need to reach anyway.

Consider another approach. Suppose the solution is to uncover the essence of virtue. Imagine what people will do once they rediscover what virtue really is. It would become obvious to them how the various virtues relate to it. It is not unrealistic to surmise that this would lead to healthy discussion. People are ready to reconsider virtue in education. Once they grasp the essence of it, they will embrace it and talk about it sensibly. Why? They will have a meaningful framework for discussion. If you suppose with me that virtue is real, that it's common to all people, that it can be integrated into education, the rest of this manual will be meaningful for you. If not, tag along. Maybe you'll change your mind.

User-Friendly Manual

This manual is supposed to be practical and applied. Read it and use it. You won't be given any more theory than you need for measuring your students. It won't become too technical. If you want a technical explanation of how the questionnaire was field tested, if you want to examine the statistics, if you want to experiment with the data, write and ask for it. I have a diagnostician's version. You can find my address in Resource G. Most teachers won't have the interest or the inclination to wade through all the jargon and technical analysis, let alone the time needed to grapple with it, but if you do, it's available for you.

Concerning your students, the results from a pencil-and-paper test can tell you a lot about them that you can't see. You might sense it, but you can't see it. They might try to hide it, but you can find out anyway. They might try to fake it, but you can detect that, too. You need that information and not just to confirm your suspicions. You need it for what you must do as a teacher. Tests are designed to go beyond hunches. If teachers intend to have an effect on the hearts of someone else's children, they will have to make an assessment, plan an approach, and explain it to the parents and sometimes to administrators. In this manual, there is a questionnaire to help you accomplish these things in a professional way.

Some may feel that teachers shouldn't mess around with their students' hearts. Nonsense! You are reaching in and molding their minds; why not help their hearts, where their attitudes are shaped, where they really need it? Most teachers want to help their students any way they can. If teachers are able to measure virtue, they will approach one class differently from another. They will approach their students individually. They will relate to administrators and parents with a measure of certainty about where their students are and explain why they are approaching them the way they are. This manual is going to provide you a few tools with which to do just that, and I am excited about it for you!

A Bird's-Eye View

Here's what you will need to reach students with rotten attitudes. First, in Part I of this manual, you will learn how to work with virtue in your classroom. Now listen, you have to get a handle on the concept of virtue. The very next chapter gives you that so you can spot it in your students, so you can measure it with the virtue assessment questionnaire, and so you can explain it to angry parents. You will find out where virtue originates inside people. You will be able to examine internal aspects of character you can't see and be able to detect external expressions of character you can see, which a good many students try to fake. This is what Chapter 2 is all about.

Once you learn where virtue comes from and how it looks, Chapter 3 will teach you how it blooms or wilts in a student's life: you know, stages of development, levels of progression, that kind of thing. Chapter 3, then, is basically considering matters of the heart, not concepts of the mind. Virtue is less of a head thing, more of a heart thing. You will come to believe, if you don't already, that teaching is more than providing furniture for the mind. You can't get away with merely teaching subject matter when your students have attitude problems. They won't stand for it, and you will find that you simply must accommodate them. You may not like it at first, but you will after you discover how effective you are becoming.

Chapter 4 focuses on measuring your students' attitudes. You may wonder, "Is it possible to measure inner attitudes?" Absolutely! If something is real, it can be measured. You say, "What about the different ways students respond to the same questions?" No problem. We can adjust for that. "Then, what about those who are faking it, those trying to test out better than they actually are, and what about those who are not really bad—but, to be cool, want to test out badly—what about them?" These things are a little more trouble to detect, but we have ways to tell if they are misrepresenting themselves and to what extent. And you will learn how to measure all of this in Chapter 4.

As you can tell, Part I is the hard part. After that, it really gets fun, so be patient. It's okay. It's a virtue. And don't skip over Chapters 2 through 4. You can't get by without them. Part II is how to deal with the data you get when you test your students' virtue. It's all about interpreting the results of the information they provide. It's also about detecting the way they respond. And it's about unlocking the mysteries of classroom problems.

Chapter 5 helps you understand the results of testing virtue in your students. It provides student response norms. It tells you how to adjust when students answer with emphasis or uncertainty. It provides a scoring key and analysis worksheets, so you can make sense of the data you have gathered. You can do this manually yourself or you can send the questionnaires in and have the computer do the work for you. See Resource G.

Chapter 6 gives you the ability to recognize response patterns after the results are scored. Besides measuring levels of virtue, which is our primary goal, you must be able to discover when students misrepresent themselves. You will also want to know if the results are skewed by a positive or negative response pattern. And you will want to know to what extent their virtue is internal or external. In Chapter 6, these things are displayed through actual examples so that you can develop the ability to recognize response patterns and make sense of them.

Chapter 7 enables you to figure out your students. It gives you the capacity to understand classroom dynamics. It helps you turn bad situations into meaningful learning experiences. The focus of this chapter is on the relationship between virtue and knowledge. There are principles of virtue and knowledge that—if violated—will produce problems in your classroom. Knowledge and virtue work great together in education, if one is kept in proportion to the other, if virtue is given priority, and if knowledge is assimilated by virtue.

The second part of the manual, then, helps you interpret what is going on in your classroom. Part III looks at restoring what's broken. Today, your students' lives are not just filled with problems, they are broken. It may frustrate you to have to repair broken lives when you should be teaching subject matter, but that's the state of things. It's a sad day, but there is sure and certain hope for you in this little handbook.

Chapter 8 reveals to you how these young lives break apart and what you can do to put them back together again. There are cyclical patterns of behavior that students fall into that they must overcome. You will be able to help them because by the time you get this far in the manual, you will have pinpointed where your students are, and you will have come to understand the internal and external elements of virtue. This chapter gives you the super glue that will help you bond these elements together so that their tender young lives will not tragically break apart anymore.

Chapter 9 gives you concrete ways to prepare their hearts for a transfusion of virtue. You can prepare their hearts by helping them assess negative feelings, by helping them change perspective, by helping them determine what is right, and good, and appropriate, and by deepening their desire to do so. These things are very difficult for many students—next to impossible without guidance. Strange thing. It doesn't take much time. Yet it does take considerable expertise. But by the time you finish working with this chapter a little bit, you will be able to prepare the hearts of your students to receive virtue.

Chapter 10 offers eight principles for instilling virtue in a broken heart. These principles are pretty foreign to teenagers, and they are best understood by them when you live them out before their eyes. So don't be bothered by the shift in focus from students to teachers in this final chapter. Teachers are not the problem. But if you want to become the solution, you will be more effective if virtue is fully functional in your life.

That's all there is to this little manual. It's easy to tell you about it. You have the hard part: putting it to work on a daily basis. These things have been tested and used in the classroom. They work. But don't take my word for it. If you want to reach students with rotten attitudes, try bringing virtue back into education. Live a life of noble character that expresses a selfless, sacrificial, loving kindness toward your students and just watch their rotten attitudes change.

2

How to Think About Virtue

Once you've developed a taste for Texas-style chili, nothing beats a bowl of red. But no matter how hard a sell it gets, most people won't eat chili, and today, most people turn away from virtue. Up to this point, I've done my best to solicit your interest. You've received your invitation to the feast, Texas barbecue, to be sure, but you'll find none better. You've glanced over the picnic table, brushed past the gingham, and you're staring into the cast-iron kettle. It's simple fare but satisfying. So in this first part of the manual, just grab a bowl and help yourself country style. It may take some getting used to, but you'll find it well worth your while, if you stay with it.

Virtue is wanting to do what you have to do.

There are three parts to this manual, each having three chapters. This is Part I. It's about measuring virtue. Historically, people have never dealt precisely with virtue. It's always been little more than a notion—a fuzzy notion to most. Now, to measure something, you must first have a mental concept of it. In this initial chapter of Part I, you will discover where virtue originates inside people, what it's made of, and how it holds together. But because virtue is something you can't see, this is all conceptual.

Let me state right off, this concept of virtue is hypothetical. It's a guess. Hold on, don't get nervous. It's an educated guess and a good one. It's constructed to include internal and external elements in matching pairs. Hunh? Slow down, pardner. Here's what I mean. If virtue is genuine in a person's life, it will be expressed in inner character as well as in outward conduct. In other words, there will be activity that you can observe, but it will be prompted by corresponding attitudes that you cannot see. When building a hypothetical construction, it's extremely important to have solid conceptual building blocks: good, sound, workable ideas. If you're still half interested, I know you're getting nervous about how "elusive concepts" can actually be used to measure something. Concepts often start out fuzzy and stay that way, I know. Nevertheless, this is a concept of virtue that everybody can accept and readily apply. Stay with me.

This concept has been designed to cross cultural barriers and span academic disciplines yet remain simple enough for children to understand. Plain and simple, virtue is devotion to duty. More simply, virtue is wanting to do what you know you have to do. Oversimplifying it, "have to" is duty, "want to" is desire, and virtue is what brings the two together to make a good choice. See, the concept of virtue does

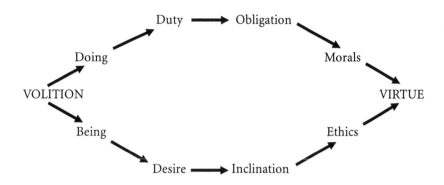

Figure 2.1. Volitional Construct of Virtue

not have to remain fuzzy. If you transfuse this from your life to your students, you can reach even those with rotten attitudes!

Teenagers have a hard time wanting to do what they have to do. That's why so many of them are miserable so much of the time. I have a plaque on my wall with a statement by Goethe that reads, "It is not doing the things we like to do, but liking the things we have to do that makes life blessed [happy]." Virtue is what bonds duty and desire together. In your classroom, virtuous students are those who know they are there to learn, who have committed themselves to work hard at it, and enjoy themselves while they are doing it. Do such students exist? Sure they do, but they are hiding.

Conceptualizing virtue this way is like holding objects up to a mirror or looking at a landscape reflected on a placid lake. You see two of everything. There are objects, and there are reflections. In this case, attitudes are the objects, activities are their reflection. Virtue has matched pairs of elements if it's the genuine article. Whenever you talk about virtue, these elements come up in matching pairs: being and doing, desire and duty, inclinations and obligations, personal ethics and social morals. In essence, all we are talking about are internal attitudes and external actions: character and conduct.

The Elements of Virtue

Philosophers, psychologists, and moralists talk about the things that constitute virtue all the time. They use different terms peculiar to their disciplines, but they talk about the same kind of things, which can readily be pieced together once they are seen in relation to each other. Notice in Figure 2.1 the external elements of virtue (the upper loop in the figure) and their internal counterparts (the lower loop in the figure). Also, as you study the figure, begin considering if it is possible for people to make choices that do not involve virtue. We will hammer that out later.

If a bloodhound could, he would always track virtue back to choice; at least that's the way Aristotle saw it (Rackham, 1945), and so does Meilaender (1984) in his *Theory and Practice of Virtue.* So let's begin with volition, the seat of decision making inside of a person. Volition, or choosing, consists of being and doing, if we can believe Studdiford (1967) and Meilaender (1984, p. 7). It is expressed in terms of character and conduct, according to Muirhead (1969, p. 22). We are talking about what you actually end up doing because of who you really are. Desire and duty are expressions of being and doing as they relate to virtue (Rée, 1973, p. 75). When you do what is right with the right motivation, you outwardly express inner virtue. But a single expression of virtue does not a virtuous person make.

> **You will understand your students better if you understand that they never act out of character.**

Truly virtuous people have developed a strong sense of what ought to be done and a deep yearning to do it. Moralists call these two compatible volitional elements *inclinations* and *obligations* (Muirhead, 1969). Inclinations and obligations are what have become more or less established in people through the choices they have made up to that point in their lives. Inherent in the concept of virtue is the element of what is right and good and appropriate. Proper inclinations establish personal ethical systems. Improper choices weaken them. A proper sense of obligation enables people to live within social mores. An improper sense of obligation, or lack of it, causes people to be socially dysfunnctional.

When all these volitional elements are present and accounted for, functioning in harmony, with external doing driven by internal being, with desire conforming to duty, virtue is established in a person's life. That's all there is to virtue. Having said that, we must also add that it is literally impossible to track virtue when you try to consider the myriad choices people make each day, let alone how different people interact with one another in various social settings. Yet understanding virtue becomes manageable when you consider overall attitudes. You can even track overall attitudes in small groups of students if you are astute. And you can become more astute by carefully considering the matching pairs of elements that constitute virtue.

The Elements of Being and Doing

Being Drives Doing

Let's take a closer look at the parts of virtue in pairs, considering each internal part and its external counterpart. First, being and doing. Being always drives doing. It may not seem like it, but it does. Even if students act contrary to the way they normally act, there is something about their being that causes them to do so. On the other hand, doing always influences being. Children sense, when they pretend, that if they do certain things, that *makes* them what they want to be. My son Peter wears cowboy boots and a cowboy hat in order to be a cowboy. If you ask him who he is, he will say, "I am a cowboy, can't you see? I put on my cowboy boots and my cowboy hat!" Pretending shapes what a child will become later in life. In a sense and to a certain degree, doing influences being. But being always drives doing.

Let's suppose that Billy Joe is torn inside. He wants to do what is right . . . sometimes. But he also likes to mess around. Typical teenager. In English class, a subject he doesn't like, he sits with trouble makers. They goof off. In history class, a subject that he likes, he is attentive and respectful, even helpful to his teacher. Another student, who is in both classes, *kindly* points this out to him by calling him a "fake." He hates his duplicity but is not sure which is genuine. In actuality, both are.

You will understand your students better if you understand that they never act out of character. You generally don't have enough time to get to really know each and every student or even one very well. Many students make compartments in their lives, but that's who they really are . . . fragmented people. Teachers may only see one compartment and be shocked when they see another, thinking their student is acting out of character. They aren't, that's who they actually are.

Sometimes, under pressure, Jerry will lie. He does not normally lie, but if he doesn't have time to think something through, he might lie to protect himself or favor himself. He might blame the pressure he is under. He might blame a person who oppresses him. He might even blame an illness. No matter. He has done something because of who he is. This is invariably true. I'm arguing with you. We are hammering out the dents now. Consider again, if it is possible for people to make choices that do not involve virtue. I am contending that whatever Jerry does, he does because of who he is. Are you with me? If not, go back and reconsider these things thoughtfully. You don't have to agree, you just have to catch my drift.

> What we have done indicates who we were and influences who we are becoming.

Doing Influences Being

This implies that what we do indicates who we are at that moment, and what we do at a particular time influences who we are becoming. This sounds contradictory, but it really just means we are constantly changing, and choices direct that change. If we make good choices, our virtue is strengthened. If we make bad choices, our virtue is weakened. In either case, we are no longer exactly who we were before the choice was made. This is why I insist that being and doing are bound together in volition.

Within most young people, there are conflicting interests that influence their choices. This is who they really are, whether they realize it or not, whether they like it or not. Conflicting interests indicate students who are still trying to establish who they will become, what direction they will take, either bad or good. But conflicting interests also indicate exactly who that person is at that particular moment. What conflicting interests do not indicate is what course will be taken. People quit struggling when they become established in either virtue or vice. Most high school students are still struggling with conflicting interests. Nevertheless, what students do truly indicates who they are and also actually influences who they will become.

> People quit struggling when they become established in either virtue or vice.

The Elements of Desire and Duty

Compatible Components

Historically, many who have debated the essence of virtue have seen duty and desire in opposition to each other, but I don't "gee and haw" (agree) with them. I find the two naturally coming together when people make proper choices. What people want to do and what they have to do need not be mutually exclusive. Personal desires need not conflict with personal responsibilities. Many times they do, but they need not. In virtue, duty and desire are special kinds of *have to* and *want to*. They follow from being and doing.

Duty and Obligation

I don't want to overstate the obvious, but, in making the connection between doing and duty, I must stress that duty carries with it nuances of doing what is right and good and appropriate. You know this, but it's important to emphasize because duty implies moral obligation. There is a compelling feature to it. The idea of obligation, of course, immediately raises questions: Why should anyone be obligated to anyone else? And if obligation is dependent on what is right, good, and appropriate, why do people think in terms of right and wrong at all?

The Obligation to Society

The answer to the first question is so obvious it is easy to overlook. We are obligated to one another, if for no other reason, because we are social beings. What you do affects me. What I do affects you. We cannot survive without helping one another. So we make arrangements to help each other and endeavor not to hurt each other in the bargain. This, all by itself, produces obligations. Therefore, we are obligated to one another because we are social. This leads us to the next question, but the answer is not so obvious as the first. If duty is dependent on what is right, good, and appropriate, why do people concern themselves with these things anyway?

The Obligation to Freedom

There are many ways that people establish what is right, good, and appropriate. It is not my purpose here to explore those ways, but people do establish these things individually and collectively, and they have a sense of responsibility to themselves and others for what they hold to be right, good, and appropriate. One reason people think in these terms is because humans are not fixed beings like animals are.

Human beings differ from animals because they think in terms of time before and time beyond themselves. They do not act according to instinct, they make laws and police them. They can do wrong, change, and do right. And they can do right, rebel, and do wrong. Animals do animal things for animal reasons. It is not immoral for a lion to kill his supper. A house cat cannot rebel and act like a dog; you never hear a cat barking. They are fixed creatures. Human beings are not. For this reason, almost every human choice is either moral or immoral.

Nonmoral People

There are few nonmoral choices with people. That's because there are no nonmoral human beings and few nonmoral conditions in life. Here are a few exceptions: children who are too small to make choices, children old enough to make choices but not old enough to be held accountable because they don't understand, and people whose faculties do not function or have disintegrated. These aren't likely to cover all the exceptions, but you get the idea. However, because people are social beings, and because they do not make fixed choices, the choices they do make are either moral or immoral. Here are a couple of exceptions.

I know of one old man whose grandchildren and great-grandchildren loved and respected him, even though he was reduced to grinning and growling. He could make a few choices, but his family did not hold him to them. He had become functionally nonmoral. His body had broken down. He had had a series of strokes, and who knows what else, and could hardly function. It would have been absurd for them to correct him for making bad choices. They knew it. They loved him in spite of the fact that his body no longer served him. They understood all this, young and old, with little said about it.

Some extremely handicapped people also fall into this category. I recall visiting a young man in a convalescent community of sorts. He had been in an awful automobile accident. His body had long healed, but a good part of his brain had been removed. It left him staring off into space, waving one arm around, almost continuously, for the rest of his life. He made no choices. He was a moral being who had been rendered morally dysfunctional. His condition had become fixed, rendering him functionally nonmoral.

Nonmoral Issues

Now, there may be nonmoral issues, such as which way to take to school, but once even such an issue is acted on, it becomes either moral or immoral. Gary, a student, might decide to take a way that leads past an adult theater so he can stir up selfish appetites and make plans for later, whereas Mr. Ledbetter, his teacher, takes a way that leads past old Miss Fisher's house so he can stop to take out her trash. Mrs. Rundle may go out of her way to see if she can pick up any students on the way so she can spend some time talking with them and show a little unexpected kindness, whereas one of her students, Priscilla, takes the fastest way so that she can get there before everyone else to show them how conscientious she is.

Even a nonmoral issue becomes moral when acted on by a moral being. Here's why: People do what they do for reasons. Behind our actions lie reasons for what we do. Obviously, it's good if we do good for good reasons. But if we do anything for a bad reason or even something bad for a good reason, it's bad. Sure, it's possible to do bad for a good reason. Take the example of students cheating on one of your examinations. The reason? They want to do well in your class. It's bad to cheat, no question, but it's also good for them to want to do well in your class.

By the way, teachers would do well to remember both the good reason and the bad deed in dealing with those who cheat. Nevertheless, doing bad for a good reason is still wrong. However, it's even worse to do bad for a bad reason, such as students who steal answers to an examination and sell them to other students so they can buy drugs and waste their lives. Yet, when discovering those who do bad for a good reason, you should discipline them for what they did wrong, but you can also praise them for wanting to do well.

> **Even a nonmoral issue becomes moral when acted on by a moral being.**

Duty without noble desire is forced, rigid, and impossible to sustain.

However, it's easy to exact punishment and overlook encouragement, especially if you stay angry about what your students have done. Yet, if you fail to praise them for wanting to do well after you discipline them for doing wrong, you've passed up a great opportunity to nurture their desire, and you leave them disheartened. Don't get me wrong; it's not your fault they are disheartened over what they have done, but you can help them if you want. No one will expect you to do this. It's extra, which is what you are looking for to strengthen your own heart's desire.

We have digressed. But we have been arguing that even a nonmoral issue becomes moral when acted on by a moral being, because people do what they do for reasons. Yet, even should one of your students do something without apparent reason, it is not neutral. There is no neutrality for moral creatures. They may not have given something much forethought, either because they were lazy, or hasty, or irresponsible, but all of these are wrong, never neutral. Even when reason-driven beings abandon the use of their reason, it is immoral.

Desire and Motivation

So much for duty, but what of desire in all of this? Basically, desire is the inner motivation that moves us toward what we do not have and wish we did. Duty without desire soon becomes drudgery. In this context, desire is the enlivening, invigorating, sustaining spirit that makes compliance with duty virtuous. Desire can stir selfish appetites and selfish ambitions, but desire can also be noble and prompt a yearning for what is right, good, and appropriate. Duty without noble desire is forced, rigid, and impossible to sustain. Noble desire sacrifices selfish appetites and ambitions to meet the needs of others. It does not shrink back from duty. It delights in it.

The Power of Noble Desire

If you tell Patty she has to be quiet, she will not normally want to. If you tell Caleb he has to go out and play, all of a sudden, he wonders if he really wants to. But it works the other way too. Children who have to eat their vegetables, later like to eat vegetables—sometimes. Other variables can factor in: George Bush's broccoli, for instance. Duty does funny things to desire. It has a way of destroying it when the heart's attitude is not right.

But desire also does funny things to duty. If Sammy really wants to look into a microscope and you tell him sternly that he has to . . . right this minute, or suffer the consequences, he will smile and think you are teasing him. And he will not feel forced or oppressed. When desire aligns with duty, there is no problem. *Want to* is much more powerful than *have to*. Desire devours duty for dessert when it's healthy and strong, but when it isn't . . . well, let's consider Rob.

The Problem With Corrupted Desire

Rob has fed selfish desires with drugs for a long time. His father finally found out. Embarrassed, he tried to force Rob to stop using drugs by being rough with him, even mean-spirited. It didn't work. His heartbroken mother took the approach of loving appeal. It had no effect. Rob's desire was polluted. His own happy, hopeful, inner desire once could have turned him away from drugs. And . . . it still would, if only somehow it could be rekindled. It can. I know you're thinking, "Okay, so tell me how." First things first.

The point for now is that joyful desire is immensely stronger than selfish desire. It is stronger than a mean-spirited, intimidating command and even stronger than a loving appeal. Nothing can touch noble desire when it is established. But it is rarely established in the young. And, when it is there at all, it is usually pretty fragile. This manual will show how it becomes corrupted and how it can be restored once it has. Here's one of many ways teachers can absolutely crush the desire to do what is right in the hearts of their students.

Crushing Noble Desire

Ten-year-old Sally approaches Mr. Curmudgeon and, before she can even tell him why she came, he tells her to go back to her desk and stay there. She returns to her desk but leaves a puddle under her chair for the rebuke. Get the picture. Teacher tells student to stay put. Student wets pants because she feels obligated to do so. How incredibly tragic! Mr. Curmudgeon imposed his will on Sally's. He, apparently, regarded neither her personal inclinations nor her sense of obligation, just so long as her body stayed in her seat.

This does not mean students have no obligation to their teachers. It just means that Mr. Curmudgeon violated not only Sally's sense of obligation but that of everyone in that class and incited their inclinations against him. The problem is, he didn't even realize what had taken place with the rest of his students. They immediately put themselves in Sally's place, felt her hopelessness and humiliation, and were outraged at how insensitive and overbearing their teacher could be. I know; I was one of those students.

Later, Mr. Curmudgeon would puzzle over why his students did not *want to* behave. He apparently saw no connection with a single incident involving one student and the many discipline problems that followed. Incidents such as this overpower a young person's fragile inner desire to do what should be done. Such sweet-spirited desire should be nurtured, not crushed. Nurturing that inner desire to do what is right, good, and appropriate is what keeps students from corruption. But before we can talk about how to nurture virtue, we must know what it is and how it works.

> **A virtuous person has developed a strong sense of what ought to be done, and a deep yearning to do it.**

Interaction Between Duty and Desire

Duty and desire influence each other, just like being and doing do. But whereas the internal always drives the external with being and doing, not so with desire and duty. Either desire or duty can drive the other. It's not so straightforward. Desire can be conformed to duty by either external or internal stimuli, but duty can also be imposed on desire. The interaction between duty and desire is like one of those gizmos where you have a half a dozen balls hanging next to each other by strings.

If you pull one from either end and let go, it will impel the one on the opposite end. But you can also pull the balls from both ends and let go at the same time, and they will both have an effect on the other. That's the way it is with duty and desire when they differ.

Something or someone external to the person can convey a sense of duty. This can have a variety of effects. For instance, the principal of your school can impose a dress code on the student body without regard for the way students feel about it. You might think this can only seem oppressive to students. But it can yield varying responses. For instance, desire can act independently of duty. Students can blow off authority and do whatever they want. They can resist being regulated. They can wear whatever they want, without regard for the dress code, doing only what they wish to do. When they do so, they produce conflict and open themselves up to thoughts of anger and rebellion, to say nothing about corrupting their sense for what is right, through willfulness.

Outward conformity without inner compliance can last for years. It is not virtue! It just looks like it.

Duty can also be obeyed without any desire behind it. Students may follow the dress code but not willingly. They may not like it. Inside, they may be rebellious, looking for a way to get around it, waiting for a time when they can justify throwing it off. This is secret resistance: outward conformity without inner compliance. It can last for years. It is not virtue! It just looks like it. You might detect it yet be tempted to overlook this kind of problem because such students do not make any waves, but it is a virtue problem. And if you wait until they become vocal and visible, they will be extremely difficult to deal with.

On the other hand, desire can negate the oppression of duty. Desire is invincible when it willingly conforms to what is required. Students can decide that they will willingly comply with the dress code because it is appropriate for the classroom, it shields them from temptation, and it nurtures a sense of decency. It is not likely that they will, in a day like today, without instruction and encouragement, but they can. And, funny thing, when they do, they will not feel oppressed by the principal's dress code.

Teachers should be careful not to categorize students as they attempt to figure out what they really want to do.

There can be different degrees of any of these, of course. Students can try different positions, shifting from one to the other with all kinds of experimentation. Teachers should be careful not to categorize students as they attempt to figure out what they really want to do. Students will feel pushed even faster in a direction they may be heading but to which they are not really committed. This does not mean that rebellious students should not be disciplined. It does mean that before teachers write off students, they can give them some guidance and latitude to help bring them around while they are experimenting.

Referring back to Figure 2.1, Desire and Duty are the most essential elements in this conceptualization of virtue. The rest are peripheral. It is intuitive that Desire and Duty come from Being and Doing. Being and Doing could be left out. The next two elements, Inclinations and Obligations, are extensions of Desire and Duty. When Desire and Duty become established, they become Inclinations and Obligations, respectively. These elements could be left out. The same is true for Personal Ethics and Social Morals. They naturally extend from Inclinations and Obligations. They could be left out also. But the foundational elements are Desire and Duty. With that in mind, let's look at the next matched pair of elements, seeing them as extensions of Desire and Duty.

The Elements of Inclinations and Obligations

Inclinations are more than just desires. Desires may be fleeting. Inclinations are those desires that are at least somewhat set. If a student is inclined to be diligent, much of that person is already involved. Students' desires may vary daily. But their inclinations have been around for awhile and form a more or less fixed part of who they are. Some students are inclined to be argumentative. If you state πr^2, they will insist it is round. Others are inclined to be passive. If you challenge them, they will just smile. Neither one takes time to ponder their reaction to you, they are just so inclined.

Intentional and Unintentional Inclinations

Inclinations involve repeated choices. They may involve determination but may stop short of it, too. Some inclinations stem from a disposition received from their ancestors. Justin had only vague and distant memories of his father. His mother thought it best to leave it that way. When Justin reached his teens, he began drinking, just like his father. He repeatedly drank until he was drunk. He didn't determine this was something he would do. He did not establish it as a goal. Neither did he chart a course to accomplish it. Nevertheless, he had a definite inclination to drink by the time he was 16.

But inclinations can also be formed by watching and weighing the actions and attitudes of others. When it comes to virtue, this is the best way to teach it: by living it. It is better caught than taught. A lot of your students will study people more than they will subject matter. Often, those who won't study books are good students of people. They may study the wrong kind of people, but often only because they get a clearer and therefore more compelling picture from them.

Consider Natasha. She's a foreign exchange student. She's not afraid to study and does pretty well with the language, but it's still a struggle for her. She understands what is spoken more readily than she can herself express, but she watches people intently. You frequently find her watching you. She is learning about people in the United States. She has no problem with academics in this country, but what she is really studying are actions and attitudes. You catch her cocking her head to one side and watching out of the corner of her eye while the class laughs at a mistake another student has made.

When you've come alongside to help another student who is struggling and you finish and turn toward your desk, you find her observing you. She quickly turns back to her work. You are intrigued, but you shouldn't be. Most students do this, though they have learned over the years to be more discreet. You notice Natasha because she can't hide it so well, because she's so captivated by the freedom here, and because she studies so intently. But this is typical of teenagers. They watch, and they weigh what is going on around them and develop inclinations from what they see. You hope Natasha will be inclined toward virtue from watching you and not toward negative attitudes from some of your students.

> A lot of your students study people more than they study subject matter.

> Is the picture you are presenting as clear and compelling and clever as that of your class clown?

But how clear is the picture you are presenting? Is it as clear and compelling and clever as that of your class clown? Today, many virtuous people are hiding their virtue, and the picture they present is muddled and confusing. On the other hand, some openly virtuous people are under such attack for what they believe and demonstrate, they present a mean-spirited, defensive picture. Not very compelling. Yet when uncluttered, virtue can be very winsome to your students' inclinations.

The Hidden Agenda of Obligations

If you do not nurture inclinations in your students, corresponding obligations will seem oppressive.

Inclinations are quite distinct from obligations. Inclinations are inside and very near, and we know them almost intuitively. We have little trouble understanding our inclinations. We may have difficulty discovering them, but once we have, they are not difficult to comprehend. Obligations are different. They are perceived. Most often they come from outside, and a lot of times, something is lost in the transmission.

Obligations are to students what grades are to learning. You may tell your students that grades are not as important as what they learn, but everything they do comes under the scrutiny of "The Grader." This strongly affects them. So do obligations. If you do not nurture inclinations in your students, corresponding obligations will seem oppressive.

Students are under obligation when you give an assignment. There is a certain measure of responsibility placed on them. It is expected that they will perform what was asked of them, in a timely manner, and to a certain degree of proficiency. If they are so inclined, they will turn in the assignment with a good attitude. If their inclinations lie elsewhere, they either will not turn in the assignment or do so with a bad attitude.

Usually, such obligations carry three notions: (a) you, as the teacher, have the authority to obligate your students; (b) what you ask to be done is right, good, and appropriate; and (c) they are required to respond to what you impose. If you have no authority, if what you require isn't right, good, and appropriate, if it shouldn't involve them, they can rightfully refuse. If you do have authority, if you require what is good, if it properly involves them, then there should be no hesitation on your part to ask and no hesitation on their part to comply. Virtue constrains both teachers and students.

Let's suppose your math class is getting bored. Purely hypothetical. Spring has sprung. Everyone wants to be outside. You decide to take your class outdoors. There is a flower bed out in front of the school. It is grown over with weeds. It has irritated you that someone hasn't done something about it. You are suddenly inspired to make a project of that flower bed with your students. Most are immediately enthusiastic. But Rusty, one of the leaders of the class, doesn't want to weed and plant and begins to influence a few of the others, whom you sense would have otherwise enjoyed it.

You perceive your plan is in jeopardy and challenge Rusty to either join the group or report to the principal's office. Rusty, usually respectful and responsive, surprises you by going to the principal's office. Later that afternoon, you find yourself discussing the matter with your principal. He agrees that you have authority to obligate your students. He allows that it was not a bad idea. He even concedes that it is wrong for students to resist their teacher's authority, but he points out that your authority does not extend over such matters as the care of the flower bed. Rusty was under no obligation to participate in your project. You must apologize to him before the entire class.

Same situation, same class, but in this case, you lead your class past the weed bed, wisely leaving it to the maintenance crew, and position your students out on the grass, having them step off geometric patterns. While you are teaching them the fine points of an isosceles triangle, your principal walks by and observes your work. At the faculty banquet, you receive a commendation for your creativity. Your colleagues admire you, and your students love you. Why? You have cultivated their inclinations to conform with your obligations, inside your jurisdiction, in a way that was right, good, and appropriate.

The Elements of Ethics and Morals

Personal Ethical Systems

Internal ethics and external morals form the final pair of elements constituting virtue. On the internal side, there is a progression extending from inner being through desires, establishing inclinations, and developing into individual ethical systems. These ethical systems begin in people's innermost beings. They are cultivated as individuals experiment with what they want to do. Early in life, people usually begin to follow self-centered desires, developing inclinations into dispositions. These form an ethical system of how they will operate. When a full range of inclinations is established, ethical systems function as a guide for what people do.

Exclusively following inner desires to develop an ethical system leads young people to self-centered reasons for doing what they do. This is a mark of immaturity. People expect that small children will be selfish and seek to guide them to consider other people. But selfish inclinations develop early, and many young people do not receive much guidance. Consequently, their ethical systems are anything but ethical, even though they are trying to do what they think is best. Their ethical systems may or may not be in keeping with prevailing social mores. Nevertheless, such external morals may also influence the development of their inner ethical systems, or consciences.

Social Mores

The external side of things presents an arena for experimentation and provides feedback so people can adjust their personal ethical systems. Their conduct is a reflection on their character. Someone else's obligations can regulate their inclinations. Social morals may influence personal ethics. Things outside of people can lead them from selfishness to concern for others. And keep in mind that external morals can come from a variety of places. It is important to consider how social morals work together and against each other.

Social morals tend to revert to what is right. Yet, at any give time, on any given issue, social morals can be corrupt—often are.

Social morals are dynamic; they change and flex with whim. Two things should be understood from this: First, social morals frequently shift under the influence of a highly vocal and visible minority. Second, right cannot necessarily be defined by the majority, though odds are in their favor. Society has a built-in capacity to keep things right, to revert to what is appropriate. Consequences for doing wrong eventually follow, and people who have been wronged let others know about it. But sometimes, wrong is made to look good, and if it is, society may try it for awhile. Nevertheless, when the consequences of wrongdoing become apparent, society will eventually adjust, if it is free to do so.

All of this is to say that social morals are often out of kilter, being pushed and shoved by fad and fancy. Take the death penalty, for instance. In times past, it seemed good to repeal it. Today, many are rethinking that. By and large, social morals tend to revert to what is right. Yet at any given time, on any given issue, social morals can be corrupt—often are. The process of social morals moving off course and readjusting to what is right takes time. And there is a lot of uncertainty about what is right during that exchange. This creates no little confusion about what is right much of the time, on many of the issues.

Joe's personal ethical system is developing and changing almost daily. His family and church give some input, his friends and his teachers do, too, but inside is where it really develops. In the school parking lot, his friends are doing drugs and he is not. Crystal asks him "Why not?" He gives a number of reasons, trying to convince himself. He says, "I'd get in trouble. My dad would find out. Besides, don't you remember that video we saw in Mr. Rodriguez's class?" These are all reasons that influence him. What he doesn't say is that, inside, two things are really bothering him. He is afraid of what might happen, and he has a sense that it is wrong. But he doesn't know how to explain such things to his friends, and he is not sure, himself. Yet this is where he really lives, struggling with being and doing, desire and duty, inclinations and obligations, personal ethics and social morals.

Summary

It should have become obvious to you through this discussion that virtue is a dynamic construct. It changes all the time. Every time people change their minds, make a choice, feel differently about something, their prevailing attitudes about life are strengthened or weakened. Teenagers change a lot. They check things out. They experiment. They adjust, readjust, and try again. The older people get, the less they change. This is unfortunate if they become settled in corruption. It's good if virtue becomes established. But the thing to remember with young people is that they are changing. When you assess their attitudes, when you try to understand them, keep in mind that what you see is not likely to be all of who they are nor who they will become.

This conceptualization of virtue respects differences among people yet is easy to apply. It has been designed to cross cultural barriers and span academic disciplines yet remain simple enough for children to understand. Plain and simple, virtue is devotion to duty. It is wanting to do what you have to do. Better yet, it is the willingness to do what you know you should do. It is conforming your desires to what is required. It is aligning inclinations with obligations. It is adjusting your personal ethical system so that you can function as a social being should, with regard for and respect for others.

Things to Review and Remember From Chapter 2

1. Conceptually, virtue begins as a choice, and expresses both inner attitudes (being), and outward actions (doing). It is good character expressed in good conduct.

2. Virtue has two essential elements: duty and desire. It involves conforming what you want to do (desire) with what you have to do (duty).

3. A virtuous person has developed a strong sense of what ought to be done (obligation) and a deep yearning to do it (inclination).

4. The conscience functions as a guide for what people do (ethics). Social mores present an arena for experimentation (morals). The context of social morals provides feedback for people to adjust their personal ethical systems. Societal obligations regulate personal inclinations.

5. In your classroom, virtuous students are those who know they are there to learn. They have committed themselves to work hard at it. And they enjoy themselves while they are doing so.

3

How to Make Virtue Operational

Mesquite trees get their start from beans, which seem to take hold better if they pass through cows. Immediately, they send down a long taproot that's very hard to grub out if you don't like them taking over your pasture. Shortly, they sprout a bunch of scraggly branches covered with thorns, which cows avoid. They grow for a number of years and then produce those long, hard, string beans from which they start. Last, they grow quite large and produce hardly any beans or leaves. Texans then chop them down for barbecue. That's their progression, the way they operate, how they function.

Now that you have a concept of virtue in your mind, I have to get a little bit technical on you. Yeah, I hate it too. But we have to move from an abstract concept to reality somehow. The most practical step is to make the concept functional, or operational, for you to use in your classroom. Otherwise, the time you gave to the last chapter will be wasted. To operationalize the concept, we need to chart the progression of virtue from its earliest expression to its most elevated. In other words, recognizing what virtue looks like in your students, from its lowest level to its highest, makes the concept work for you.

Domains of Learning

Because our conceptualization of virtue is based on volition and involves a student's attitudes, it's better to work within the framework of the affective domain instead of the cognitive domain. What did I just say? You probably hate hearing definitions as much as I hate offering explanations. But this won't last long. So, hold on, don't jump to the next chapter. It's going to get better, I promise, but not for a few moments.

Cognitive. Affective. Psychomotor. Good learning involves all three domains simultaneously. But it's very difficult to coordinate these together in a meaningful way. Educators usually keep them separated so they are more manageable. So much of what you and your students do in the classroom is cognitive; head stuff—thinking, reflecting, considering, speculating—mental activity, that kind of thing. It's a primary part of the curriculum. But, interestingly enough, it can be done almost to the exclusion of the other two domains.

Psychomotor. Tongue in cheek, this is what students are supposed to save for physical education or do on the ball field. It's physical activity. Yes, it incorporates thinking. Yes, it involves choosing. Yes, it includes feelings. But it is hands-on involvement, so to speak. The arts and crafts and shop classes do this. It's a regular, though secondary, or adjacent, part of the curriculum for most educators. For many students, it is the only thing that keeps them in school.

Affective. So little of what is done by design in the classroom is affective. The affective domain concerns heart matter—intentions, influences, attitudes, feelings, conscience, volition, that sort of thing. Until recently, it has been the forgotten element in the curriculum. This is the domain in which we have conceptualized virtue. To avoid reinventing the wheel, I decided to build on the well-known taxonomy of educators Krathwohl, Bloom, and Masia (1964), which is extremely well-suited for this purpose.

Taxonomy of the Affective Domain

The success of Benjamin Bloom's (1956) Taxonomy of the Cognitive Domain prompted the development of a similar framework for the affective domain (Krathwohl, Bloom, & Masia, 1964). Their desire was to measure educational objectives both in terms of behavior and in relation to a broad classification system. Such a framework provides "a convenient system for describing and ordering test items, examination techniques, and evaluation instruments" (p. 5). And Purcell (1968) found that the abbreviated approach of using the continuum of an established taxonomy for ordering test items was as satisfactory as the item-pool approach. So I took advantage of Krathwohl, Bloom, and Masia's work and followed Purcell's advice.

Krathwohl, Bloom, and Masia's (1964) objectives for the affective domain emphasized more than mere feelings and emotions. Their focus was on the entire range of affective behavior, which varied "from simple attention to selected phenomena to complex but internally consistent qualities of character and conscience" (p. 7). The cohesive feature of their continuum is the process of internalization, which they distinguish from socialization. They see socialization referring to "the acceptance of the contemporary value pattern of the society," whereas they see internalization "referring to the process through which values, attitudes, etc., in general are acquired" (p. 30). They describe the process of internalization in the following manner:

> As internalization progresses, the learner comes to attend to phenomena, to respond to them, to value them, and to conceptualize them. He [or she] organizes his [or her] values in a value complex which comes to characterize his [or her] way of life. (p. 44)

This brief description of the levels of the Taxonomy reveals an internal structure that continually modifies behavior, from openness to examine matters of value all the way to embodiment of a worldview. Not only that, Krathwohl, Bloom, and Masia (1964) maintained that "the stages of the affective domain are seen as consistent with an empirically and theoretically based point of view on conscience" (p. 44). In addition, they specifically designed the Taxonomy in broad enough terms to include any philosophic or cultural orientation. These features make the *Taxonomy* particularly pertinent for my purposes and yours.

Substantiating My Approach

I have used the rationale and continuum of the Taxonomy to develop and order items on a questionnaire for measuring virtue, which you will see in the next chapter (Yawn—stay with me). Larry Mikulecky (1976) substantiated the hierarchical structure of the levels of Krathwohl, Bloom, and Masia's (1964) Taxonomy through statistical analysis (blink-blink, boring—don't fade out yet). Mikulecky included every level of the Taxonomy and, through item analysis, demonstrated that each item score correlated at a level of .60 or higher with the total score of items reflecting the Taxonomy stage appropriate to each item (Hmmm. Not bad numbers). He also tested the Taxonomy's hierarchy using Kaiser's scaling of Guttman's Simplex, checking the goodness-of-fit, and reported significant findings of .80 and above (pretty impressive!). These solid findings were deemed sufficient to warrant the use of the Taxonomy for operationalizing virtue in the affective domain. Following this path worked (whew! glad that's over with).

Next, you will find an abbreviated adaptation of Krathwohl, Bloom, and Masia's (1964) Taxonomy of the Affective Domain. The levels in the Taxonomy are organized around the process of internalization, which Gress & Purpel (1988) described as "the inner growth that occurs as the individual becomes aware of and then adopts the attitudes, principles, codes, and sanctions that become a part of him [or her] in forming value judgments and in guiding his [or her] conduct." (pp. 268-269) This taxonomy forms the backdrop for my taxonomy of virtue, which makes my concept of virtue functional or useful in a practical sense.

Taxonomy of the Affective Domain

As mentioned earlier, this taxonomy is a careful, though abbreviated, adaptation of Krathwohl, Bloom, and Masia's (1964) taxonomy derived from *A Taxonomy of Educational Objectives: Handbook II, The Affective Domain,* and is taken from James R. Gress and David E. Purpel: *Curriculum: An Introduction to the Field,* copyright 1988 by McCutchan Publishing Corporation, Berkeley, CA 94702. Permission granted by the publisher.

1.0 **Receiving:** Here, the concern is that the individual be sensitized to the existence of certain phenomena and stimuli—that is, that he [or she] be willing to receive or to attend to them.

    1.1 Awareness: Unlike knowledge, here the concern is not so much with a memory of, or ability to recall, an item or fact as it is. Given an appropriate opportunity, the individual will merely be conscious of something. He [or she] will take into account a situation, phenomenon, object, or state of affairs.

1.2 Willingness to receive: Here, the concern is with the willingness to tolerate a given stimulus, not to avoid it. Like awareness, it involves neutrality or suspended judgment toward the stimulus.

1.3 Controlled or selected attention: At a somewhat higher level, the concern is with differentiation of a given stimulus or aspects of a stimulus, perceived as clearly marked off from adjacent impressions.

2.0 **Responding:** At this level, the concern is with responses that go beyond merely attending to the phenomenon. It involves doing something with or about the phenomena beyond merely perceiving it.

2.1 Acquiescence in responding: This behavior might be best described by the word *obedience* or *compliance*. There is a passiveness so far as the initiation of the behavior is concerned. There is more the element of reaction to a suggestion and less of the implication of resistance or yielding unwillingly.

2.2 Willingness to respond: This level involves the capacity of voluntary activity. The element of resistance is replaced with consent.

2.3 Satisfaction in response: Here, satisfaction accompanies consent. The behavior is accompanied by an emotional response, generally of pleasure, zest, or enjoyment. [Krathwohl et al. had trouble placing this category, even questioning its inclusion.]

3.0 **Valuing:** Behavior at this level is sufficiently consistent and stable to have taken on the characteristics of a belief or an attitude.

3.1 Acceptance of a value: At this level, the concern is with ascribing worth to a phenomenon, behavior, object, etc. A person is sufficiently consistent in their response to something that others can identify the value and is sufficiently committed that he [or she] is willing to be identified with it.

3.2 Preference for a value: Behavior at this level implies not just the acceptance of a value to the point of being willing to be identified with it, but the individual is sufficiently committed to the value to pursue it, to seek it out, to want it.

3.3 Commitment: This level involves a high degree of certainty. The ideas of *conviction* and *certainty* help convey further the level of behavior intended.

4.0 **Organization:** With successive internalization of values, situations arise for which more than one value is relevant. Thus, the necessity arises for (a) the organization of the values into a system, (b) the determination of the interrelationships among them, and (c) the establishment of the dominant and pervasive ones. This category is intended as the proper classification for objectives that describe the beginnings of the building of a value system.

4.1 Conceptualization of a Value: At this level, the individual sees how the value relates to those that he already holds or to new ones that he is coming to hold.

4.2 Organization of a Value System: Here, the individual brings together a complex of values, possibly disparate values, into an ordered relationship with one another. Ideally, the ordered relationship will be one that is harmonious and internally consistent.

5.0 Characterization by a Value or Value Concept: At this level of internalization, the values already have a place in the individual's value hierarchy, are organized into some kind of internally consistent system, have controlled the behavior of the individual for a sufficient time that he [or she] has adapted to behaving this way, and an evocation of the behavior no longer arouses emotion or affect except when the individual is threatened or challenged.

5.1 Generalized Set: The generalized set is that which gives an internal consistency to the system of attitudes and values at any particular moment. It is selective responding at a very high level. It is a predisposition to act in a certain way. It is a basic orientation that enables the individual to reduce and order the complex world about him or her and to act consistently and effectively in it.

5.2 Characterization: At this level, the emphasis is on internal consistency of attitudes, behaviors, beliefs, or ideas. (pp. 268-272)

Now that you have had a chance to study the Taxonomy of the Affective Domain, compare it to the following Taxonomy of Virtue, which I patterned after it. Afterwards, I will illustrate it, part by part, from examples drawn from an educational setting. This should make the concept of virtue workable for you. In other words, you should then not only be able to play with it in your mind, you should be able to see how it operates in your classroom and begin to start identifying the development of virtue in your students lives.

Taxonomy of Virtue

1.0 Examining

1.1 Is Aware: At this level, students will entertain thoughts of obligation.

1.2 Tolerates: At this level, students will receive instruction about what they should do.

1.3 Attends: At this level, students will distinguish what is expected of them from what is not.

2.0 Experimenting

2.1 Obeys: At this level, students will comply with what is required of them.

2.2 Participates: At this level, students will actively participate in what is productive and beneficial.

2.3 Enjoys: At this level, students will enjoy doing what they know they should do.

3.0 Establishing

3.1 Accepts: At this level, students will accept what they should do as right.

3.2 Prefers: At this level, students will prefer to do as they should.

3.3 Commits: At this level, students will commit themselves to do what is good.

4.0 Evaluating

4.1 Identifies: At this level, students will clearly distinguish between good, better, and best.

4.2 Correlates: At this level, students will attach degrees of importance to what they do.

4.3 Ranks: At this level, students will differentiate between what is good, better, and best and prioritize them.

5.0 Embodying

5.1 Conforms: At this level, students will conform their lives to what is required of them.

5.2 Regulates: At this level, students will regulate their lives by their value systems.

5.3 Revises: At this level, students will remain open to make revisions so that their lifestyles more closely conform to the way they look at life.

Classroom Examples of the Levels of Virtue

Okay, you've made it through the tough part of this chapter. The rest should be fun. We are now going to examine the levels of virtue through classroom examples. The early part of our virtue taxonomy will have long been formed in the lives of many of your students by the time you have them in class. You generally won't see it. It will have begun at home, for many, before they ever started their formal education. This is as it should be. But for the sake of example, let's trace the levels of the taxonomy of students in their teenage years. That way, as you have occasion to refer to this discussion, it will be with examples to which you can relate.

Level One: Examining Virtue

1.1 Is Aware: At this level, students will entertain thoughts of obligation.

Jose is a fighter. A scrapper. Only those who do not know him mess with him. He is thin and wiry and not very tall. But he is fast, and he is fierce. He grew up on the streets, and with him, it was "Take care of number one, first. Nothing else matters." For Jose, it was a matter of survival. School never held any meaning for him.

He tolerates it now because everyone else does, and he doesn't know any better yet. Besides, it gives him contacts.

He began dealing drugs in junior high. He never did them himself. His brothers told him that those who did drugs were stupid. Jose is a very intelligent young man, but he has no scruples. He would knife someone without a second thought. Knives are quick and quiet and suit his abilities. He can smile, get close, cut quickly, and vanish before anyone knows what happened. And Jose is in your class.

He does not look vicious to you. You look at him and he smiles. But you realize that you never know what he is thinking. He does not cause trouble, but you notice he never does his homework, either. Yet a lot of kids in your school do not. When you test his virtue, you are surprised that he has none. You would not have guessed it. He has fooled a lot of people. But he has no sense of obligation to anyone.

You decide to befriend him. You see him in the hallway and call him by name. The next day, you give an assignment to be done in class. You stop at his desk and help him. After awhile, you pat him on the back. He seems troubled by your friendliness, even a little suspicious, but he obviously enjoys the attention. He is questioning inside, for the first time in his life, if he should really try in school. He is at level 1.1. He is entertaining thoughts of obligation to you. Such thoughts seem very strange to him.

1.2   Tolerates: At this level, students will receive instruction about what they should do.

You sense Jose's struggle. You give him space for a week or so. One day, as you lecture, you say in a friendly way, "Isn't that right, Jose?" Uncharacteristically, Jose answers in a belligerent way. You don't react. You are tempted to think your efforts for him are futile. But after class, you approach him and ask, "Everything OK?" He snarls "Yeah, I gotta get outta here. See ya." You quickly respond, "Hold on a minute. Can we talk?" He shrugs, "I guess so."

He sits in a chair by your desk, looking down, as you state: "Something's wrong. What is it?" He looks up defiantly, "What do you care? I'm not sure I even like you anyway." Honestly, you say, "I care about all my students. That's why I teach, but I care especially for those who struggle. Tell me what's troubling you." Jose is silent for what seems like a long time. You wait. Finally, he looks up and says, "I don't know. I usually don't think about it."

You can tell he doesn't know how to put into words what is happening in his life, so you say, "A young man your age should be thinking about the things that trouble him, shouldn't he?" He ponders your point—seriously considering it—and replies, "Yeah, I probably should." You sense you have taken him about as far as he is willing to go, so you conclude, "Good, then think about it. Tomorrow we'll talk again, OK?" He forces half a smile and agrees, "OK," glad to leave without having to say much. He is at level 1.2. He is willing to receive instruction about what he should do.

1.3   Attends: At this level, students will become aware of what is expected of them.

The next day, after class, Jose is the first one out the door. He avoids you like the plague. You just smile whenever you see him and give him more space. A couple of weeks pass, and he finally stays after class. He flops in the chair next to your desk and says, "I've been thinking about it." You coyly ask "What?" and smile. He returns your smile and says, "What's troubling me?" You respond, "OK, what?"

He goes on to tell you he's dealing drugs, and sometimes, people get hurt. You think for a minute and say, "Do you know what you need to do about it?" He thinks for a long minute and says with a question, "Give it up?" You say, "Of course. And . . . " He hesitates and says, "Stay away from my brothers?" You say, "Good thinking, Jose. You have some difficult decisions to make. And it will be even harder to carry them out. But you won't be troubled inside if you do." He is at level 1.3. He is becoming aware of the implications of what he should do.

The school year is almost over, and you wish you could have accomplished more with your students, as always. But then you look into Jose's eyes, and you nod to the sparkle you see there. He smiles, and you say to yourself, "Jose is examining the issues of virtue right now in his life. Whatever else happens, for this much, I'm grateful." It has been a good year after all.

Level Two: Experimenting With Virtue

2.1   Obeys: At this level, students will comply with what is required of them.

After examining the issues of virtue, students may begin experimenting with them. Here's one way Level Two looks when you see it lived out. Cindy had been yelled at all her life. Her mother never disciplined her, she just exploded whenever Cindy didn't live up to her expectations, which was more often than not. She idolized her father, who never yelled at anyone and who treated her like a princess. In fact, that was his nickname for her.

At the beginning of Cindy's junior year in high school, her father died suddenly of a heart attack. Her mother became very morose and quite difficult to live with. To this point in her life, Cindy had no value system of her own. It had been, without thinking, her father's. Although she would not reexamine her father's values, now that he was gone, she began to experiment with them. Her mother's tirades drove her back to the beginning of Level Two. She used to sit in the front row of your class and participate. Now, she sits quietly in the back, watching.

You, of course, know little of what is taking place inside Cindy. But you have observed a change in her attitude and also noticed her move to the rear of the room. You attempt to draw her back into the class by asking her opinion. She does not refuse, but there is a long silence before she responds. Then, she answers very slowly and quietly. She acts half numb to what is going on around her and seems like she is in a fog. You wonder if she has started using drugs. Other students in the class glance at her quizzically. She is at Level 2.1. She complies with what she should do, but that is all.

*2.2   Participates: At this level, students will actively participate in what is
        productive and beneficial.*

Over the next couple of months, Cindy fades in and out. Sometimes, she seems attentive—other times, miles away. After class one day, you tease her, "Earth to

Cindy, Earth to Cindy. Come in, Cindy. Cindy, are you there?" She half smiles and walks past you out of the classroom. You sigh and wonder, "What is it I can do to get through to her?" You decide to have a gathering in your home on Friday after Thanksgiving. You invite a number of students in whom you have a special interest. Some students don't come, but Cindy does and so do a few others. You play some games and then have some pumpkin pie and vanilla ice cream.

As the conversation lags, you suggest that each person share with the rest something for which they are particularly grateful and why. You begin by relating something about each student for which you are thankful. The rest of the students readily respond. One says she appreciates how understanding her boyfriend is. Another says how grateful he is that you are an easy grader. You assign him an "F" for trying to influence the teacher, and everyone laughs. Then it's Cindy's turn. She quietly says, "I'm thankful for my father." And she immediately bursts into tears and heart-wrenching sobs.

You quickly offer more pie and ice cream to whoever wants to go into the kitchen and get some. All leave except you and Cindy. You sit next to Cindy and ask, "Tell me what's bothering you." She pours out her heart to you. You comfort her, and after a few minutes, you rejoin the group in the kitchen and resume the festivities. Monday, when you ask a question in class, Cindy is among those who raise their hands and volunteer to answer. She answers incorrectly, but she is actively involved once again. She is at Level 2.2. She is actively participating in what is expected of her.

2.3   Enjoys: At this level, students will enjoy doing what they know they should do.

Cindy reports, after Christmas break, that things are better at home. Her mother is still hard to live with, but a man named Preston has begun calling on her mother, and she goes out with him quite often, which gives Cindy some relief. She is doing her homework regularly and begins to stay after class to talk with you about it. You comment that she is doing very well and would make a good teacher some day. She says, "I'm beginning to really enjoy your class." She is at Level 2.3. She is enjoying doing what is required of her.

Level Three: Establishing Virtue

3.1   Accepts: At this level, students will accept what they should do as right.

Greg is a good boy from a good home. At first, you think he is the ideal student. He is cheerful, responsive, and cooperative, and he has a good learning attitude. He is pretty consistent from day to day in doing his assignments and differs from many of your students in this respect, but you notice he is somewhat noncommittal. When others in the class goof off, he becomes amused and will laugh with them. And although he does not join in, he does not resist either, and, furthermore, does not seem bothered by it. You determine he has not quite established virtue in his life.

You are troubled by Greg, not because he is a bad boy but because you want to see him take a stand for what is right, good, and appropriate. So you determine that the next time there is some commotion in class, you will look first at Greg to study his reaction. You will not accuse him or say anything to him, but you will let him know that you are curious about his response to what is wrong.

The next day, as you are writing an assignment on the board with your back to the class, someone zings a pencil past your ear. Some in the class smirk, others laugh, but you turn and look directly at Greg. He is startled. He stops laughing immediately, realizing that his laughter implicates him with the others. He approaches you after class to tell you he had nothing to do with the pencil incident. You tell him, "I know." But say nothing more. He walks away puzzled.

Over the course of a few weeks, you continue observing Greg after the same fashion. You watch his laughter change to a smirk, and then a slight frown. As he changes, you no longer look at him as long, nor even first. Inside, you smile. You know that with others, this would not have been effective, but Greg . . . he's yours. You have helped him realize what was happening inside. He is standing with you now. He is at level 3.1. He accepts what he should do because it is right.

3.2   Prefers: At this level, students will prefer to do as they should.

But the year is far from over for you and Greg, and now, you yearn for him. You consider his growth. You want him to actively prefer what is right and pursue it. You are not content to let him coast. So, at lunch hour one day, he walks into the library. You are there researching a lesson plan. You look up as he passes. You smile and hush a "Hello, Greg" to him. He smiles and nods as he meanders past.

You ponder over some books that would fit Greg's situation. He is taken aback a little when you approach him, but his ready smile encourages you to make the offer to him. "Greg, are you interested in earning a little extra credit in my class?" He considers your question for a moment and replies, "Sure." You continue probing him, "It will take some work. You don't have to do it. You are doing well enough right now to get a "B" in my class, but I want the best for you."

Sensing that you are more serious than he is, he reflects for a moment, and says, "OK." You say, "Great! Research this question: 'What is the value of taking initiative?' Are you still interested?" Intrigued, he says "Sure." You say, "Come on, I'll show you how to get some resources." He is at level 3.2. He is beginning to prefer to do as he should.

3.3   Commits: At this level, students will commit themselves to do what is good.

It has been 2 weeks since you gave the extra credit assignment to Greg. You stop him one day and ask, "How's the paper coming, Greg?" He looks somewhat discouraged, so you inquire, "Having trouble with it?" He says, "Well, not trouble with the topic, trouble with the work. From my study, I've learned how to get going, but I get tired of it before very long."

You suggest, "Greg, let's set a date to turn it in, and then you make that a commitment. Do you understand what it means to willingly make a commitment? It's different than going along with a commitment that someone else has made for you, like just being here in school. It means that your honor is at stake. It means that you consider yourself bound by your word to do what you say. It means that others depend on you because you have stated your intentions. Are you willing to stake your reputation and make a commitment?" Rising to the challenge, Greg says, "I sure am." You fix a date with him, and he turns in a very fine paper . . . on time. He is at level 3.3. He has committed himself to do as he should.

Other students notice the special attention you are showing to Greg. Some complain to their parents, but you explain that you are willing to help them if they are willing to work hard. You try to reach every student and explain that each student is at a different place, that you are trying to discover where each is and offer them the chance to go further if they are interested.

Level Four: Evaluating Virtue

4.1   Identifies: At this level, students will clearly distinguish right from wrong.

You will not find many teenage students beyond Level 3 but probably more than you think will be within Level 4. Freeda is one. She's a very attractive black girl and very vocal. And she has an incredible sense of justice. She is a champion in search of a cause. You find it easy to admire her, and you are filled with hope for what she will become. She is flowering early in life, and it is a delight to watch her unfold.

Freeda is on the Student Council. You have been appointed to meet with this group of students after school. They have a complaint: not with you, you discover, but with the principal, your friend. It seems they want to have political clubs on campus and hold debates. The principal has had a long-standing rule against forming political organizations at the school. Freeda is incensed. In her heart, she knows that it would be good to develop positions and exchange ideas about politics. You sense her frustration but perceive that her zeal is clouding the issues for her and for others.

It is difficult for the Council, under Freeda's influence, to see any reason the principal should be so narrowly focused. She says, "He has no right and no reason to deny us this privilege." You listen to Freeda's articulate presentation of the advantages of her idea and have to admit there is much merit in what she says. The Council erupts in applause for Freeda as she finishes her remarks. But you know she needs to be able to discern between what seems right because of intense desire and what is really right.

You calm them and explain that their principal was in college when there was much political unrest and saw the turmoil it brought to the study atmosphere. She counters, "But there is no political unrest now!" You say, "Good point, but he does have reason, and as principal, he does have the right." There is a long pause. The room is quiet, so you continue. "And if you are going to accomplish anything, you would do well to consider both of those things along with your idea."

You follow up: "Students, the intensity you feel for something good does not automatically make it right to do nor does it make it appropriate at this time." Freeda rejoins, "But it does not necessarily make it wrong either." You concur. "I agree, but there might be more to consider than the depth of your desire." You enjoin the Council to put themselves in the principal's position to see if they can gain insight into the authority he has to make such decisions and his reason for doing so. The meeting is adjourned until the following week.

The students discuss it throughout the week. You can tell because they quit talking and smile when you walk past them. But you are glad they are thinking and interacting. Thursday comes, the Council meets. Freeda opens by saying, "We agree that the principal has the authority to make a decision in the best interests of the school, and he has a reason that seems good to him. He is right to do what he is doing, but we see no reason not to present arguments in favor of our position and to dialog with him about it."

You are thrilled, and you tell them so: "It is really wonderful to have a good idea and the intense desire to accomplish it. But it is noble to take into consideration those around you as you do it. The difference between your attitude this week and last is that of respect and consideration, and that gives you the right to make an appeal and the inner ability to make it effectively." Freeda says, "Thank you for showing us how to do the right thing in the right way." She is at level 4.1. She clearly distinguishes right from wrong, even when confronted with conflicting positions.

4.2   Correlates: At this level, students will attach degrees of importance to what they do.

After discussing how to approach the principal with their requests instead of making demands, the Council is satisfied, and the meeting is adjourned. You make arrangements for the principal to meet with the Council the following week. There is a lot of excitement among the students through the week in anticipation of this meeting. When they gather in his office, the students are stunned to discover how gracious and understanding their principal is. He thoughtfully considers their requests, their appeals, and their attitudes. Then changes his policy. They walk away amazed and humbled. Freeda sums it up for the group as they leave, "It sure would have been different had we gone in there angry."

Freeda concludes in her heart, *It was clearly more important to consider this man, his responsibilities, and his reputation than our cause. Our cause was good, but to present it properly was more important. And our attitudes at first were so bad. How could I have been so blind? Had we continued angry and arrogant, we could have ruined the effectiveness of this wonderful man at school, and our proposal would probably have been rejected. He would have seen our bad attitudes and concluded that we would stir up trouble. And he would have been right.* Freeda is at level 4.2. She is properly attaching degrees of importance to what she is doing.

4.3   Ranks: At this level, students will differentiate between what is good, better, and best and prioritize them.

At the next meeting, Freeda insightfully says, "We saw how crucial it was for us to consider what was most important. I think it would be good for us, now that we have permission, to list all the things that need to be done, consider who they affect, and then list them according to what is best and what is most important." She looks at you for confirmation. You add, "Freeda, that is a very thoughtful thing to do. You're right." She is at level 4.3. She is considering the distinctions between good, better, and best in light of how they affect others.

Level Five: Embodying Virtue

5.1   Conforms: At this level, students will conform their lives to what is required of them.

Michael is a genuinely ugly young man. His head is large and unevenly shaped. His wizened body seems dwarfed by it. His face is pockmarked and full of acne. His skin is very oily and so uneven that he cannot effectively shave. His hair is a dull black, wild and unruly. You feel an inner aversion toward him from the moment you see him and quickly realize that people probably find it easy to dislike Michael. You determine you are not going to be one of them.

While talking with other teachers in the faculty lounge, you discover that Michael is a computer genius, a prodigy. He has incredible programming skills. You also find out that he is a straight "A" student, has been as far back as anyone can remember. He does not look like, nor act like, an intelligent person, though he is strangely quiet and self-assured. He does not communicate very much, but his quick eyes seem to miss nothing.

Michael is in your class. He does not seem preoccupied with trying to please you, like so many other top students do. No one sits around him, but he does not seem bothered by it. There seem to be no traces of self-pity. If he was ever bitter, it doesn't show now. He rarely volunteers information but, when asked, is encyclopedic in his knowledge. He is not particularly emotional, but you do notice that he smiles with his eyes.

The more you get to know him, the more you find how remarkable a person he is. You are intrigued by him. In spite of his physical immaturity, he is wise beyond his years. You wonder what it is that you, as a teacher, have to offer him. He is already at 5.1, at least. He readily conforms his life to what is required.

5.2   Regulates: At this level, students will regulate their lives by their value system.

Michael seems neither confined nor out of control in any area of his life. You determine to get to know him better. Discipline and self-control seem second nature to him. Unlike so many other teenagers, he is not upset with himself, others, or even his circumstances. For him, right is not something to find and do, it is living. You decide to ask him if you are perceiving him properly and if so, what has made the difference in his life.

At lunch, you see him sitting on the grass, back against a tree, reading. You ask if he would like to go for a walk and talk with you. He readily complies. You open what turns out to be a most incredible conversation by saying, "You are always alone. Does that bother you?" He responds simply, "No, not really." You follow up by probing, "Do you like people?" "Yes, of course, but people aren't really drawn to me, for obvious reasons," he answers, his eyes smiling.

You inquire, "Do people treat you that badly?" He responds, "Yes, they often taunt and tease and sometimes become very mean." You ask, "Why aren't you bitter after such ridicule and rejection?" He thinks for a moment and then says, "I find that suffering in silence helps my outlook on life." You are awestruck by this strange perspective. As you ponder what he has just said, he goes on to explain. "Instead of becoming introspective and feeling sorry for myself, I study those around me." He continues, "This kind of broadens my perspective." He tells you that his loneliness encourages him to be what he should be. He is not pressured to conform by those around him. And he adds that the pain he feels helps him not to be selfish. Instead, he has learned to consider what others need.

You are stunned by the simple truth of what he is saying. He concludes by suggesting that pure motives give him a calm confidence that helps him accept rejection. You ask him, "Where did you learn this?" He shrugs his answer. "By remaining silent when I hurt and thinking about things instead of complaining." He is demonstrating level 5.2. He regulates his life by his value system rather than external pressures or influences.

5.3   Revises: At this level, students will remain open to make revisions so that their lifestyles more closely conform to the way they look at life.

You are silently thinking as you walk, "What a wonderful person; ugliness has made him a very attractive young man." You wish he were more willing to share with fellow students, that he would develop a willingness to reach out and make friends. You say, "It is really good to see how you have turned pain into strength of character. But it seems inconsistent to me that, although you obviously think of helping others, you do not actively reach out and make friends, especially with the inner confidence you possess."

He ponders your words as you continue strolling past the cafeteria. You begin to think he was not listening to you, but then he says belatedly, "You're right, thank you. I'll do it." He is at level 5.3. He is open to make revisions so that his lifestyle more closely conforms to the way he looks at life. He is remarkably mature for his years. You are inwardly relieved that you initially decided not to misjudge him by his appearance. What a privilege to get to know such a fine young man!

You ask him what he knows about virtue. He says "Not much." You say, "Oh, yes you do. You just don't know you do." Then you get an idea. "I hear you can write computer programs." He says, "A little." You pose a question. "How about if we develop some software to help students face situations that require them to make good choices." He says, "That's a great idea!"

Several months later, a group of students gathers around Michael in the computer lab. You watch his smiling eyes while he explains how his new computer game works. He has reached out to others and now has a number of genuine friends. He smiles toward you, telling them that you gave him the idea for the game they are playing. You tell them you enjoyed every minute of it.

Summary

The concept of virtue is now more than just an abstraction. It has become operational for you. You now have the ability to use it in your classroom to identify where your students are. With a little practice and with the help of the Loehrer Virtue Assessment Questionnaire (LVAQ), you will be able to diagnose the virtue structure of many of your students. But keep in mind that rarely are the levels pure and fixed in teenagers. They are frequently not straightforward. There are some good reasons for this.

Virtue structures in people are received (absorbed through exposure) from parents or guardians. Keep in mind, the structures they receive may not be complete or without problems. Then, they are modified through interaction with society: sometimes through persuasion, sometimes through coercion, sometimes through intimidation. Then, when teenagers come to the point of making this adopted, modified structure their own, they alter it. They may only modify it a little bit, or they may overhaul the whole thing, for better or worse. They may jump backward and start a level over. They may throw some part out. Or they may keep an incomplete or weakened structure, just as they received it, considering it normal.

But wherever they are, at least now you have a framework for thinking about these things. And you have the capacity to begin analyzing your students with respect to the virtue structures that direct their lives. Hopefully, you have seen the importance of considering the affective domain in teaching. The levels of virtue were derived from an educational taxonomy in use for over 30 years. These levels move from entertaining thoughts of obligation to a willingness to sacrifice in the service of others. It would prove helpful for you to cogitate for a moment about where some of your students might fall along this continuum.

Things to Review and
Remember From Chapter 3

1. The concept of virtue becomes usable in the classroom when operationalized in the affective domain. Affect involves things such as feelings, influences, intentions, choices, attitudes, and conscience.

2. Krathwohl, Bloom, and Masia's (1964) Taxonomy of the Affective Domain forms the basis for establishing five progressive levels of virtue.

3. Level One: Examining—involves entertaining thoughts of obligation, a willingness to receive instruction about what should be done, and an awareness of the implications of what is expected.

4. Level Two: Experimenting—focuses on compliance with what is required, actively participating in what is productive and beneficial, and enjoying doing what should be done.

5. Level Three: Establishing—accepts what should be done as right, prefers doing what is good, and commits to doing what is appropriate.

6. Level Four: Evaluation—includes clearly distinguishing right from wrong; attaching degrees of importance to what is good; differentiating between what is good, better, and best; and properly prioritizing these things.

7. Level Five: Embodying—consists of continually conforming personal desires to what is required, self-regulation by a well-balanced value system, and an openness to make revisions to more closely conform to a healthy worldview.

4

How to Measure Virtue

If you ask a Texan how the cow ate the grindstone, he or she will glibly tell you, "Slow and by degrees." Up to this point, you have formed a mental picture of what virtue is. You have also learned to identify the progression of virtue in your students, right? Now you need something to actually measure each student so that this identification process becomes more than just a hunch on your part, as you watch it happen, slow and by degrees.

Wouldn't it be great if you could just measure their virtue like measuring their height? You know, just line them up against a wall and say, "Step right up. Hmm. Five feet, four and a half inches. Mark that down. Next." You can, with the questionnaire in this manual, and in about the same amount of time. It only takes about 10 minutes to administer the test! Let's take a look at how the test was built so that it will mean something to you when you begin to use it.

Construction of the Questionnaire

I know that as a teacher, you are familiar with testing and instrumentation. To create the LVAQ (pronounced *el-vak* and shown in Form 4.1), statements were designed to reflect the levels of the Taxonomy of Virtue introduced in the previous chapter. Then, numbers were assigned to a response pattern so that your students' virtue structures could be measured. Enh! Sounds pretty boring I know, but the reason I had you study the taxonomies in the last chapter is that they give structure to the questionnaire. The response pattern part of the questionnaire allows you to give numbers to the answers of your students and thereby to actually measure their attitudes. And that is a pretty incredible thing, if you stop and think about it.

All your students have to do is just read a statement and then circle a response, such as *Strongly Disagree, Disagree, Uncertain, Agree, Strongly Agree*, only the response pattern is abbreviated. So they just circle one of the following after having read the statement: SD D ? A SA. To score the LVAQ, "SD" gets a 1, "D" gets a 2, "?" gets a 3, "A" gets a 4, "SA" gets a 5. If the question is stated negatively, the numbers are reversed: "SD" gets a 5, "D" gets a 4, and so on. Simple as pie. Slicker than a

Form 4.1 Loehrer Virtue Assessment Questionnaire[1]

Please fill in the following blanks: Name: (print clearly) _____

Gender: Male ____ Female ____   Race: (specify) _____

Age: 13 ____ 14 ____ 15 ____ 16 ____ 17 ____ 18 ____ 19 ____ Other (specify) _____

Grade: 7 ____ 8 ____ 9 ____ 10 ____ 11 ____ 12 ____ Other (specify) _____

Instructions: Your responses should honestly describe your personal experience. You are not expected to spend a great deal of time responding to these statements. Your first response is best. Please circle the letters that best indicate the extent of your agreement or disagreement with each of the following statements.

SD = Strongly Disagree; D = Disagree; ? = Uncertain; A = Agree; SA = Strongly Agree

1. I can remember "playing sick" to get out of something.	SD D ? A SA
2. I maintain my priorities so that I can do what is best.	SD D ? A SA
3. I often refuse to do what I know is right.	SD D ? A SA
4. I do what I should, even if friends reject me for it.	SD D ? A SA
5. I frequently insist on my own way, even if I sense I might be wrong.	SD D ? A SA
6. I have never intensely disliked anyone.	SD D ? A SA
7. I am fully committed to change whatever keeps me from doing what I should.	SD D ? A SA
8. I find it hard to really enjoy myself when doing daily chores.	SD D ? A SA
9. I am an example of wholehearted dedication to duty.	SD D ? A SA
10. I feel uneasy because I won't help when I know I should.	SD D ? A SA
11. I sometimes try to get even, rather than forgive and forget.	SD D ? A SA
12. I am consistently true to what is best.	SD D ? A SA
13. I resist establishing values in my life so I can be free to be who I am.	SD D ? A SA
14. I gladly respond without hesitation when something is required of me.	SD D ? A SA
15. I am tired of those in charge trying to show me a better way.	SD D ? A SA
16. I never resent being asked to return a favor.	SD D ? A SA
17. I am fully committed to do what I know I should.	SD D ? A SA
18. I have trouble telling right from wrong.	SD D ? A SA
19. I can easily distinguish between good, better, and best.	SD D ? A SA
20. I get angry when those in authority insist I do things their way.	SD D ? A SA
21. I sometimes feel resentful when I don't get my way.	SD D ? A SA
22. I openly defend what is right.	SD D ? A SA
23. I rebel when someone talks to me about doing what I should.	SD D ? A SA
24. I immediately confess and make it right whenever I do something wrong.	SD D ? A SA
25. I am afraid of what others might think if I do as I ought.	SD D ? A SA
26. I have almost never felt the urge to tell someone off.	SD D ? A SA

greased pig. A scoring form and scoring guidelines are provided in Resources C and D.

In constructing the LVAQ, I designed 20 virtue items, each containing both elements of Desire and Duty. Memory check. You haven't forgotten these essential elements from Chapter 2, have you? Here's a statement taken from the questionnaire: I often refuse to do what I know is right.

Notice first, the element of Duty: doing what is known to be right. Second, notice the element of Desire or in this case, the lack of it: refusal. Every item contains both of these elements. When students respond to one of these statements, they are answering a question that prompted the design of that statement. In other words, I had a question in my mind that I wanted them to answer. But because I couldn't just ask everyone that question in the same way and get comparable answers, I designed a statement that answers the question, letting them circle a response.

Why is it important to ask the question in the same way and get comparable answers? Well, statistically speaking, that sameness allows researchers to check the validity and reliability of the questionnaire for wide and dependable use and enables them to establish norms for interpreting your students' responses. If you want to make sure the test consistently measures what it is supposed to measure for this age group, these constraints help it happen.

Now, look again at the LVAQ statement. You can readily tell that this particular item is stated negatively. Instead of saying, "I often choose to do what I know is right," the statement is directed the other way: "I often refuse to do what I know is right." As your students read the questionnaire, the direction of the items will be switched from positive to negative so that they won't fall into a set way of responding, such as totally agreeing or disagreeing with every item. Also, the 10 lower-level statements are stated negatively to accommodate those who will score lower. And the 10 higher-level statements are worded positively to accommodate those who will score higher. And they are all mixed up to keep the students from detecting what is going on or from being distracted by any observable order.

The next thing I had to think about was the basis of orienting each statement. Remember our elements of Being and Doing? Ten items were designed to focus on Being, and 10 on Doing so that you could tell if students' attitudes were in keeping with their actions: their character with their conduct. In other words, you can compare the number of Being items answered virtuously with the number of Doing items that students answered virtuously. They should correspond quite closely. In fact, the testing done in the questionnaire's development revealed a correlation between Being and Doing items of .675, highly significant.

I used the Likert Scale approach (SD D ? A SA) for three reasons: It is particularly well-suited for measuring attitudes, it is relatively easy to construct, and reliability can often be achieved with fewer items. After spending so much time building the questionnaire, I honestly could no longer see the forest for all the trees. So I asked some colleagues to help refine what I had done.

Hey, this isn't hash, and it isn't hamburger helper. This is fine cuisine. The chefs have worked hard. They have a great deal of expertise. The recipes have been tried, tested, and refined to the point . . . well, they are simply magnifique! Let's look into the kitchen. I'll introduce them to you.

Panel Evaluation of the LVAQ

A preliminary form of the questionnaire was given to a panel to evaluate the orientation of the items and the theoretical structure of the instrument. The panel was selected from professionals known for their expertise in disciplines related to this study. Dr. Don A. Brown of Educational Diagnostics in Englewood, Colorado, was selected for expertise in educational research. Dr. John Carter of Rosemead School of Psychology, Biola University, was selected for expertise in the area of psychology. Dr. William Michael of the University of Southern California was selected for expertise in educational measurement. Dr. Robert Radcliffe of Western Conservative Baptist Seminary was selected for expertise in the area of philosophy and ethics. And Dr. Frederic Wilson of Wheaton College was selected for expertise in the area of moral education.

The primary purpose of the panel was to evaluate the LVAQ as it related to the theoretical and operational frameworks underlying the questionnaire. In other words, the panel members were to assess the content of the items and the framework behind them to determine if the questionnaire was consistent with the theory on which it was built. There were some 20 pages of recommendations provided from the panel's efforts, which were collated in preparation for the revision of the instrument. After fully considering the rating of the items by the panelists, their comments while taking the test, and their suggestions for improving it, the instrument was revised and pilot tested. It was then validated through field testing for use among junior and senior high public school children.

You're still leery? I don't blame you. Before I try a new restaurant, I want to hear from some people who have sampled from its menu, especially if there are exotic items on it and especially if I am going to take someone special there. In the same way, before you order an ice cream cone, you have to decide what flavor you want, right? Especially if someone is pushing something new. There may be 31 flavors, but before you select Hawaiian True Fru Fru you will probably want to sample it to make sure that it's going to be good. You're skeptical? You should be. You have to eat it. Here are some samples of our data.

Public High School Samples

Three samples were taken: the first, a sample of junior high summer school students from the Waco Independent School District, taken with the gracious permission of Mr. George Dupree. This was the pilot test. The second sample consisted of the entire student body of the Frost Independent School District (FISD), consisting of Grades 7 through 12, through the special assistance of Principal Gordon Lockett. This sample forms the heart of this study. A third sample was taken from the high school Physical Education classes of the Joshua Independent School District under the direction of their teacher, Mr. Jack Wilson. This sample was a follow-up study.

The results were convincing. Coefficient alpha reliability estimates were consistent and high (.78 and higher). Construct validity was established through item analysis and also a high correlation between the Being and Doing items (.675). Criterion validity was established by correlating student attitudes, behavior, and academic performance. These criteria were assessed by teachers, and in some cases, by detention and suspension records. Content validity was established through the work of the panel. And I am pleased to say we had good numbers in all of this. This means you can expect the questionnaire to perform well for use in your classroom. The Hawaiian True Fru Fru is not bad. Try it!

Now let's examine the LVAQ a little more closely. I have three purposes in doing this. First, so you will feel more confident when you use it and explain it to students, parents, other teachers, and administrators. Second, so you'll be prepared to interpret what you've measured, when it comes to that point. And third, so you can learn more fully about virtue: how it looks, how it works, how you can use it, how you can live it. I realize that with many tests, you just administer them, get the results, and go on. But I have a twofold task before me: to reintroduce virtue to our society and to help teachers in a technological society measure it. It's the "killing-two-birds-with-one-stone" approach. So, let's get out the microscope and put our good eye on it.

Please keep in mind that virtue is a dynamic construct. As such, it constantly changes with the myriad choices made each day. Yet the changes are not abrupt, and I have found that the structure remains stable enough for measurement to be meaningful. But bear in mind that the results of this test are not intended to be definitive or conclusive. Consequently, they do not provide proof for issuing a judgment. This is not a fear-prompted disclaimer. It's emphatically true! Do not hold your students' feet to the fire over your interpretation of the results. That is not the purpose of the test. It is a beginning point for evaluation and discussion with the student, his or her parents, and perhaps administrators. If by some remote chance you've been daydreaming, please go back and read this paragraph over again. I have to tell myself this repeatedly.

The LVAQ is built on the foundation of a volitional (choosing) concept of virtue and its five-level operational structure, which we discussed earlier. Recall that the concept of virtue is twofold, because choosing is seen as an expression of being and doing. And remember, the operational structure has five levels of virtue patterned after the Taxonomy of Virtue introduced in the last chapter.

The framework to follow includes five levels of progression, from examining to embodying, with questions progressing through each level. This framework will do two things for you. It will display how each item was developed and how it fits into the Taxonomy of Virtue. In this sense, the framework is didactic; it will teach you about virtue. But it will also indicate how a statement on the LVAQ provides an answer to a corresponding question in the framework, once a student responds to it. In that sense, it is diagnostic; it will enable you to assess virtue.

The following framework will list each item on the questionnaire, the question behind it, and comments explaining its construction and significance. I am intentionally following the same format for describing each item. It will seem somewhat repetitious to you as you initially read over it, but it will be helpful later as you use it for referencing a certain item. An analytic table also will follow, which is an abbreviated way of doing this same thing, but it will not have the item itself, the framework behind it, or comments explaining it. It will prove more useful after you become familiar with the framework.

I've kept a secret from you. This is a quick-scan, reference chapter. It's a look-it-over, get-familiar-so-you-can-refer-back-to-it chapter. Sorry; I didn't want you to know until now. It's hard to make this stuff entertaining, and if I had told you from the beginning, you would have jumped to the next chapter quicker than scat. But you can familiarize yourself with what follows and leave it for later reference. Wait! That only includes down through this framework. After that, you have to read carefully again. Is it a deal?

Developmental Framework of the LVAQ

Level 1: Examining

23. Openness: Is the student willing to think about what is required of him or her?

23. I rebel when someone talks to me about doing what I should.

Item 23 is negative in its direction, as are the first 10, to accommodate those who are in the process of establishing virtue. It is ranked 1st, or lowest, on an ascending scale of 20. Each virtue item contains elements of Duty and Desire. In this case, Desire, or lack of it, because the item is negative in direction, can be seen in "rebelling" and Duty, in "doing what should be done." This statement is doing based. It focuses on an action (rebelling) that is performed under specific circumstances (when someone talks to me). It is the first item on Level 1. The Examining Level includes a willingness to entertain thoughts, to receive instruction, and to become aware of the implications of duty. But here the focus is on openness, to begin to entertain thoughts of obligation to those in authority.

The struggles at this lowest level on the spectrum usually occur early in life, most likely during the "terrible two's." In these younger years, there is a mutual give-and-take between children and parents. Parents provide for and protect their children, who in turn do what they are told. If they don't, they are corrected or should be. Most children find out pretty early that crime does not pay and are usually quite willing to think about doing what is required of them. When high school students refuse to do as they are told, it usually means they are intentionally undoing what was once established. I said, "Usually." We know this is not always the case. Many juvenile delinquents establish rebellious attitudes very early in life and are never seriously challenged. Challenging the rebellious calls for considerable creativity. We want to win them, not alienate them further.

15. Tolerance: Is the student willing to trust those in a position to give direction to his or her life?

15. I am tired of those in charge trying to show me a better way.

Item 15 is negative in its direction to accommodate those who are in the process of examining virtue. It is ranked 2nd on an ascending scale of 20. Each virtue item contains elements of Duty and Desire. In this case, Desire, or lack of it, because the item is negative in direction, can be seen in "being tired" and Duty, in "being shown a better way." It is being biased. *I am tired* is a state of being. This item is second on Level 1. As such, it concerns a willingness to examine virtue for the purpose of considering what part it will play in life. The Examining Level includes a willingness to entertain thoughts, to receive instruction, and to become aware of the implications of duty. But here, the focus is on a certain amount of tolerance or the willingness of students to trust their teacher to explain what is expected of them.

Willingness to trust those in charge at this lower level is almost second nature to children because of the parent-child arrangement. Small children naturally trust those in a position to give them direction, unless they have been hurt. Trust is something they have to unlearn, which means that adults, parents for the most part, must give them reason to unlearn it by betraying that trust. It is grievous to think about how this happens. Child abuse, neglect, and molestation are obvious, even glaring, ways. But the same results can happen by playing favorites, rejecting personality differences, performance-based acceptance, and shame-based discipline. Think about it.

20. Submission: *Will the student allow someone who should to give direction to his or her life?*

20. I get angry when those in authority insist I do things their way.

Item 20 is negative in its direction to accommodate those who are still in the process of examining virtue. It is ranked 3rd on an ascending scale of 20. Each virtue item contains elements of Duty and Desire. In this case, Desire, or lack of it, because the item is negative in direction, can be seen in "getting angry" and Duty, in "those in authority insisting on their way." It is doing based. *Getting angry when . . .* is a specific activity, something that is done in a specific situation. Item 20 is the third item on Level 1. As such, it concerns a student's willingness to examine virtue so as to consider what part virtue will play in his or her life. The Examining Level includes a willingness to entertain thoughts, to receive instruction, and to become aware of the implications of duty. But here, the focus is on submission. This implies that the individual will be willing to yield to directions given by an authority figure, such as you.

The implication here is that those in authority have the right to insist that things be done the way they ask. In the military, they say, "Rank has its privileges." This means that there are certain rights that accompany responsibility. It is the duty of those who are under authority to do what they are asked and to do it the way they are told. Those who get angry, even though they do what is required in the specified way, make it difficult for others to enjoy their work, both those in charge and those subordinate. Of course, it is understood that those in authority assume responsibility not to abuse their authority by asking those under them to do what is wrong or to ask in an offensive or overbearing way.

Nevertheless, teenagers often rankle under this arrangement for several reasons. First, because they have spent so many years under other people. This is especially true for secondborn children and for those under stern parents. Also, teenagers are in transition between being subordinate and being in charge. This creates a real dilemma about when it is appropriate for them to submit and when they should demonstrate they are ready to accept responsibility. Furthermore, they face the problem of establishing (Level 3) their own value system. This can cause them no little grief, especially if those in authority will not give them sufficient freedom to experiment (Level 2).

18. Selection: *Can the student differentiate what is required from what is not?*

18. I have trouble telling right from wrong.

Item 18 is negative in its direction to accommodate those who are still in the process of examining virtue. It is ranked 4th on an ascending scale of 20. Each item contains elements of Duty and Desire. In this case, Desire, or lack of it, because the item is negative in direction, can be seen in "having trouble" and Duty, in "telling right from wrong." It is being based (having trouble reflects a condition). This statement is the last on Level 1. As such, it concerns a student's willingness to examine virtue to consider what part virtue will play in his or her life. The Examining Level includes a willingness to entertain thoughts, to receive instruction, and to become aware of the implications of duty. But here, the focus is on the capacity a student has to assess what should or should not be done.

It is surprising that some students will demonstrate no ability at all to distinguish right from wrong. It's kind of like babies who reach for fire because it is fascinating, without any sense of what it will do to them. Some students seem morally void of any natural caution. It is like their smoke detector is faulty. Most students will have varying degrees of discernment. But some will not be able to tell the difference between right and wrong by themselves. How can you help them begin to make this distinction? By setting firm guidelines, by allowing them the freedom to fail, by maintaining consistent discipline, and by communicating understanding and compassion to them.

Level 2: Experimenting

3. Obedience: *Is the student open to try to do what he or she should?*

3. I often refuse to do what I know is right.

Item 3 is negative in its direction, as are the first 10, to accommodate those who are in the process of establishing virtue. It is ranked 5th on an ascending scale of 20. Each item contains elements of Duty and Desire. In this case, Desire, or lack of it, because the item is negative in direction, can be seen in "refusing" and Duty, in "doing what is known to be right." The item is doing based. *Refusing to do* something is an activity. Item 3 is the first Level 2 item. The Experimenting Level involves compliance, active participation, and even experiencing enjoyment from doing one's duty. As such, it concerns a willingness to test the outcome of doing what is right. Item 3 focuses on obedience.

You must make a clear distinction in your thinking here. At this level, we are not talking about a willingness to just do what is right but a willingness to *test* doing what is right. When you view behavior at this level, it will often look like more than it is. To experiment indicates a willingness to test something out until the evidence is in. Experimentation also has a purpose. Once the evidence is in, a decision is made to accept or reject doing something that has already been tried. The desired result, of course, is that students continue doing as they ought, but they can obviously do otherwise.

Suppose a student has been obedient the entire semester. Then all of sudden, he or she becomes rebellious. This could confuse you, if the student were only experimenting and you were under the impression that obedience was established in his or her life. But if test results showed that virtue was not established, that he or she was still experimenting, you would not be surprised and would search for a way to encourage him or her to work through experimentation and move on to establishing virtue. If the student accepts your advice in his or her weakened condition, you should expect to find him or her obedient one day and not the next. This is a sign of experimentation. Do not be concerned. Experimentation means trial and error. During this process, remember to set firm guidelines, allow failure, maintain consistent discipline, and communicate understanding and compassion.

10. Contentment: Does the student feel a sense of accomplishment after doing what is required?

10. I feel uneasy because I won't help when I know I should.

Item 10 is negative in its direction, as are the first 10, to accommodate those who are in the process of experimenting with virtue. It is ranked 6th on an ascending scale of 20. Each item contains elements of Duty and Desire. In this case, Desire, or lack of it, because the item is negative in direction, can be seen in "unwillingness" and Duty, in "helping when I know I should." It is being based. *Feeling uneasy* is a state of being. It is the second Level 2 item. The Experimenting Level involves compliance, active participation, and even experiencing enjoyment from doing one's duty. As such, it concerns a willingness to test the outcome of doing what is right. Here, the focus is on contentment.

Unwillingness to help when duty requires it usually indicates a lack of contentment. A student who does not feel inner contentment is likely to be concerned with his or her own needs rather than helping someone else. The issue with contentment is that it should follow as a consequence of obedience. However, those who really struggle with obedience might not feel it. This will be a big hurdle for them. The feeling of accomplishment from having done what was required should begin to convince them of the innate goodness of virtue. This is not as strong a feeling as that of satisfaction, but it is enough reinforcement to encourage them to try being conscientious.

5. *Conscientiousness: Is the student actively involved in doing what he or she should?*

5. *I frequently insist on my own way even if I sense I might be wrong.*

Item 5 is negative in its direction, as are the first 10, to accommodate those who are in the process of experimenting with virtue. It is ranked 7th on an ascending scale of 20. Each item contains elements of Duty and Desire. In this case, Desire can be seen in "insisting" and Duty, in "sensing wrong." It is doing based. *Frequent insistence* looks at repeated action. It is the third Level 2 item. The Experimenting Level involves compliance, active participation, and even experiencing enjoyment from doing one's duty. As such, it concerns a willingness to test the outcome of doing what is right. Here, the focus is on conscientiousness.

Conscientiousness indicates a certain amount of involvement and intensity. Its opposite requires a stubborn resistance to the inner call of the conscience. After experimenting for awhile with obedience, seeing its benefits, and experiencing the contentment that comes from it, it is difficult not to continue. If a student is at this point and resists going further, the internal struggle will be incredible. Do not be disturbed. It simply means that virtue is very compelling. It is winning the student away from selfish desires.

On the other hand, if the student answers this question virtuously, it indicates that experimentation has led him or her to try intense involvement. Conscientious experimentation with what is right, good, and appropriate might appear as strong virtue. If you look at such a student's test results and see that he or she is only at the level of experimentation, you might question the test's validity because of how conscientious he or she appears. You might be even more surprised a few weeks later to find such a student quit trying and turn to trouble. Yet it is in perfect keeping with where that student is. He or she is experimenting. And the results of this experimentation, no matter what they are, can lead the student to go in either direction.

8. *Satisfaction: Does the student enjoy doing as he or she ought?*

8. *I find it hard to really enjoy myself when doing daily chores.*

Item 8 is negative in its direction, as are the first 10, to accommodate those who are in the process of experimenting with virtue. It is ranked 8th on an ascending scale of 20. Each item contains elements of Duty and Desire. In this case, Desire, or lack of it, because the item is negative in direction, can be seen in "finding enjoyment difficult" and Duty, in "doing daily chores." It is being based. *Lack of enjoyment* is a state of being. Doing daily chores is definitely an activity, but in this case, it provides a condition under which a state of being is assessed. It is the last Level 2 item. The Experimenting Level involves compliance, active participation, and even experiencing enjoyment from doing one's duty. As such, it concerns a willingness to test the outcome of doing what is right. Here, the focus is on satisfaction.

The strongest evidence that can accumulate through experimentation is the enjoyment of having done what was right. This will register itself in a number of ways: by discovering that it made someone else happy; by realizing that it accomplished something beneficial, even if no one ever knew about it; by sensing the inner conviction that it was the right thing to do, even if it was misunderstood or not perceived as such.

The feelings that follow obedience are very persuasive. Look for ways to confirm these feelings in your students. Feelings of gratification will powerfully reinforce their efforts to establish virtue in their lives. Experiencing satisfaction is the ultimate in experimentation. Resistance often means a student is in his or her final struggle at the experimentation level before becoming established in virtue. Encouragement is extremely important at this point. Condemnation for failing is immensely destructive. I mention this because, in their struggle, your students might become very discouraged and angry. You could find it quite easy to react to such emotions and try to shame them into changing. Sometimes, shame will bring immediate change, but it will not last, and it can promote resentment.

Level 3: Establishing

13. Acceptance: Are the student's inclinations divided between right and wrong?

13. I resist establishing values in my life so I can be free to be who I am.

Item 13 is negative in its direction, as are the first 10, to accommodate those who are just beginning to establish virtue. It is ranked 9th on an ascending scale of 20. Each item contains elements of Duty and Desire. In this case, Desire, or lack of it, because the item is negative in direction, can be seen in "resisting" and Duty, in "establishing values." It is doing based. *Resisting* is something that is done repeatedly. Item 13 is the first Level 3 item. The Establishing Level includes an acceptance of, a preference for, and a commitment to duty. As such, it indicates a willingness to stand for what is right. Here, the focus is on acceptance.

This is not mere mental assent. After intense experimentation, the student at this point is truly embracing duty with heartfelt desire. It may not yet be wholehearted acceptance, because that is a process that extends from this level on through the last level of embodying virtue. But its beginnings are here. It is a delusion for the student to think that to resist establishing values brings freedom. The opposite is true. To resist embracing the desire to do what is right enslaves people to selfish appetites and ambitions. It may seem like freedom to a student when he or she can do whatever he or she feels like doing, but it is nothing more than slavery to selfishness.

25. Confidence: Is the student confident enough to do what is right in the face of opposition?

25. I am afraid of what others might think if I do as I ought.

Item 25 is negative in its direction to accommodate those who are in the early stages of establishing virtue. It is the last negative item. It is ranked 10th on an ascending scale of 20. Each item contains elements of Duty and Desire. In this case, Desire, or lack of it, because the item is negative in direction, can be seen in "fearing" and Duty, in "doing what ought to be done." It is being based. *Being afraid* is a state of being. It is the second Level 3 item. The Establishing Level includes an acceptance of, a preference for, and a commitment to duty. As such, it indicates a willingness to stand for what is right. Here, the focus is on confidence.

Confidence attends the settled result of the acceptance of virtue as a way of life. It is an attitude that recognizes opposition for what it is and faces it anyway. It is the realization of inner strength. And it is wonderfully confirming to one in the early stages of establishing virtue. It does not necessarily bring discernment with it. It may lack the caution and foresight of prudence. But it is secure enough to do what is right when challenged to do otherwise.

4. Preference: Does the student prefer to do what he or she should?

4. I do what I should, even if friends reject me for it.

Item 4 is positive in its direction to accommodate those who are establishing virtue in their lives. It is the first positive item of the second half of the framework. In other words, the last 10 items are all positive. It is ranked 11th on an ascending scale of 20. Each item contains elements of Duty and Desire. In this case, Desire can be seen in "preferring duty over rejection" and Duty, in "doing what should be done." Item 4 is doing based, as is obvious from *I do what I should.* It is the third Level 3 item. The Establishing Level includes an acceptance of, a preference for, and a commitment to duty. As such, it indicates a willingness to stand for what is right. Here, the focus is on preference.

Preference should not indicate lack of resolve to you here. Instead, it means a choice in light of other possibilities. It indicates a weighing of possibilities. It means saying no to others. It means the heart is finding delight in one choice over another. Well-reasoned choices may be lacking. Discernment may be lacking. But what is believed to be good will be preferred. The emphasis is not on strength or discernment, but on a deepening desire to do what is right in the face of conflicting inclinations. There may be opposing interests, but not many, because the heart is becoming emotionally bound to what is right.

17. Commitment: Has the student become committed to do what is required?

17. I am fully committed to do what I should.

Item 17 is positive in its direction to accommodate those who are establishing virtue in their lives. It is ranked 12th on an ascending scale of 20. Each item contains elements of Duty and Desire. In this case, Desire can be seen in "being fully committed" and Duty, in "doing what should be done." It is being based. Being *fully committed* is a condition of the heart. Item 17 is the last Level 3 item. The Establishing Level includes an acceptance of, a preference for, and a commitment to duty. As such, it indicates a willingness to stand for what is right. Here, the focus is on commitment.

Commitment indicates strength of character. It indicates wholehearted resolve. If what is right is known, it will be done. At this point, it can even mean unquestioning commitment. This is because at this level, discernment is not of paramount importance. Understanding may be lacking. But what is seen is maintained. Later, after the next level of evaluation, questioning will become important. At the final level, as embodying virtue grows, openness to reconsider is a part of noble virtue.

Level 4: Evaluating Virtue

22. Protection: Has the student evaluated what is right to the point of certainty?

22. I openly defend what is right.

Item 22 is positive in its direction, as are the last 10, to accommodate those who are in the process of embodying virtue. It is ranked 13th on an ascending scale of 20. Each item contains elements of Duty and Desire. In this case, Desire can be seen in "openness" and Duty, in "defending what is right." Item 22 is doing based. *Making an open defense* is a sustained activity. This item is the first Level 4 item. The Evaluating Level includes a willingness to distinguish duty from dereliction, to assign degrees of importance to duties, and to order them according to priority. As such, it includes a good amount of wisdom. Here, the focus is on protection.

Protectiveness contains elements of possession and preservation. "I have made this mine, I will preserve it." Protectiveness preserves what is right because of the inner conviction that it is morally wrong to remain silent. It is taking personal responsibility for the reputation of what is right, realizing that doing nothing betrays what is true. It is a preservation of what is right for the very sake of righteousness. It is evaluation's first step because of the certainty required. Such evaluation is based on a commitment to what is right (the step just prior to this) but also on a basic understanding of what it is. It is more of an inner sense or intuition than a clearly defined conceptual understanding.

A student at this level might sometimes seem contentious, but if so, he or she will be contentious for what is right and just . . . in his or her mind. Even though you are tempted, you should avoid arguing with such a student, even if he or she needs correction. Zeal for what is right is likely to overshadow a low level of discernment. He or she might perceive your opposition as an assault on what is right and think you are opposing virtue. Instead, you should affirm the student's stand for what is right and then offer a shift in emphasis or a change in direction or an adjustment in focus. A minor modification in a spirit of gentleness is powerfully persuasive. Careless confrontation with one zealous for what is right might leave you on the wrong side of right in the mind of your students.

19. *Differentiation:* *Can the student discern between good, better, and best in terms of what he or she should do?*

19. *I can easily distinguish between good, better and best.*

Item 19 is positive in its direction to accommodate those who are in the process of evaluating virtue. It is ranked 14th on an ascending scale of 20. Each item contains elements of Duty and Desire. In this case, Desire can be seen in "ease of ability." The ability to distinguish is enhanced by the desire to distinguish. Duty can be seen in "distinguishing between good, better, and best." Item 19 is being based. In this case, *easily distinguishing* is an ability, a quality of being. It is the second Level 4 item. The Evaluating Level includes a willingness to distinguish duty from dereliction, to assign degrees of importance to duties, and to order them according to priority. As such, it includes a good amount of wisdom. Here, the focus is on differentiation and not just between right and wrong, like the previous step.

Initial distinctions between right and wrong begin at the final step of examining virtue (Level 1). At that lowest level, there is little moral discernment. The ability to make an assessment between right and wrong develops with exposure to those who are in a position of knowing and forms the basis for experimentation (Level 2). The first step of evaluation (Level 4), just prior to this one, deals with the inner ability to discern right from wrong. As soon as a student has developed that ability with certainty, he or she begins to differentiate between good, better, and best. Commitment, along with assuming responsibility as protector of what is right, calms inner struggles and promotes clearer thinking about making such distinctions. Students at this level will amaze you with the clear insights of an uncluttered mind and the acute intensity of an unwavering will.

2. *Organization:* *Has the student organized his or her life around his or her priorities to do what is right?*

2. *I maintain my priorities so that I can do what is best.*

Item 2 is positive in its direction to accommodate those who are in the process of evaluating virtue. It is ranked 15th on an ascending scale of 20. Each item contains elements of Duty and Desire. In this case, Desire can be seen in "maintaining priorities." Priorities will not be maintained over time without the desire to do so. Duty is seen in "doing what is best." This item is doing based. *Maintaining priorities* is something that is done. Item 2 is the third Level 4 item. The Evaluating Level includes a willingness to distinguish duty from dereliction, to assign degrees of importance to duties, and to order them according to priority. As such, it includes a good amount of wisdom. Here, the focus is on organization.

Item 2 indicates not only a high level of accomplishment but also implies consistently maintaining it. Organization calls for the sorting and rearranging that comes from a developed ability to evaluate. Yet the focus is not just on organization skills but rather, a considerable aptitude for moral judgment—enough, at least, to sustain a righteous way of life. To attain this level in life is no small matter for adults, let alone adolescents.

Yet some of your students will attain this level. You might even feel threatened at times. Don't be concerned if you feel this way. It's a natural reaction. Just don't allow such feelings to influence how you treat them. You might feel a desire to "keep them in place below their teacher." Here are some temptations you might face: "<u>Older</u> is wiser. Teachers are superior to their students. I can't be outdone by my students. I should be an example to them, not them to me." Dismiss such notions. They're foolish. They will make you appear angry, hypocritical, and untouchable before your students. They will recognize it at once and reject you for it.

12. Consistency: Does the student generally maintain his priorities to do as he or she should?

12. I am consistently true to what is best.

Item 12 is positive in its direction to accommodate those who are evaluating virtue. It is ranked 16th on an ascending scale of 20. Each item contains elements of Duty and Desire. In this case, Desire can be seen in "consistency." Consistency cannot be sustained apart from desire. Duty can be seen in "remaining true to what is best." Item 12 is being based. *Loyalty* is a state of being. In this case, it reflects a general attitude. It is the last Level 4 item. The Evaluating Level includes a willingness to distinguish duty from dereliction, to assign degrees of importance to duties, and to order them according to priority. As such, it includes a good amount of wisdom. Here, the focus is on consistency.

Consistency indicates a considerable amount of discernment, because it involves evaluation at every turn to maintain personal priorities to do what is right. It means constant surveillance. It means continual analysis, assessment, and adjustment. It means unwavering devotion to duty. There will be mistakes. There will be errors in judgment. There will be occasional incongruities. But, in general, over time, the life will be marked by consistency. And it will be characterized by an ability to evaluate situations for what they are, an ability to assess the outcome for what it should be, and an ability to discover the best path to get there.

Level Five: Embodying Virtue

14. Responsibility: Has it become second nature for the student to do as he or she should?

14. I gladly respond without hesitation when something is required of me.

Item 14 is positive in its direction, as are the last 10, to accommodate those who are in the process of embodying virtue. It is ranked 17th on an ascending scale of 20. Each item contains elements of Duty and Desire. In this case, Desire can be seen in "gladly responding without hesitation" and Duty, in "when something is required." Item 14 is doing based. *Responding* is an activity. It is the first Level 5 item. The Embodying Level includes a willingness to conform all activities to one's value system, to regulate all of life by it, and to remain open to new duties. As such, it reflects a highly disciplined yet highly flexible way of life. Here, the focus is on responsibility.

Some students will try to copy virtue at this level, but the difference will be obvious. Those who copy will appear to be working hard at being responsible, whereas it will obviously be second nature to those who are genuine. A moment's hesitation when asked to do something, a downcast look, a sigh, all indicate those who are striving to be responsible, to attain to a high level of virtue. Those who truly embody virtue, when asked to do something, gladly respond without hesitation. There is a lift in their voice, a twinkle in their eye, and a sense of anticipation. It's fun to watch.

9. Demonstration: Would other people agree that the student is living as he or she should?

9. *I am an example of wholehearted dedication to duty.*

Item 9 is positive in its direction to accommodate those who are in the process of embodying virtue. It is ranked 18th on an ascending scale of 20. Each item contains elements of Duty and Desire. In this case, Desire can be seen in "wholehearted dedication," and Duty in this case is obvious. It is being based. In this instance, being an example reflects not an activity but a general attitude behind a way of life. It is the second Level 5 item. The Embodying Level includes a willingness to conform all activities to one's value system, to regulate all of life by it, and to remain open to new duties. As such, it reflects a highly disciplined yet highly flexible way of life. Here, the focus is on demonstration.

Demonstration involves others being aware as well as the student. It also means lack of concern that others know or holding personal awareness without arrogance or self-preoccupation. Falsified virtue quickly denies virtue with false modesty. Those whose virtue is genuine know they cannot deny it without being untruthful. Instead, they are quick to give credit for what has become established as a way of life for them. They realize that without the considerable patience of parents, teachers, and other meaningful role models, they would not have developed the way they have. Because they are filled with gratitude, they quickly express it and selflessly point to others. Neither are they afraid to be role models, because others were for them. For them, it's a demonstration of responsibility.

24. Regulation: Does the student regulate his or her life by what he or she knows he or she should do?

24. *I immediately confess and make it right whenever I do something wrong.*

Item 24 is positive in its direction to accommodate those who are in the process of embodying virtue. It is ranked 19th on an ascending scale of 20. Each item contains elements of Duty and Desire. In this case, Desire can be seen in "immediacy" and Duty, in "confession and restitution." Item 24 is doing based. *Confession* and *restitution* are activities. This is the third Level 5 item. The Embodying Level includes a willingness to conform all activities to one's value system, to regulate all of life by it, and to remain open to new duties. As such, it reflects a highly disciplined yet highly flexible way of life. Here, the focus is on regulation.

Highly virtuous people are not those who never make mistakes or do anything wrong. They will make mistakes and do things wrong just like everyone else. What makes them different is the way they respond when they do. Those who fake virtue will tend to deny wrongdoing, unless it is somehow fashionable at the moment to admit it, and will never seem to find a way to make restitution. Those who do not care about virtue will readily admit wrongdoing but will either be proud of it and make no restitution or, if ashamed, will not want to change or will feel powerless to do so. Virtuous people realize when they do something wrong that they need to make adjustments in their lives. They stop doing wrong. They openly acknowledge it as such. Realizing the consequences of their errors, they quickly figure out a way to make them right. Nor do they worry after it's over. They have done what they could, and now they are on to other things.

7. Revision: Does the student remain open to become more consistent in doing as he or she should?

7. I am open to change anything that keeps me from doing what I should.

Item 7 is positive in its direction to accommodate those who are embodying virtue. It is ranked 20th on an ascending scale of 20. Each item contains elements of Duty and Desire. In this case, Desire can be seen in "openness to change" and Duty, in "doing what should be done." It is being based. In this case, being open to change is a general attitude. This is the last Level 5 item. The Embodying Level includes a willingness to conform all activities to one's value system, to regulate all of life by it, and to remain open to new duties. As such, it reflects a highly disciplined yet highly flexible way of life. Here, the focus is on revision.

Revision can be a tiresome thing but not to those at this level. It provides excitement for them, a challenge, an opportunity for improvement. They are glad when others point out faults. They will first ponder the criticism, agree, then say "thank you." Then they begin devising ways they can revise their approach to life. Many human beings actually hate those at this level, because such people force them to see themselves for who they really are. People can tolerate them as heroes after they're dead, but are usually repulsed by them when they are around. Don't be surprised if you naturally do not like such people. This may not be a problem for you if you know someone like this from a distance, but watch your resentment rise, the closer you get.

As promised, Table 4.1 is an analytical table of virtue, which summarizes the framework given in the previous discussion. Besides acquainting you with the structure of virtue, the framework has been designed for you to refer to when looking at the individual results of a student's test. Keep in mind that it is not good to conceive of the levels as strictly progressive. One does not complete the first before progressing to the next or maintain one level simply because it has been attained. These levels are not strictly contrived as developmental. A pass can be made from bottom to top, with an item or two in each, then strengthened or weakened on the next pass, with all manner of variation. Nonetheless, structurally, virtue breaks down as shown in Table 4.1.

Table 4.1 Virtue Items Analytical Table

Item number	23	15	20	18	3	10	5	8	13	25	4	17	22	19	2	12	14	9	24	7
Item rank	1	2	3	4	5	6	7	8	9	10	11	12	13	14	15	16	17	18	19	20
Item direction	–	–	–	–	–	–	–	–	–	–	+	+	+	+	+	+	+	+	+	+
Item basis	D	B	D	B	D	B	D	B	D	B	D	B	D	B	D	B	D	B	D	B
Virtue levels	Examining				Experimenting				Establishing				Evaluating				Embodying			

NOTE: B = Being; D = Doing.

As you have seen, there are 20 virtue items on the instrument. Six other items, adapted with permission, are from the Marlow-Crowne Social-Desirability Scale. This is why every fifth item number in the Virtue Items Analytical Table (Table 4.1) is missing (1, 6, 11, 16, 21) and why the range of item numbers in the table extends beyond 20 in number. These six items are included in the questionnaire to detect those who, for various reasons, misrepresent themselves. You should realize that some of your students will take the test in such a way as to confound your attempts to measure them. Most of the time, they will not do this knowingly, but you must be aware of what they are doing so that you can properly interpret their scores.

Response Sets

There are certain ways that students respond to tests that can confuse your interpretation of the results. By and large, they involve the various ways people perceive a test and then react to it. You already realize your students will answer differently, but there are some things you can look for. For example, some students will tend to acquiesce to a test. Others will seek to answer positively, whereas others will wish to respond negatively. Some will choose the most desirable answer. There are a number of response patterns you should know about.

Some students are more passive than others. They will sense the way a question is worded and, without considering themselves—which is what you want them to do—will acquiesce to the direction of the question. Acquiescence is the tendency to follow the pattern of the test items rather than their content. The results of such a response obviously tell you nothing about a student's virtue.

Other people enjoy being agreeable and will tend to answer affirmatively when asked questions. They will try to read the question in such a way as to be able to answer positively. They might desire to be supportive. They might be seeking to put their best foot forward. Who knows all of the reasons? Maybe, they are just optimistic. Usually, this kind of response still tells you about their virtue, but they will tend to have more uncertainty (more question marks circled), because half the items on the questionnaire are stated negatively to move them away from a fixed response set.

The reverse is also true. Some of your students will tend to answer negatively. They might want time to think things over. They might be reluctant to give information about themselves. They might resent being moved by the suggestibility of a question—to answer as they feel it leads them to answer. They might just feel protected by a negative answer. It is, therefore, important to help them avoid these patterns as much as possible and at the same time, be able to identify it when they do so.

Mueller (1986) recommended that a balance be maintained between positively and negatively worded items to avoid the possible effect of "acquiescence response set" (p. 73). I decided that this would also help detect those seeking to answer only positively or negatively. Therefore, I reversed the direction on alternate questions so that, if a student answered all questions positively or negatively, you could readily detect it.

Another problem you will face is that some students will be uncertain about what you want to know, or whether they want you to know it, or if they even understand, and they will need to be able to express that uncertainty. I felt that students should not be forced to answer something about which they are unsure, by limiting the possible selections available to agreement or disagreement. It's okay if they hem and haw a little bit. Some will want to swagger, others will be more timid—you know, express themselves with greater or lesser degrees of intensity—so I included response options of strongly agree and strongly disagree. This approach is typical for a Likert-type scale. But a further word needs to be said first concerning uncertain responses and then about emphatic responses.

Should students answer a lot of questions by indicating they are uncertain, they are either unwilling or unable to relate to you what you are asking. It might be revealing to question them further about their responses. Whatever the case, the number of question marks circled is valuable information. The total number on each test should be compared with the rest of your students' results (typically, about three per test). Uncertain responses also might reveal areas where virtue is being broken down in a previously attained level. Now, let me say a word about emphatic responses.

Some students will answer by strongly agreeing or strongly disagreeing. This does not indicate that you should reject their answers. Neither does it mean their answers necessarily indicate strong affirmation or strong disagreement. It may only mean they like to express themselves forcefully. Conversely, there are those who will avoid expressing strong answers altogether, even if they hold something very strongly. They are just more reserved in the way they express themselves. However, these are exceptions.

You should also be alert to indications that a student's answers are not to be taken seriously. For example, one student signed the name Adolf Hitler on the top of his or her test. His or her answers should be examined carefully. Another indication that a respondent's answers might not be taken seriously is a few likely answers at first with the rest all the same. Extraneous comments, derogatory remarks, doodling, all indicate that the student's answers should be closely examined to determine if they have represented themselves accurately. Yet none of these indicators necessarily invalidates their responses. Students may answer every question to the best of their abilities, but with extra time afterward, or while directions are being given, they may doodle. Nevertheless, such indicators should prompt you to more closely examine each response.

Social Desirability Items

Donlon (1974) reported a serious problem of response distortion in self-report tests. If respondents were able to determine the desired response, they could then respond in an acceptable manner, thereby misrepresenting themselves. He stated,

> While development of instruments has a straightforward logic and requires little technical theory or body of knowledge, the gist of the methods is perceivable by the respondent, and the distortion of responses, either consciously or unconsciously, is the greatest single problem in working with them. (p. 27)

To accurately measure something inside of your students, beyond your hunch, you really have to rely on them to report it to you. You intuitively know that some will misrepresent themselves. It would be helpful to know who, so you can find out why.

I have found from extensive testing that the less virtuous people are, the more likely they are to represent themselves correctly. It's true! It doesn't seem like it, because virtue and misrepresentation do not go together. But there are a couple of other things that must be considered. First, very unvirtuous people don't care who knows. They have no reason to cover up. They are going to do what they want anyway, and it usually doesn't matter to them who knows about it. What's more, they frequently hate those who fake it. These things provide them strong reasons not to misrepresent themselves. In fact, they consider themselves better than those who fake something they are not, and it's likely they are right.

Second, those who are somewhat virtuous and want to be still more virtuous will frequently misrepresent themselves. Even more so will those who are trying to be virtuous and want others to think they are. In talking with those who misrepresented virtuous responses, I found that they scored higher than the norm on virtue but wanted to be even higher or have others believe they were. This stands to reason, if you think about it. Some who are not highly virtuous either want to be or want others to think they are or think others want them to be, and so they will misrepresent themselves.

Figure 4.1 shows the kinds of categories I have seen in testing student virtue and talking with teachers and students. It's not likely to give you all the categories, but most of those you will see.

Notice that those who score low might misrepresent average virtue but not high. Later in life, sociopaths will do so but hardly ever as teenagers. Also notice that those who score high may misrepresent average virtue but not low.

With all of this misrepresentation going on among teenagers, we decided to include questions that would detect it if students misrepresented themselves from the Marlowe-Crowne Social-Desirability Scale (Crowne & Marlowe, 1980). The *social desirability response set* is understood to be the tendency for test takers to respond to test items in a socially acceptable way instead of in keeping with their beliefs and preferences.

Surprisingly, the less virtuous people are, the more likely they are to represent themselves correctly.

Low Score

| Clearly representing low virtue |
| Low virtue misrepresenting average virtue |
| Average virtue misrepresenting low virtue |
| Clearly representing average virtue |
| Average virtue misrepresenting high virtue |
| High virtue misrepresenting average virtue |
| Clearly representing high virtue |

High Score

Figure 4.1. Sample Categories of Student Virtue

This means that some people will select the most desirable answer, not because it represents who they are but because it reflects what they wish they were or want to become. It may also indicate a desire to please or to respond positively to what is expected of them. Mueller (1986) recommended establishing good administrative rapport with your students to reduce this likelihood. And Summers (1976) recommended that the extent of this influence be determined, for the sake of validating the questionnaire. Besides, the risk for this kind of response set seems even greater with virtue as content for the test items.

Summary

Consequently, the LVAQ was designed to account for such response sets. If a student answers with all positive responses or all negative responses, his or her answers should be highly suspect, because the direction of the LVAQ questions has been alternately stated positively, then negatively. In other words, one question will measure higher virtue when answered positively, and the next question will measure higher virtue when answered negatively. Also, items to detect social desirability have been interspersed among those items measuring virtue. These mechanical features will enable you to discern, with greater precision, the data your students provide.

Conclusion

In conclusion, the LVAQ was developed by following the pattern of a taxonomy well known in educational circles, by submitting it to a panel of experts for revision, and through extensive field-testing and refinement for use with adolescents at junior and senior high school levels. It has shown a high degree of reliability and validity through statistical analysis, and the results have been confirmed by written reports and dialogue with teachers and administrators in various public high school settings. Now that you have become acquainted with it in Part I of this manual, I invite you to put it into practice. Part II is designed to help you accomplish this.

Things to Review and Remember From Chapter 4

1. Virtue is a dynamic construct. As such, it changes with the myriad choices made each day.

   a. The changes are not abrupt, and the structure of the construct remains stable enough for measurement to be meaningful.

   b. The results of the LVAQ (pronounced "el-vak") are not intended to be definitive or conclusive.

   c. The purpose of the test is to serve as a beginning point for evaluation and discussion with the student, his or her parents, and perhaps administrators.

2. There are 20 virtue items on the LVAQ.

   a. Half of the 20 virtue items are oriented toward character assessment (Being) and half toward the assessment of conduct (Doing).

   b. Each virtue item contains elements that measure a student's inclinations (Desires) and his or her sense of obligation (Duty).

   c. The virtue items are ranked on an ascending scale, progressing through five levels:

   • Level 1: The Examining Level includes a willingness to entertain thoughts, to receive instruction, and to become aware of the implications of duty. As such, it concerns a student's willingness to examine virtue to consider what part it will play in his or her life.

   • Level 2: The Experimenting Level involves compliance, active participation, and even experiencing enjoyment from doing one's duty. As such, it concerns a student's willingness to test the outcome of doing what is right.

   • Level 3: The Establishing Level includes an acceptance of, a preference for, and a commitment to duty. As such, it indicates a willingness to stand for what is right.

   • Level 4: The Evaluating Level includes a willingness to distinguish duty from dereliction, to assign degrees of importance to duties, and to order them according to priority. As such, it includes a good amount of wisdom.

   • Level 5: The Embodying Level includes a willingness to conform all activities to one's value system, to regulate all of life by it, and to remain open to new duties. As such, it reflects a highly disciplined yet highly flexible way of life.

    d. These levels should not be thought of as strictly progressive or developmental in nature.
- A student does not complete the first level before progressing on to the next or maintain one level simply because it has been attained.
- A pass can be made from bottom to top, with an item or two in each, then strengthened or weakened on the next pass, with all manner of variation.

3. There are set ways that students respond to tests that can confuse your interpretation of the results. These response patterns involve their perceptions and reactions to tests.

    a. Acquiescence Response Set: This is a passive response. Students will sense the way a question is worded and, without considering themselves, will acquiesce to the direction of the question.

    b. Positive Response Set: This response is an attempt to be agreeable. Students will tend to answer affirmatively when asked questions. They will try to read the question in such a way as to be able to answer positively. They might desire to be supportive. They might be seeking to put their best foot forward. They might just be optimistic in their outlook on life.

    c. Negative Response Set: This response is an attempt to be careful. Students might want time to think things over. They might be reluctant to give information about themselves. They might resent being moved by the suggestibility of a question—to answer as it leads them to answer. They might just feel protected by a negative answer.

    d. Social Desirability Response Set: This response is prompted by a desire to be socially acceptable instead of representing personal beliefs and preferences. Students will select a socially desirable answer, not because it represents who they are but because it reflects what they wish they were or want to become. There are six social-desirability items on the LVAQ designed to detect those who misrepresent themselves.

Note

1. Items 1, 6, 11, 16, 21, and 26 are from Crowne and Marlowe (1980/1964).

5

The Students of Frost
Independent School District

To this point, you have considered the concept of virtue: how it was conceived and constructed. You recall, . . . the elements of Being and Doing, . . . Duty and Desire, right? You also examined how the concept was adapted for use in education. Remember the taxonomies? Of course you do. And you studied the framework in which the conceptual construct operates with students—that's correct, the five levels of virtue. Furthermore, you have examined how the questionnaire was patterned after the conceptual construct and operational framework and have discovered how it was designed to measure virtue. Now, you will be able to observe how it actually performed with students. And though I don't want you to overdose on details, this chapter has some compelling numbers that not only give credibility to the study but enable you to assess your students' virtue.

Don't get me wrong, I'm not trying to make a silk purse out of a sow's ear, but by the time you finish this chapter, you will be familiar with scoring trends among high school students so you can make sense of your own students' scores. For instance, you will get a feel for normal response patterns. You will be able to rank their scores, both for the Virtue subtest and for the Social-Desirability subtest (measuring misrepresentation). Beyond that, you will learn how to make mental adjustments for students who respond with emphasis or uncertainty or both. And finally, you will see an actual example of the difference implementing the LVAQ can make over time.

Initial Sample

The data you are about to review came from a sample taken from a high school with 162 students. It is located deep in the heart of Texas, about 50 miles south of Dallas as the crow flies. The town is typical of the heartland of Texas, where just about every bend in the road has a community of 500 to 600 people. Mr. Gordon Lockett, Frost High School Principal, and Mr. Jim Revill, the FISD Superintendent, were kind enough to allow me to obtain data from their students and teachers. The

Table 5.1 LVAQ Mean and Standard Deviation Scores

Sample	Cases	Mean	SD
Waco Independent School District Pilot Group	69	65.406	6.563
Initial Frost Independent School District Group	140	65.664	10.131
Joshua Independent School District Physical Educations Group	115	63.774	10.491
Follow-up Frost Independent School District Group	140	67.157	8.643

162 students included both Junior and Senior High Schools, where Junior High consisted of seventh and eighth grades, and senior high consisted of grades 9 through 12.

There were 12 teachers administering the test to the entire school. One hundred forty students actually took the test, 22 being either absent or tardy for the first period of the day, when the test was offered. Students had no prior knowledge that the test would be given. The sample was inclusive and random, in that every student had the opportunity to participate, no one being included or excluded for any particular reason. It took approximately 15 minutes, but students were allowed whatever time they needed to complete the test. A copy of the administration instructions for the questionnaire, given to the teachers, may be found in Resource B. In addition, the same test was administered to Frost High School 2 years later, under the same conditions, to determine what impact, if any, the cultivation of virtue had had.

Scores, Ranges, and Distributions

Statistical information shown in Table 5.1 was obtained by using Statview (1988) and Microsoft Excel (1991) on a Macintosh computer. The mean virtue score for the initial Frost sample (1994) was 65.664. This was consistent with the mean for the pilot data, which was 65.406, taken from a sample of students representing over a dozen schools in the greater Waco, Texas, area taken in 1993 during summer school with the gracious permission of Mr. George Dupree. It was also consistent with a posttest sample (63.774) taken from physical education classes with the assistance of Mr. Jack Wilson in the Joshua Independent School District in the Fall of 1994. The mean for the Frost High School follow-up in 1996 was 67.157. All mean scores were about 10 points lower than those of adults previously tested. Dr. Douglas Winn (1993) used the LVAQ to measure those enrolled in adult education at five junior colleges in Texas. Their mean score was 75.409, which was the same (75.275) as adults previously tested nationwide (Loehrer, 1991).

The initial FISD scores ranged from 36 to 92, quite broad for the size sample that was taken. The follow-up FISD scores ranged from 45 to 95. A normal distribution is indicated when two thirds of the scores fall between (−,+) one standard deviation from the mean, and when 95% of the scores fall between (−,+) two stan-

Table 5.2 LVAQ Normal Distribution

Frost Independent School District Sample	1 SD Mean	Count	Percentage	2 SD Mean	Count	Percentage
Initial	56-75	102	73	45-86	132	94
Follow-up	59-76	102	73	50-84	133	95

Table 5.3 LVAQ Gender Frequency Distribution

Gender	Count	Percentage	Range	Mean	SD
Female	66	47.1	51-92	67.667	9.999
Male	74	52.9	36-87	63.878	9.997

dard deviations from the mean. In Table 5.2, you can see that the samples taken from Frost did just that.

These numbers indicate a random sample with a normal distribution and tell you that we have an adequate representation of our target population of high school students. Is that bad or good? It's good, because it lets you know what high school students will do in general, so you can use it without wondering if it will work with your students. That should give you confidence to use the LVAQ and be comfortable about the way it performs.

Descriptive data for Age, Grade, and Ethnicity are insufficient at the present to provide reliable information, but early indications are that grade and ethnicity do not influence scores. Age doesn't seem to, either, but I want to add a word of clarification. Young teens are as capable of scoring high in virtue as are older teens—or adults, for that matter—nor are low scores necessarily found with those younger. Neither is there any indication that *all* people naturally become more virtuous the older they get. However, the norm with adults is 10 points higher than with adolescents, suggesting that growth comes with age, for most people. Although there weren't enough students in each group for age, grade, and ethnicity to establish anything yet, there were enough students to do so with the gender categories, as you can see in Table 5.3.

A curious feature is that the lower limit for the range of scores for females is considerably higher than for males. This seems to fit reality for high school students. Females are generally more virtuous than males. And whereas the data show that both have the capacity to score quite high, males as a group tend to extend their range of scores considerably lower. Teachers readily observe this in classroom behavior and attitudes. The mean scores for males and females also indicate this. Notice also that the females ranged a little higher than the males, and let me add that, when they did, they displayed a greater tendency to misrepresent themselves. The gender sample was large enough and stable enough to expect that this would hold true for other samples. Next, let's consider in Table 5.4 the distribution of scores and norms.

Table 5.4 LVAQ Virtue Range Frequency Distribution

Virtue Range	Initial Count	Initial Percentage	Follow-Up Count	Follow-Up Percentage
20-49	5	4	4	3
50-59	29	21	21	15
60-69	61	43	63	45
80-79	29	21	42	30
80-100	16	11	10	7

Table 5.5 LVAQ Virtue Range Possibilities

Answer Abbreviations	Rank Descriptions	Answer Value	Total Score
SA/SD	Lowest	1	20
A/D	Low	2	40
?	Uncertain	3	60
A/D	High	4	80
SA/SD	Highest	5	100

NOTE: A = Agree; D = Disagree; ? = Uncertain; SA = Strongly Agree; SD = Strongly Disagree

Next, let's compare these range trends with range possibilities, which extend from 20 to 100. Notice the relatively even distribution of scores for the initial group compared with the upward shift of the follow-up group. Now, look at the range possibilities in Table 5.5.

If people answered every question the lowest they could on the virtue subtest, their virtue score would be 20; they would get 1 point for every answer. This means that they would have to answer emphatically (*Strongly Agree* or *Strongly Disagree*, depending on whether the item were stated positively or negatively), as well as low, to score the lowest they could. If people answered low on every virtue question but did not answer emphatically, they would have a score of 40; they would get 2 points for every answer. If people were uncertain about every virtue question, they would have a score of 60, because circling a question mark on the test gets a 3, and 3 times 20, the number of virtue items on the questionnaire, equals 60. If people answered every virtue question on the high side but avoided being emphatic about it, they would have a score of 80. And if people scored high on every virtue question and did so emphatically, they would obviously have a score of 100. Let's look at the same thing for the Social-Desirability subtest, measuring misrepresentation.

The range possibilities for the Social-Desirability (misrepresentation) subtest extend from 6 to 30. Because there are six items, if people answered the lowest they could, their misrepresentation score would be 6. This means that they would have to answer emphatically (*Strongly Agree* or *Strongly Disagree*, depending on whether the item were stated positively or negatively), as well as low. If people answered low on every misrepresentation question but did not answer emphatically, they would have a score of 12; they would get 2 points for every low answer. If people were uncertain about every misrepresentation question, they would have a score of 18,

Table 5.6 Misrepresentation Range Possibilities

Answer Abbreviations	Rank Descriptions	Answer Value	Total Score
SA/SD	Lowest	1	6
A/D	Low	2	12
?	Uncertain	3	18
A/D	High	4	24
SA/SD	Highest	5	30

NOTE: A = Agree; D = Disagree; ? = Uncertain; SA = Strongly Agree; SD = Strongly Disagree

Table 5.7 Misrepresentation Comparisons

Misrepresentation Score	Low Virtue (20-60)		Middle Virtue (61-70)		High Virtue (71-100)	
	Count	Percentage	Count	Percentage	Count	Percentage
Low (6-16)	35/41	85.4	28/48	58.4	24/51	47.1
Uncertain (17-19)	1/41	2.4	10/48	20.8	8/51	15.6
High (20-30)	5/41	12.2	10/48	20.8	19/51	37.3

because circling a question mark on the test gets a 3, and 3 times 6, the number of misrepresentation items on the questionnaire, equals 18. If people answered every misrepresentation question on the high side but avoided being emphatic about it, they would have a score of 24. And if people scored high on every misrepresentation question and did so emphatically, they would obviously have a score of 30.

The implications of these possibilities on individual scores should also be considered. Because students tend to score a little on the high side (the middle score is 60, whereas the average score is about 65), and because they tend to answer fewer questions emphatically by a 2 to 1 ratio, when someone has a virtue score in the 20s or 30s, it is extremely rare. But a virtue score in the 80s or 90s is not so rare, for two reasons: first, people tend to answer on the high side and second, there is a tendency to misrepresent a high score, and if students are able to do so, they usually do it pretty well. Notice the increased tendency to misrepresent higher scores in Table 5.7.

One of the first things you should notice when scoring your students' tests is their tendency to answer one way or another. I have taken into consideration the different ways people tend to respond to tests and have shuffled the order of the items on the questionnaire to help students avoid merely responding in set patterns, rather than indicating who they really are and what they really do. So if they do answer all questions with uniformity, this should indicate to you that they are not really giving you useful information, they are merely following a set response pattern. Also, comparing the frequency of their responses with the norm and noticing their tendencies will help you interpret their scores. Some will want to answer emphatically, others will carefully avoid strong answers, and these tendencies may have more to do with their personalities than a particular item on the questionnaire.

Table 5.8 Overall LVAQ Response Norms

Strongly Disagree	Disagree	Uncertain	Agree	Strongly Agree
3	7	3	9	4

Table 5.9 Uncertain Response Norms

Misrepresentation	Virtue	Total
.4	2.6	3

LVAQ Response Norms

It will prove helpful when evaluating a student's responses to have a feel for how others have responded. Table 5.8 presents the overall norms for this sample. Recall that, after reading an item on the questionnaire, the respondent is invited to circle one of the abbreviated answers (SD D ? A SA).

The first thing to detect from the overall norms is that there is a 2-to-1 ratio for responses on the disagreement side (3:7) and on the agreement side (4:9). That is to say, there are two *Disagree* responses for every *Strongly Disagree* response, and there are likewise two *Agree* responses for every *Strongly Agree* response. Also you should notice that there are relatively few uncertain responses, 3 out of 26, meaning that students respond to about 88% of the questions with certainty. Last, observe that there is a slight tendency to respond more on the agreement side (13) than the disagreement side (10). Okay, so much for the overall results. Let's consider just the virtue items on the questionnaire as seen in Table 5.9. There were 20 of them.

If you are wondering which LVAQ items students had more or less uncertainty about, the following table gives a frequency distribution of uncertain responses, item by item. For instance, a student may have had only one uncertain response, but it was with a question that caught your interest. You might wonder if it was particularly troublesome for students in general. By consulting Table 5.10, you might gain some additional insight.

For example, Item 18 caused considerable uncertainty. Item 10 did not. Item 18 reads, "I have trouble telling right from wrong." Because the statement is quite intelligible, and because it is generally not too troublesome for teacher types, you might be surprised that it caused the most consternation among teens, but it reflects a change among our youth, many of whom are adrift in a sea of relative values. This can be remedied, as you will see when you compare the follow-up test results at the end of this chapter, which were taken 2 years later. Item 10 reads, "I feel unwilling to help, even when I know I should." This is a pretty straightforward statement, but those who are not as in touch with their feelings might think it holds a considerable element of uncertainty. Not so for youth! This item held the least amount of uncertainty for highschoolers of any of the statements. More data will certainly stabilize these preliminary results, but it's enough to start the wheels turning. Now let's consider some virtue norms for highschoolers in Table 5.11.

Table 5.10 LVAQ Items and Uncertain Response Frequency Distribution

Item Rank	LVAQ Item	Uncertain Count
1	23	20
2	15	7
3	20	14
4	18	45
5	3	13
6	10	6
7	5	9
8	8	15
9	13	24
10	25	14
11	4	19
12	17	20
13	22	18
14	19	12
15	2	22
16	12	33
17	14	20
18	9	41
19	24	25
20	7	13

Notice that what is true for the overall test is true for the virtue items: namely, that there are half as many strong responses, or a 2-to-1 ratio, on both the disagreement side (2:5) as well as on the agreement side (3:7). Also, notice again the slight tendency to agree more than to disagree (10:7). Last, notice, too, that most do not have much trouble with uncertainty: only 3 out of 20. Now, let's look more closely at just the Social-Desirability items, those that measure misrepresentation.

Misrepresentation Response Norms

This part of the test, though the smallest (six items), is in some ways the most important. Without the capacity to determine if the virtue scores are genuine, they would always be suspect. Because virtue is a socially desirable thing, some will want to fake it for various reasons. Low scores on the Social-Desirability subtest indicate the extent to which students accurately represent themselves. The lower that students score on the social-desirability items, the more readily their virtue scores may be interpreted. Conversely, higher scores indicate the extent they misrepresent themselves; their virtue scores may not be interpreted with confidence. The norms are presented in Table 5.12.

Here, we see that the 2-to-1 ratio we saw among virtue items is maintained. Actually, the norm is not 0 for uncertainty, it is .4, and for the 20 virtue items, it is

Table 5.11 Virtue Response Norms

Strongly Disagree	Disagree	Uncertain	Agree	Strongly Agree
2	5	3	7	3

Table 5.12 Social-Desirability Response Norms

Strongly Disagree	Disagree	Uncertain	Agree	Strongly Agree
1	2	0	2	1

Table 5.13 Misrepresentation Classification

Number of Negative Responses	Count	Response Percentage	Classification
0	0	0	Pure misrepresentation
1	8	5.7	Probable misrepresentation
2	19	13.6	Possible misrepresentation
3	23	16.4	Questionable
4	49	35.0	Possible representation
5	34	24.3	Probable representation
6	7	5.0	Pure representation

2.6, so the ratio is roughly similar (compare with Tables 5.8 and 5.9). Nevertheless, uncertainty for these items was pretty low. To get a feel for how these items measure misrepresentation, consider this: If students scored anywhere from 1 through 3 on an item, they would be answering on the low side; they are not misrepresenting themselves. I include 3 because if they are uncertain (a 3), they still haven't *chosen* to misrepresent themselves. If they scored a 4 or 5, they would be indicating misrepresentation. To grasp the significance of this, simply count how many misrepresentation responses students have, to see how they rank in Table 5.13.

LVAQ Rankings

You should observe that there are considerably more on the representation side, category for category, as there are on the misrepresentation side. This indicates that most students accurately represent themselves but that there is a sizable element that choose to misrepresent themselves and that these items are demonstrating the capacity to reveal them. Now, let's consider in Table 5.14 the misrepresentation rankings. The lower students score on these Social-Desirability items, the more likely their scores represent their virtue. Conversely, the higher they score, the more likely their scores misrepresent their virtue.

From this, you can see there are at least twice as many on the Unlikely side as there are on the Likely side, depending on exactly how you look at it. The Unlikely

Table 5.14 Misrepresentation Rankings

Score	Count	Percentage	Classification
6-10	7	5.0	Extremely unlikely
11-13	32	22.8	Very unlikely
14-16	48	34.3	Unlikely
17-19	19	13.6	Uncertain
20-22	20	14.3	Likely
23-25	11	7.9	Very likely
26-30	3	2.1	Extremely likely

Table 5.15 Virtue Rankings

Virtue Score	Group Count	Group Percentage	Group Classification
20-50	8	5.7	Very low
51-55	12	8.6	Low
56-60	21	15.0	Moderately low
61-70	48	34.3	Average
71-75	25	17.8	Moderately high
76-80	13	9.3	High
81-100	13	9.3	Very high

side has 87 in its ranks, or 62%. There are 19 in the Uncertain category, or about 14%. On the Likely side there are 34, or 24%. Overall, this means that about three quarters of those tested did not misrepresent themselves. When students have high misrepresentation scores, the most that may be said is that their virtue scores indicate the extent that virtue is desirable to them, for whatever reasons. Now let's look at the virtue rankings in Table 5.15.

First, notice that, category for category, there is a very close correspondence. The obvious bell-shaped curve confirms that this sample is representative of high school students. The full range of scores lends additional support. This means that this classification system gives you a relative reference point for understanding your students' responses. When you consider how the Social-Desirability subtest effectively distinguishes those who represent themselves from those who do not, the LVAQ scores become a meaningful assessment of the extent of your students' virtue.

Follow-Up Sample

Having seen that we can effectively measure our students' virtue, we naturally question next, Can we actually instill virtue in them so that it makes a measurable difference? Tables 5.16 and 5.17 suggest that we can. For this information to become meaningful, it helps to convert the percentages in the tables to real-life people. Let's take Item 23, for example. There is a 10% shift away from unvirtuous responses, half responding virtuously, the other half with uncertainty. This means that 14 fewer students indicated rebellion when challenged to do what they should. Seven out of 140 knew with certainty that they were no longer rebelling. Seven were uncertain. Just think about having five fewer attitude problems to deal with per 100 students, and you suddenly grasp the significance of what can happen with your students. And keep in mind that this information was gathered just 2 weeks before the end of the school year for both samples. You *know* what that means: teachers at their wits' end; students with spring fever, gearing up for vacation. But in this case, it also meant a year of measurable improvement in reaching students with rotten attitudes.

I am going to comment on these tables, level by level, to spare you the time it takes to study them. To get the most from my comments, consult the table after reading my analysis, and picture in your mind actual students whose lives are being changed. The shift in Virtue Level 1, the Examining Level, indicates that those with attitude problems are not reacting to their teachers as much or influencing as many other students (read Items 23 and 15, then consider that we are talking about rebelliousness and resentment in 15 students). At this level, there is also a significant increase in the ability to discern right from wrong (read Item 18, and reflect that some 60 students—what an increase!—no longer have trouble telling right from wrong.) In addition, a few less students are harboring anger (read Item 20, and ponder that there are about five students who are not reacting to their teachers as much as before). The percentages may seem small at first, but when you consider that actual students are reporting these things about themselves, something good is happening somewhere, and it happens to be between teachers and students.

When considering Level 2, Experimenting with Virtue, our students' responses indicate that those with attitude problems are being allowed to experiment (read Item 3, and realize that some 16 students no longer refuse to do what they know is right; then read Item 10, and reflect that 14 are now willing to help when they know they should). The downside is that with greater freedom to experiment, more students will insist on their own way, even if they sense they might be wrong (read Item 5, and consider that 8 students who would not have insisted on their own way before are at least now considering it). Teachers should not be troubled by this, unless they want their students to remain children for the rest of their lives. School is a great place for them to experiment, and part of that experimentation includes the opportunity for them to insist, even if they might be wrong. Nevertheless, their insistence to use that freedom indicates a lack of virtue. Yes, it would be better if they patiently waited for appropriate opportunities to experiment rather than being insistent. But it would also be better if teachers allowed them even more space for trial and error than they already had. Perhaps this is why so many teens have trouble enjoying themselves when fulfilling their responsibilities (read Item 8, and consider that an additional 21 students—pretty significant!—indicated that they need more desire to do what they know they should do). This increase brings the total up to 64%. This means that 90 out of 140 students found it hard to enjoy themselves when performing routine responsibilities. The connection between en-

Table 5.16 Initial and Follow-Up Virtue Response Comparison (in percentages)

LVAQ Items	*Virtuous*		*Unvirtuous*		*Uncertain*	
Virtue Level One: Examining	94V	96V	94U	96U	94?	96?
23: I rebel when someone talks to me about doing what I should.	46	51	40	29	14	20
15: I am tired of those in charge trying to show me a better way.	46	51	49	39	5	11
20: I get angry when those in authority insist I do things their way.	31	30	59	57	10	13
18: I have trouble telling right from wrong.	38	82	30	11	32	7
Virtue Level Two: Experimenting	94V	96V	94U	96U	94?	96?
3: I often refuse to do what I know is right.	54	66	36	23	9	11
10: I feel unwilling to help, even when I know I should.	64	74	32	14	4	11
5: I frequently insist on my own way, even if I sense I might be wrong.	49	43	45	44	6	13
8: I find it hard to really enjoy myself when doing daily chores.	41	29	49	64	11	8
Virtue Level Three: Establishing	94V	96V	94U	96U	94?	96?
13: I resist establishing values in my life so I can be free to be who I am.	44	44	39	32	17	24
25: I am afraid of what others might think if I do as I ought.	54	58	36	28	10	14
4: I do what I should, even if friends reject me for it.	61	61	26	21	14	17
17: I am fully committed to do what I know I should.	59	61	27	16	14	23
Virtue Level Four: Evaluating	94V	96V	94U	96U	94?	96?
22: I openly defend what is right.	78	71	9	9	13	19
19: I can easily distinguish between good, better, and best.	86	81	6	10	8	9
2: I maintain my priorities so that I can do what is best.	76	79	9	10	16	11
12: I consistently remain true to what is best.	51	56	26	21	24	24
Virtue Level Five: Embodying	94V	96V	94U	96U	94?	96?
14: I gladly respond without hesitation when something is required of me.	50	50	36	25	14	25
9: I am an example of wholehearted dedication to duty.	33	42	38	29	29	29
24: I immediately confess and make it right whenever I do something wrong.	37	27	45	41	18	32
7: I am fully committed to change whatever keeps me from doing what I should.	82	56	9	25	9	19

joying work (later in life, job satisfaction?), and being allowed to experiment should not be ignored.

At the third level, Establishing Virtue, we find students exhibiting less peer dependence (read Item 25 and realize that six students are no longer afraid of what others will think, if they do what they are supposed to do, and another five have moved from fear to uncertainty, a few to the point of experiencing rejection—read Item 4). This is no small jump, even for a big frog. In addition to this, they are in the process of exchanging self-autonomy for social values (read Item 13, and contemplate that 10 teenagers are making this shift). Beyond that, they are becoming

Table 5.17 Initial and Follow-Up Virtue Response Assessment

Level 1: Virtuous	Level 1: Unvirtuous	Level 1: Uncertain	Level 1: Assessment	
23. 5% more virtuous	11% less unvirtuous	6% more uncertainty	U → V & ?	Gaining
15. 5% more virtuous	11% less unvirtuous	6% more uncertainty	U → V & ?	Gaining
20. 1% less virtuous	2% less unvirtuous	3% more uncertainty	V & U → ?	Gaining
18. 44% more virtuous	19% less unvirtuous	25% less uncertainty	U & ? → V	Gaining
Level 2: Virtuous	Level 2: Unvirtuous	Level 2: Uncertain	Level 2: Assessment	
3. 11% more virtuous	14% less unvirtuous	2% more uncertainty	U → V	Gaining
10. 11% more virtuous	18% less unvirtuous	7% more uncertainty	U → V & ?	Gaining
5. 6% less virtuous	1% less unvirtuous	6% more uncertainty	V → ?	Losing
8. 12% less virtuous	15% more unvirtuous	3% less uncertainty	V & ? → U	Losing
Level 3: Virtuous	Level 3: Unvirtuous	Level 3: Uncertain	Level 3: Assessment	
13. 1% more virtuous	7% less unvirtuous	6% more uncertainty	U → ?	Gaining
25. 4% more virtuous	8% less unvirtuous	4% more uncertainty	U → ? & V	Gaining
4. 1% more virtuous	4% less unvirtuous	4% more uncertainty	U → ?	Gaining
17. 2% more virtuous	11% less unvirtuous	9% more uncertainty	U → ?	Gaining
Level 4: Virtuous	Level 4: Unvirtuous	Level 4: Uncertain	Level 4: Assessment	
22. 6% less virtuous	0% (same)	6% more uncertainty	V → ?	Losing
19. 5% less virtuous	4% more unvirtuous	1% more uncertainty	V → U	Losing
2. 3% more virtuous	1% more unvirtuous	4% less uncertainty	? → V & U	Gaining
12. 5% more virtuous	5% less unvirtuous	0% (same)	U → V	Gaining
Level 5: Virtuous	Level 5: Unvirtuous	Level 5: Uncertain	Level 5: Assessment	
14. 0% (same)	11% less unvirtuous	11% more uncertainty	U → ?	Gaining
9. 9% more virtuous	9% less unvirtuous	1% less uncertainty	U → V	Gaining
24. 10% less virtuous	4% less unvirtuous	14% more uncertainty	V & U → ?	Losing
7. 26% less virtuous	16% more unvirtuous	9% more uncertainty	V → U & ?	Losing

committed to do what they know they should (read Item 17, and reflect that 15 students are moving toward full commitment in that regard).

By the way, most of your unnoticed students are at this level, and what is happening here pictures their growth pattern. If you look at how the percentages shift, you'll see what I mean. For every single Level 3 item, you will see the same pattern: substantial movement from unvirtuous responses to uncertainty, with a few kind of sliding on in to a virtuous response every now and then. Their growth is slow and steady and hardly noticeable. It moves toward virtue, mainly through uncertainty, with a few—very quietly—sneaking in through the back door. If you hide and watch, you might catch them in the act. Pick out a wallflower student sometime, and try it.

It should be no surprise that Level 4, Evaluating Virtue, should hold such high response percentages. First, because, of all the five levels, this is the most cognitive, the most conceptual, the most easily given to explanation, which is what most teachers prefer to teach . . . content, right? Second, because evaluation is the most readily demonstrated level to students by their teachers. Third, because virtuous evaluation is the sole surviving remnant of our culture's strong moral heritage. Students can still breathe it in from society, on a clear day.

The high response percentages at this level indicate a well-developed capacity to evaluate moral and ethical issues among most of these students. However, some ground has been lost to confusion (read Item 19, and ponder that seven additional students struggle with moral discernment). Not only that, some students are questioning if it's worth it to fight for what is right (read Item 22, and contemplate that nine students are no longer certain they would stand against those who oppose what is right). Yet what is lost in discernment and confidence before others is gained in personal steadfastness (read Item 2, and consider that four more people are keeping their priorities straight; then read Item 12, and realize that seven more students are able to say they are not swayed by bad influences).

At the highest level, Embodying Virtue, we observe relatively lower percentages than at Level 4, which is what we would expect, but that doesn't diminish the significance of the gains and the losses. First, there is a subtle shift in favorable attitudes toward fulfilling responsibilities (read Item 14, and reflect that 15 students no longer refuse to respond when required to do so. They may not be glad about it, they may hesitate, but they no longer refuse). Not only that, some are willing to see themselves as examples and role models (read Item 9, and consider that 13 more students see themselves as examples of dedication to duty). Now for the losses. There is an increasing reluctance among these students to own up to wrongdoing and its consequences (read Item 24, and ponder that as many as 20 more students are not willing to promptly own up to wrongdoing and make restitution). This is no small matter.

Now let me say a word about this last item, Item 7. It was reworded after the first testing because it was not difficult enough for its level. It used to read, "I am open to change anything that keeps me from doing what I should." This wording did not seem to clearly require the high level of virtue given in the taxonomy, so I strengthened it to read, "I am fully committed to change whatever keeps me from doing what I should." This is very likely what accounts for the large shift you see.

To keep all of these gains and losses in perspective, I must tell you that they only represent an overall shift of six percentage points. In other words, after you let the gains and the losses cancel each other out, there was only a net movement of 6%. That does not seem like much. However, that shift was away from unvirtuous responses. More specifically, there was a 3.2% shift to virtue and a 2.74% shift to uncertainty. You probably noticed this definite upward trend throughout the spectrum of responses. I factored out Item 7 because it couldn't be compared due to the rewording of the item to make it more difficult. Now, in Tables 5.18 and 5.19, let's compare the responses from the Social-Desirability subtest, the misrepresentation items.

When we average the changes in percentages of the Social-Desirability items, we readily observe that the shift was not from representation to misrepresentation, it was from representation to uncertainty. In other words, of the 5.12% overall shift from representation, 4.64% went to uncertainty, and only .48% went to misrepre-

Table 5.18 Initial and Follow-Up Social-Desirability Response Comparison (in percentages)

Social-Desirability—Misrepresentation	94R	96R	94M	96M	94?	94?
1: I can remember "playing sick" to get out of something.	61	51	32	36	6	13
6: I have never intensely disliked anyone.	65	61	31	29	4	10
11: I sometimes try to get even, rather than forgive and forget.	61	53	34	39	4	8
16: I never resent being asked to return a favor.	14	21	77	66	9	13
21: I sometimes feel resentful when I don't get my way.	53	46	39	41	8	13
26: I have almost never felt the urge to tell someone off.	84	76	12	19	4	6

Table 5.19 Initial and Follow-Up Social-Desirability Response Assessment

96 S-D: Representation	96 S-D: Misrepresentation	96 S-D: Uncertain	96 S-D: Assessment	
10.00% less representation	3.57% more misrepresentation	6.43% more uncertainty	R → M & ?	Losing
4.29% less representation	2.14% less misrepresentation	6.43% more uncertainty	R & M → ?	Losing
8.57% less representation	5.00% more misrepresentation	3.57% more uncertainty	R → M & ?	Losing
7.14% more representation	11.43% less misrepresentation	4.29% more uncertainty	M → R & ?	Gaining
6.43% less representation	1.43% more misrepresentation	5.00% more uncertainty	R → ? & M	Losing
8.57% less representation	6.43% more misrepresentation	2.14% more uncertainty	R → M & ?	Losing

sentation. This just means there was more uncertainty about the items in the second testing than there was in the first. All in all, we can conclude that there was a 3% increase in virtue, along with a 3% increase in uncertainty, without any more misrepresentation.

What accounted for these shifts? There are a number of variables that probably influenced the changes in the intervening 2 years since the first test was given. Some students graduated, some moved away, some moved in, some dropped out, some were expelled, others moved up from lower grades. But these do not diminish the overall significance of the gains that were made, because these variables probably offset each other. We are free to make that assumption because we had a random and representative sample, with a normal distribution. This just means that if some unvirtuous students graduated or were expelled or moved, others probably came up from the lower grades or moved into the school district to offset the differences. All right then, what accounted for this shift, modest as it is?

After we initially tested the school, Principal Lockett began to implement what you are learning from this manual. At the beginning of the second year, we trained the teachers how to bring virtue back into education. We showed them ways they could reach students with rotten attitudes. Then, they worked hard all year long, like they do every year, and it made a difference that you can measurably see. You might not think it's much, but it represents a reversal of the awful trend we have watched gradually change our schools over the last 30 years. This indicates that you *can* make a difference.

The purpose of this chapter has been to acquaint you with the sample data I obtained from the Frost Independent School District and to demonstrate how my virtue questionnaire performed. In the following chapter, you will observe how to assess the virtue of actual students. I invite you to judge the effectiveness of the scoring forms and guidelines and contemplate how you will use them with your own students as you do so.

Things to Review and Remember From Chapter 5

1. The score range limits of the LVAQ are 20 to 100. The average score for high school students is about 66.

    a. Low virtue scores for high school students range from 20 to 55.
    b. Average virtue scores for high school students range from 56 to 75.
    c. High virtue scores for high school students range from 76 to 100.

2. The score range limits of the Misrepresentation Test (Social-Desirability subtest) is 6 to 30. The average score for high school students is about 18.

    a. Low misrepresentation scores for high school students range from 6 to 16.
    b. Uncertain misrepresentation scores for high school students range from 17 to 19.
    c. High misrepresentation scores for high school students range from 20 to 30.

3. To get an idea of how one student's score relates to others, adjustments for emphasis and uncertainty should be considered.

    a. Emphasis norms follow a 2-to-1 ratio. There is usually one emphatic response for every two unemphatic responses. Emphatic responses do not necessarily indicate a stronger answer.
    b. The average amount of uncertain responses is 3 out of the 26 items. It is not at all uncommon for students to have no uncertain responses. Six or more uncertain responses should cause you to consider possible reasons for this. Uncertain responses can indicate areas of weakness in a student's virtue structure.

6

Scoring and Assessing the Questionnaire

You have now learned how the LVAQ was designed to measure virtue, I hope. Your next task? Transform the data into meaningful information. Once you become familiar with the scoring process, it will not take you any longer to score the questionnaire than it took your students to take it—about 10 minutes. You will find it helpful to work through the scoring procedures before trying to use them. Believe me. Initially, this will take you less than half an hour. To follow is a detailed description acquainting you with this important task. After you have scored a few questionnaires, it will become second nature to you and will quickly become a pleasant procedure as you see the scoring form come alive, depicting your students' virtue.

LVAQ Scoring Form

Right now, the scoring form just looks like a bunch of boxes, signs, symbols, and such. In fact, the whole page is crawling with them, for crying out loud—crowded confusion! Can't be helped. Sorry, but think about it: N. A. (Necessary Abbreviation). This chapter will acquaint you (in a painless way, I promise) with the scoring procedures. After making friends with the scoring form, you will watch me score a few (if you're patient—it's O.K., it's a virtue). Then, you can try some. Directly following, you will find the scoring form, its parts interspersed with descriptions of how they are used. This is the first time through, so just stop, look, and listen.

Number	Misrepresentation Items	SD	D	?	A	SA
1.	I can remember "playing sick" to get out of something.	5 M−	4 M	3	2 R	1 R+
6.	I have never intensely disliked anyone.	1 R+	2 R	3	4 M	5 M−
11.	I sometimes try to get even rather than forgive and forget.	5 M−	4 M	3	2 R	1R+
16.	I never resent being asked to return a favor.	1 R+	2 R	3	4 M	5 M−
21.	I sometimes feel resentful when I don't get my way.	5 M−	4 M	3	2 R	1 R+
26.	I have almost never felt the urge to tell someone off.	1 R+	2 R	3	4 M	5 M−

You can see that this first part of the scoring form contains only six of the questionnaire items, those measuring misrepresentation. No big deal. Notice from the numbers at the left that these items were regularly interspersed, every fifth, throughout the questionnaire. In the columns on the right, you will recognize the letters that were circled in response to the questionnaire (SD D ? A SA). But please note, there are also numbers (1 2 3 4 5), which give you the ability to score the questionnaire later. Following these numbers are letter indicators, which allow you to identify the response of each kind of answer: misrepresentation (M) or representation (R). The plus (+) and minus (–) signs indicate emphasis. In other words, if students expressed "strong" agreement or disagreement (SA/SD), they would be answering with emphasis. The next part of the scoring form presents the 20 virtue items. It is arranged the same way.

Number	Virtue Items	SD	D	?	A	SA
23.	I rebel when someone talks to me about doing what I should.	5V+	4 V	3	2 U	1 U–
15.	I am tired of those in charge trying to show me a better way.	5V+	4 V	3	2 U	1 U–
20.	I get angry when those in authority insist I do things their way.	5V+	4 V	3	2 U	1 U–
18.	I have trouble telling right from wrong.	5V+	4 V	3	2 U	1 U–
3.	I often refuse to do what I know is right.	5V+	4 V	3	2 U	1 U–
10.	I feel unwilling to help even when I know I should.	5V+	4 V	3	2 U	1 U–
5.	I frequently insist on my own way even if I sense I might be wrong.	5V+	4 V	3	2 U	1 U–
8.	I find it hard to really enjoy myself when doing daily chores.	5V+	4 V	3	2 U	1 U–
13.	I resist establishing values in my life so I can be free to be who I am.	5V+	4 V	3	2 U	1 U–
25.	I am afraid of what others might think if I do as I ought.	5V+	4 V	3	2 U	1 U–
4.	I do what I should even if friends reject me for it.	1 U–	2 U	3	4 V	5V+
17.	I am fully committed to do what I know I should.	1 U–	2 U	3	4 V	5 V+
22.	I openly defend what is right.	1 U–	2 U	3	4 V	5 V+
19.	I can easily distinguish between good, better, and best.	1 U–	2 U	3	4V	5V+
2.	I maintain my priorities so that I can do what is best.	1 U–	2 U	3	4 V	5 V+
12.	I consistently remain true to what is best.	1 U–	2 U	3	4 V	5 V+
14.	I gladly respond without hesitation when something is required of me.	1 U–	2 U	3	4 V	5 V+
9.	I am an example of wholehearted dedication to duty.	1 U–	2 U	3	4 V	5 V+
24.	I immediately confess and make it right whenever I do something wrong.	1 U–	2 U	3	4 V	5 V+
7.	I am fully committed to change whatever keeps me from doing what I should.	1 U–	2 U	3	4 V	5 V+

This part of the scoring form is similar to the first. However, these items are listed according to rank. Item 23 is the lowest in rank on the questionnaire; Item 7 is the highest. Notice that, whereas the response letters appear like they do on the first part of the scoring form (SD D ? A SA), as do the numbers for scoring (1 2 3 4 5), the letter indicators reflect a virtuous (V) or an unvirtuous (U) response. The plus (+) and minus (–) signs again indicate an emphatic response. The first two portions of the scoring form are offered for the purpose of transferring the responses from the questionnaire to the scoring form. The next part of the scoring form is for the purpose of recording how many of each kind of response there were.

	SD	D	?	A	SA
Norm Response Totals	3	7	3	9	4
Individual Response Totals	( )	( )	( )	( )	( )

At the top of this portion are the familiar response characters (SD D ? A SA). At the left are two categories: Norm Response Totals and Individual Response Totals. The first category gives the average number of each kind of response. In other words, the average number of Strongly Disagree (SD) responses for the test is 3. The empty spaces under these Norm Response Totals are provided for you to enter the number of each kind of response, which you can quickly tally from the first two parts of the scoring form. Keep in mind that both the misrepresentation and virtue items are intended to be included in this tally. To check yourself, after you have entered the totals, add them up. They should equal 26, the number of items on the questionnaire. If not, tally again the totals of each kind of response until they equal 26.

Why are these totals important? Some people tend to respond in set patterns (see the section in the previous chapter on response sets). Some wish to maintain a positive outlook and will respond on the agreement side much more often than most. Others tend to be negative and will respond on the disagreement side more frequently. Some tend to answer emphatically, whereas others studiously avoid emphatic responses. In addition, some will respond with considerably more uncertainty than others. If the individual you are scoring reflects any of these tendencies, you will want to make mental or written notes and factor these things into your interpretation.

If such mental adjustments do not seem scientific enough for you, send your questionnaires to us (see Resource G). We'll score them by computer and mathematically factor in the adjustments for emphasis and uncertainty (I hate scoring by hand). However, once you get a feel for how the earlier-mentioned tendencies affect scoring, you will find your mental adjustments quite adequate in giving you the approximation you need to understand your students. The next portion of the scoring form allows you to score and rank your findings. It contains two parts: first, the scoring boxes.

	Misrepresentation	Virtue
Uncertainty Count	( ) of 6	( ) of 20
Certainty Count	( ) of 6	( ) of 20
Raw Score	( ) of 30	( ) of 100
Norm Rank	( )	( )

This smaller part (beginning with Uncertainty Count) is for entering information.

Misrepresentation		Virtue	
Ranking Description	*Raw Score*	*Ranking Description*	*Raw Score*
Extremely Unlikely	6 to 10	Very Low	20 to 50
Very Unlikely	11 to 13	Low	51 to 55
Unlikely	14 to 16	Moderately Low	56 to 60
Possible	17 to 19	Average	61 to 70
Likely	20 to 22	Moderately High	71 to 75
Very Likely	23 to 25	High	76 to 80
Extremely Likely	26 to 30	Very High	81 to 100

The larger part (beginning with Ranking Description) is for consulting, after you have entered the required information.

Now, let's consider how to use these two parts of the form. First, you will want to know the extent of your students' uncertainty. Spaces are provided for this information (those with "of" in them), once you count the number of question marks (?) for misrepresentation, then for virtue. Spaces are also provided for you to tally the number of misrepresentation responses and the number of virtuous responses. Hold on there! Do not simply subtract the uncertainty count from 6 or 20, presuming that will leave you with the correct number of "Certainty" responses. Instead, tally only items marked with "M" or "M–," and enter that amount in the certainty count space. Disregard for now those items marked with "R" or "R+." Then, you will do the same for the virtuous responses, counting only items marked with a "V" or "V+," and entering that number in the certainty count space, disregarding all items marked with "U" or "U–."

Next, notice the place for Raw Score for the misrepresentation items. This requires the total of all six misrepresentation items. Whoa, big stallion! This time do not just add the numbers of the items marked "M" or "M–." Include the representation responses ("R" and "R+") as well as those indicating uncertainty (?). For instance, if the first item were "M," its numerical value would be 4. If the next were "?," its numerical value would be 3. And if the next were "R," its numerical value would be 2. The numerical misrepresentation score of these three items is 9 (i.e., $4 + 3 + 2 = 9$). After obtaining a raw score for all six misrepresentation items and entering it in the appropriate space, the norm ranking description that corresponds to that numerical score can be found in the table directly below the boxes. Once this is determined, the ranking description can be written in the Norm Rank space provided.

The same thing can be done with the virtue part of the questionnaire by adding the numerical value of all 20 virtue items and putting the total in the Raw Score box. Then, the norm ranking description that corresponds to that numerical score can be found and *written* in the Norm Rank box. When these tasks are completed, the results can be read to form an interpretive statement of your findings. For example, if the Raw Misrepresentation Score were 21, and if the Raw Virtue Score were 78, you would conclude, It is "likely" that this student misrepresented a "high" virtue score.

However, under certain conditions, you may wish to modify these findings. If the student responded emphatically more than 10 times, you might mentally lower the numerical score a bit; if not at all, you might raise it a little. If the student expressed considerable uncertainty (i.e., more than five) but answered most of the other items virtuously, you would want to mentally adjust the score higher. If more than five items were marked with uncertainty and most of the rest were unvirtuous, you would want to mentally adjust the score lower. In other words, Unvirtuous responses get a 1 or a 2. Uncertain responses get a 3. A whole bunch of 3s artificially raises a score otherwise characterized by 1s and 2s. Get it? The same is true for Virtuous responses, which get a 4 or a 5. A good many 3s artificially lower a score characterized by 4s and 5s. The next part of the scoring form provides an idea about a person's virtue structure at the time the questionnaire was taken.

Virtue Response Analysis

Item Number	23	15	20	18	3	10	5	8	13	25	4	17	22	19	2	12	14	9	24	7
Item Rank	1	2	3	4	5	6	7	8	9	10	11	12	13	14	15	16	17	18	19	20
Item Direction	−	−	−	−	−	−	−	−	−	−	+	+	+	+	+	+	+	+	+	+
Item Basis	D	B	D	B	D	B	D	B	D	B	D	B	D	B	D	B	D	B	D	B
Character	▓		▓		▓		▓		▓		▓		▓		▓		▓		▓	
Conduct		▓		▓		▓		▓		▓		▓		▓		▓		▓		▓
Virtue Levels	Examining				Experimenting				Establishing				Evaluating				Embodying			

Virtue Balance	Character (Inner Being)	Conduct (Outward Doing)
Virtue Item Count	( ) of 10	( ) of 10

This portion also contains two parts: (a) the Virtue Response Analysis Table you've already seen in Chapter 4 and (b) a Character-Conduct Balance Check. The Virtue Analysis Table provides a blank under each item for you to insert the appropriate virtue indicator from the virtue scoring boxes in the first part of the scoring form. For example, if Item 23 were marked *SD,* the virtue indicator would be "V+," which you would place in the blank below Item 23 on the Virtue Analysis Table. Notice that the only blank for Item 23 is in the "Conduct" row. The next item is 15. The virtue indicator for this item must go in the "Character" row. Once you have entered an indicator for each of the 20 virtue items, count all the Character items that have a "V" or "V+." Then count all the Conduct items having "V" or "V+." Enter the numbers in the Virtue Item Count boxes for Character and Conduct.

These numbers should closely correspond. For instance, if there were four virtuous responses for the Character items, there should also be four virtuous responses for the Conduct items. In actuality, the number of character items matched the number of conduct items in over two thirds of those tested. But it's not unusual for this correspondence to vary one point in either direction (i.e., 4-5 or 5-4, or 3-4, or 4-3), which must happen whenever there is an odd number of virtue items. However, if the character and conduct item count does not closely correspond, the reasons are significant. For example, if you have an imbalance (Character = 3 and Conduct = 6), you would conclude that a student is presenting something with his or her actions that is out of keeping with what is going on inside. Possible reasons include performance-based upbringing, a desire to please the teacher, peer dependence, and so on.

Well, that's all there is to scoring the LVAQ. And now that you have "mastered" the scoring procedures, you will want to look over the guidelines below. When you have taken a quick look, you will find some actual examples to give you an idea of the kind of differences you will encounter. Then, you will be ready to score some of your own students. After you have repeated the scoring process yourself several times, you will become quite proficient. Remember the old axiom, "Repetition is the best teacher."

On the next page, you will find a blank Scoring Form. Following that, you will find Scoring Guidelines that explain how to use the Scoring Form. The Scoring Guidelines offer steps to follow for using the Scoring Form. The part of the Scoring Form that is being explained will be represented in miniature so you can locate where you are when you use the Scoring Form. Don't enter information on the Scoring Guidelines.

LVAQ Scoring Form

Name: **School:**   **Grade:**

Race: **Gender:**   **Age:**

No.	Misrepresentation Items	SD	D	?	A	SA
1.	I can remember "playing sick" to get out of something.	5 M-	4 M	3	2 R	1 R+
6.	I have never intensely disliked anyone.	1 R+	2 R	3	4 M	5 M-
11.	I sometimes try to get even, rather than forgive and forget.	5 M-	4 M	3	2 R	1 R+
16.	I never resent being asked to return a favor.	1 R+	2 R	3	4 M	5 M-
21.	I sometimes feel resentful when I don't get my way.	5 M-	4 M	3	2 R	1 R+
26.	I have almost never felt the urge to tell someone off.	1 R+	2 R	3	4 M	5 M-

No.	Virtue Items	SD	D	?	A	SA
23.	I rebel when someone talks to me about doing what I should.	5V+	4 V	3	2 U	1 U-
15.	I am tired of those in charge trying to show me a better way.	5V+	4 V	3	2 U	1 U-
20.	I get angry when those in authority insist I do things their way.	5V+	4 V	3	2 U	1 U-
18.	I have trouble telling right from wrong.	5V+	4 V	3	2 U	1 U-
3.	I often refuse to do what I know is right.	5V+	4 V	3	2 U	1 U-
10.	I feel unwilling to help even when I know I should.	5V+	4 V	3	2 U	1 U-
5.	I frequently insist on my own way even if I sense I might be wrong.	5V+	4 V	3	2 U	1 U-
8.	I find it hard to really enjoy myself when doing daily chores.	5V+	4 V	3	2 U	1 U-
13.	I resist establishing values in my life so I can be free to be who I am.	5V+	4 V	3	2 U	1 U-
25.	I am afraid of what others might think if I do as I ought.	5V+	4 V	3	2 U	1 U-
4.	I do what I should, even if friends reject me for it.	1 U-	2 U	3	4 V	5 V+
17.	I am fully committed to do what I know I should.	1 U-	2 U	3	4 V	5 V+
22.	I openly defend what is right.	1 U-	2 U	3	4 V	5 V+
19.	I can easily distinguish between good, better and best.	1 U-	2 U	3	4 V	5 V+
2.	I maintain my priorities so that I can do what is best.	1 U-	2 U	3	4 V	5 V+
12.	I consistently remain true to what is best.	1 U-	2 U	3	4 V	5 V+
14.	I gladly respond without hesitation when something is required of me.	1 U-	2 U	3	4 V	5 V+
9.	I am an example of whole-hearted dedication to duty.	1 U-	2 U	3	4 V	5 V+
24.	I immediately confess and make it right whenever I do something wrong.	1 U-	2 U	3	4 V	5 V+
7.	I am fully committed to change whatever keeps me from doing what I should.	1 U-	2 U	3	4 V	5 V+

	SD	D	?	A	SA
Norm Response Totals	3	7	3	9	4
Individual Response Totals	( )	( )	( )	( )	( )

	Misrepresentation	Virtue
Uncertainty Count	( ) of 6	( ) of 20
Certainty Count	( ) of 6	( ) of 20
Raw Score	( ) of 30	( ) of 100
Norm Rank	( )	( )

Misrepresentation		Virtue	
Ranking Description	Raw Score	Ranking Description	Raw Score
Extremely Unlikely	6 to 10	Very Low	20 to 50
Very Unlikely	11 to 13	Low	51 to 55
Unlikely	14 to 16	Moderately Low	56 to 60
Possible	17 to 19	Average	61 to 70
Likely	20 to 22	Moderately High	71 to 75
Very Likely	23 to 25	High	76 to 80
Extremely Likely	26 to 30	Very High	81 to 100

Virtue Response Analysis

Item Number	23	15	20	18	3	10	5	8	13	25	4	17	22	19	2	12	14	9	24	7
Item Rank	1	2	3	4	5	6	7	8	9	10	11	12	13	14	15	16	17	18	19	20
Item Direction	-	-	-	-	-	-	-	-	-	-	+	+	+	+	+	+	+	+	+	+
Item Basis	D	B	D	B	D	B	D	B	D	B	D	B	D	B	D	B	D	B	D	B
Character																				
Conduct																				
Virtue Levels	Examining		Experimenting		Establishing		Evaluating		Embodying											

Virtue Balance	Character (Inner Being)	Conduct (Outward Doing)
Virtue Item Count	( ) of 10	( ) of 10

LVAQ Scoring Guidelines

These guidelines provide a simple format for scoring the Loehrer Virtue Assessment Questionnaire. Carefully follow the steps below, and then consider the implications of your findings.

For scoring purposes, "M" indicates misrepresentation, while "R" indicates representation. "V" indicates a virtuous response, while "U" indicates an unvirtuous response. Plus (+) or minus (-) signs indicate an emphatic response (SD or SA). Numbers (1 2 3 4 5) indicate the raw score for that item.

Begin scoring by placing the Questionnaire and the Scoring Form side by side and then read Step One.

No.	Misrepresentation Items	SD	D	?	A	SA
1.	I can remember "playing sick" to get out of something.	5 M-	4 M	3	2 R	1 R+
6.	I have never intensely disliked anyone.	1 R+	2 R	3	4 M	5 M-
11.	I sometimes try to get even, rather than forgive and forget.	5 M-	4 M	3	2 R	1 R+
16.	I never resent being asked to return a favor.	1 R+	2 R	3	4 M	5 M-
21.	I sometimes feel resentful when I don't get my way.	5 M-	4 M	3	2 R	1 R+
26.	I have almost never felt the urge to tell someone off.	1 R+	2 R	3	4 M	5 M-

No.	Virtue Items	SD	D	?	A	SA
23.	I rebel when someone talks to me about doing what I should.	5 V+	4 V	3	2 U	1 U-
15.	I am tired of those in charge trying to show me a better way.	5 V+	4 V	3	2 U	1 U-
20.	I get angry when those in authority insist I do things their way.	5 V+	4 V	3	2 U	1 U-
18.	I have trouble telling right from wrong.	5 V+	4 V	3	2 U	1 U-
3.	I often refuse to do what I know is right.	5 V+	4 V	3	2 U	1 U-
10.	I feel unwilling to help even when I know I should.	5 V+	4 V	3	2 U	1 U-
5.	I frequently insist on my own way even if I sense I might be wrong.	5 V+	4 V	3	2 U	1 U-
8.	I find it hard to really enjoy myself when doing daily chores.	5 V+	4 V	3	2 U	1 U-
13.	I resist establishing values in my life so I can be free to be who I am.	5 V+	4 V	3	2 U	1 U-
25.	I am afraid of what others might think if I do as I ought.	5 V+	4 V	3	2 U	1 U-
4.	I do what I should, even if friends reject me for it.	1 U-	2 U	3	4 V	5 V+
17.	I am fully committed to do what I know I should.	1 U-	2 U	3	4 V	5 V+
22.	I openly defend what is right.	1 U-	2 U	3	4 V	5 V+
19.	I can easily distinguish between good, better and best.	1 U-	2 U	3	4 V	5 V+
2.	I maintain my priorities so that I can do what is best.	1 U-	2 U	3	4 V	5 V+
12.	I consistently remain true to what is best.	1 U-	2 U	3	4 V	5 V+
14.	I gladly respond without hesitation when something is required of me.	1 U-	2 U	3	4 V	5 V+
9.	I am an example of whole-hearted dedication to duty.	1 U-	2 U	3	4 V	5 V+
24.	I immediately confess and make it right whenever I do something wrong.	1 U-	2 U	3	4 V	5 V+
7.	I am fully committed to change whatever keeps me from doing what I should.	1 U-	2 U	3	4 V	5 V+

Step One: The first step is to *transfer the responses* circled on the questionnaire (**SD D ? A SA**) to the *LVAQ Scoring Form*. Begin with the box labeled **Misrepresentation Items** at the top of the Scoring Form like that shown above. The numbers in the **No.** column on the left side of the *Scoring Form* correspond to the item numbers on the *Questionnaire*.

Highlight or circle the *box* under the appropriate response column on the *Scoring Form* that matches the response circled by the student on the *Questionnaire*. For example, if "SD" was circled for item No. 1 on the Questionnaire, then find item No. 1 on the left side of the Scoring Form and highlight or circle the box under the column labeled "SD" containing "5M-" on that same line.

Once you transfer all 26 responses (both Misrepresentation and Virtue Items) from the Questionnaire to the Scoring Form you may set the Questionnaire aside. The rest of the work will be done on the Scoring Form itself.

	SD	D	?	A	SA
Norm Response Totals	3	7	3	9	4
Individual Response Totals	( )	( )	( )	( )	( )

Step Two: Beginning at the top of the *Scoring Form,* glance down the columns and count the number of each kind of response (SD D ? A SA) for all 26 items (including both misrepresentation and virtue items), and put the *totals* on the line that says *Individual Response Totals* like that shown above.

	Misrepresentation	Virtue
Uncertainty Count	( ) of 6	( ) of 20
Certainty Count	( ) of 6	( ) of 20
Raw Score	( ) of 30	( ) of 100
Norm Rank	( )	( )

Step Three: Go back to the top of the Scoring Form and count the number of *Misrepresentation Items* answered with a question mark (?) and enter the number in the *Uncertainty Count* box under the *Misrepresentation* column like that shown above. Do the same for the *Virtue Items.*

Next count the number of *Misrepresentation Items* which have an "M" or "M-" and enter the total in the *Certainty Count* box of the *Misrepresentation* column. Then count the *Virtue Items* which have a "V" or "V+" and write the total in the *Virtue* column of the *Certainty Count* box.

After doing so, add the numbers (1 2 3 4 5) in the boxes of all six misrepresentation items and place the total in the *Raw Score* box like that shown in the *Misrepresentation* column. Do the same for all twenty virtue items. A calculator helps ensure accuracy for this part.

Finally, find the *Ranking Descriptions* in the table, like the one shown below, that match the *Raw Scores* and enter them in the *Norm Rank* boxes like those shown directly above.

Misrepresentation		Virtue	
Ranking Description	Raw Score	Ranking Description	Raw Score
Extremely Unlikely	6 to 10	Very Low	20 to 50
Very Unlikely	11 to 13	Low	51 to 55
Unlikely	14 to 16	Moderately Low	56 to 60
Possible	17 to 19	Average	61 to 70
Likely	20 to 22	Moderately High	71 to 75
Very Likely	23 to 25	High	76 to 80
Extremely Likely	26 to 30	Very High	81 to 100

Step Four: Return to the top of the page on the *Scoring Form* to the *Virtue Items* portion and transfer the *response indicators* (U- U ? V V+), one by one, to the empty boxes on the *Virtue Response Analysis* table like the one shown below.

Virtue Response Analysis

Item Number	23	15	20	18	3	10	5	8	13	25	4	17	22	19	2	12	14	9	24	7
Item Rank	1	2	3	4	5	6	7	8	9	10	11	12	13	14	15	16	17	18	19	20
Item Direction	-	-	-	-	-	-	-	-	-	-	+	+	+	+	+	+	+	+	+	+
Item Basis	D	B	D	B	D	B	D	B	D	B	D	B	D	B	D	B	D	B	D	B
Character																				
Conduct																				
Virtue Levels	Examining			Experimenting			Establishing			Evaluating			Embodying							

For example, item 23 is a *Conduct* item. You can detect this because the *Character* box is shaded in to prevent you from putting anything in it, and because the *Item Basis* for this item is a "D" for *Doing*. (Conduct is *Doing*. Character is *Being*.) So, in this case, you would put the appropriate indicator (U- U ? V V+) in the empty box below 23. And you can readily see that the next item, number 15, is a *Character* item, because the *Conduct* box is shaded.

Step Five: Finally, count the number of virtuous *Character* responses from the *Virtue Response Analysis* table like the one shown above and enter the total in the *Virtue Item Count* box like that found below. Do the same for the *Conduct* responses. Count only the responses which indicate virtue ("V" or "V+"). Do not include those responses indicated by "U-", "U", or "?".

Virtue Balance	Character (Inner Being)	Conduct (Outward Doing)
Virtue Item Count	( ) of 10	( ) of 10

The *Virtue Balance* portion of the Scoring Form (above) is for the purpose of comparing the internal and external (character and conduct) expressions of virtue. The two should correspond closely. It is insignificant if they vary by one, either higher or lower, from the other.

The rest of the chapter contains actual scored examples employing the scoring form you just learned to use. Glancing over these examples and considering the assessment that follows will enable you to do your own scoring. And after you have actually scored a few, you will find the whole process quite easy.

Name: Ken (fictitious name) **School:** **Grade:** 12
Ethnic Background: White **Gender:** Male **Age:** 1 7

No.	Misrepresentation Items	SD	D	?	A	SA
1.	I can remember "playing sick" to get out of something.	5 M-	4 M	3	2 R	1 R+
6.	I have never intensely disliked anyone.	1 R+	2 R	3	4 M	5 M-
11.	I sometimes try to get even, rather than forgive and forget.	5 M-	4 M	3	2 R	1 R+
16.	I never resent being asked to return a favor.	1 R+	2 R	3	4 M	5 M-
21.	I sometimes feel resentful when I don't get my way.	5 M-	4 M	3	2 R	1 R+
26.	I have almost never felt the urge to tell someone off.	1 R+	2 R	3	4 M	5 M-

No.	Virtue Items	SD	D	?	A	SA
23.	I rebel when someone talks to me about doing what I should.	5 V+	4 V	3	2 U	1 U-
15.	I am tired of those in charge trying to show me a better way.	5 V+	4 V	3	2 U	1 U-
20.	I get angry when those in authority insist I do things their way.	5 V+	4 V	3	2 U	1 U-
18.	I have trouble telling right from wrong.	5 V+	4 V	3	2 U	1 U-
3.	I often refuse to do what I know is right.	5 V+	4 V	3	2 U	1 U-
10.	I feel unwilling to help even when I know I should.	5 V+	4 V	3	2 U	1 U-
5.	I frequently insist on my own way even if I sense I might be wrong.	5 V+	4 V	3	2 U	1 U-
8.	I find it hard to really enjoy myself when doing daily chores.	5 V+	4 V	3	2 U	1 U-
13.	I resist establishing values in my life so I can be free to be who I am.	5 V+	4 V	3	2 U	1 U-
25.	I am afraid of what others might think if I do as I ought.	5 V+	4 V	3	2 U	1 U-
4.	I do what I should, even if friends reject me for it.	1 U-	2 U	3	4 V	5 V+
17.	I am fully committed to do what I know I should.	1 U-	2 U	3	4 V	5 V+
22.	I openly defend what is right.	1 U-	2 U	3	4 V	5 V+
19.	I can easily distinguish between good, better and best.	1 U-	2 U	3	4 V	5 V+
2.	I maintain my priorities so that I can do what is best.	1 U-	2 U	3	4 V	5 V+
12.	I consistently remain true to what is best.	1 U-	2 U	3	4 V	5 V+
14.	I gladly respond without hesitation when something is required of me.	1 U-	2 U	3	4 V	5 V+
9.	I am an example of whole-hearted dedication to duty.	1 U-	2 U	3	4 V	5 V+
24.	I immediately confess and make it right whenever I do something wrong.	1 U-	2 U	3	4 V	5 V+
7.	I am fully committed to change whatever keeps me from doing what I should.	1 U-	2 U	3	4 V	5 V+

	SD	D	?	A	SA
Norm Response Totals	3	7	3	9	4
Individual Response Totals	(3)	(16)	(0)	(7)	(0)

	Misrepresentation	Virtue
Uncertainty Count	(0) of 6	(0) of 20
Certainty Count	(1) of 6	(11) of 20
Raw Score	(12) of 30	(63) of 100
Norm Rank	(Very Unlikely)	(Average)

Misrepresentation		Virtue	
Ranking Description	Raw Score	Ranking Description	Raw Score
Extremely Unlikely	6 to 10	Very Low	20 to 50
Very Unlikely	11 to 13	Low	51 to 55
Unlikely	14 to 16	Moderately Low	56 to 60
Possible	17 to 19	Average	61 to 70
Likely	20 to 22	Moderately High	71 to 75
Very Likely	23 to 25	High	76 to 80
Extremely Likely	26 to 30	Very High	81 to 100

Virtue Response Analysis

Item Number	23	15	20	18	3	10	5	8	13	25	4	17	22	19	2	12	14	9	24	7
Item Rank	1	2	3	4	5	6	7	8	9	10	11	12	13	14	15	16	17	18	19	20
Item Direction	-	-	-	-	-	-	-	-	-	+	+	+	+	+	+	+	+	+	+	+
Item Basis	D	B	D	B	D	B	D	B	D	B	D	B	D	B	D	B	D	B	D	B
Character		V		V		V		U		V+		U		V		U		U		V
Conduct	U		V		V		V		V		U		U		U		U		U	
Virtue Levels	Examining		Experimenting		Establishing		Evaluating		Embodying											

Virtue Balance	Character (Inner Being)	Conduct (Outward Doing)
Virtue Item Count	(6) of 10	(5) of 10

After scoring Ken's test, it becomes immediately obvious that although Ken's score is average (63; the mean is 65.664) and although he has not misrepresented himself (12; a low misrepresentation score; the mean is 16.443), he has responded in quite an unusual fashion. He responded negatively to 19 of the 26 questions, answering almost 3 to 1 on the disagreement side. This is rather unusual.

Such a response to the test (i.e., his high number of negative responses) is important information. It should cause you to consider if he just had a negative attitude that day or if he was defensive. Yet his response to the first question was positive, so that's not too likely. And his responses to the rest of the questions do not seem contrived. Also, he has positive responses interspersed throughout. Yet he had no strong agreement responses at all. Neither did he have any uncertain responses. When he did answer with emphasis, it was on the disagreement side. This shows a definite predilection. It would be worth talking to Ken about this. It is likely that, had the direction of the items on the test not been reversed one from another, Ken would have disagreed with every question, perhaps even telling himself as he took it that he had discovered the key to answering correctly.

I followed up Ken's questionnaire by asking his teacher to briefly describe three things: his attitude in general, his behavior in class and his academic performance (see Resource E for an example of the form I used). When I asked Ken's teacher to tell us a little about his attitude in general, Mrs. Poulter (a fictitious name) said, "It's pretty good; he has basically worked hard all year." Of his behavior in class, she added, "It's good. But he is often tired and sleepy, especially on Mondays (probably puts in a full weekend); otherwise, he is quite attentive and participates fairly well. His attendance is excellent." As far as grades go, Mrs. Poulter related, "Ken is a solid 'B' student. He could probably do better but overall is a good student." Knowing these things about Ken, as his teacher, you would want to ask him about his negative responses.

But first notice that Ken is pretty solid through the first three virtue levels. He has successfully examined virtue, experimented with it, and established it in his life, without any uncertainty. There has even been some movement into the areas of evaluating and embodying virtue. Ken is 17. In a couple of weeks, he will graduate. You can feel good for him. He has made it through the teenage years with a good attitude and is growing into a fine young man. But why did he answer so negatively? There is nothing on his questionnaire to tell you.

When you sit down to talk with Ken about his test, he is likely to be slightly suspicious of you, or at least curious, for asking the kinds of questions you asked on the questionnaire. Before he will be very free with further information, he will probably be interested in knowing how you used what he has already given you. You would do well to begin your conversation with him by describing what the test measures and how.

You could say, "Ken, this test was designed to measure how willing you are to do what you know you should do. It also has the capacity to detect if you misrepresented yourself. For instance, Ken, some of the questions ask what almost everybody has done but that those who are misrepresenting themselves would be likely to say they have never done, like 'Have you ever stuck gum on the underside of your desk?' The other questions ask if you are the kind of person who likes doing what you should do and if you actually do what you should do when you have occasion to do it. The reason I am interested in this is that these things affect how you will handle the knowledge teachers want to give you and will help me teach more effectively."

The next thing you need to convince Ken about is that you do not consider the test to be a *complete* means of measuring much of anything (it's true!). You want to tell him it's just a place to begin and that that is why you want to talk further about this with him. You could say, "Ken, I realize there are definite limitations to what a test will tell us, but there are a few things a questionnaire will ask better and faster than I can without using one, and it will do it in a uniform way for all the students. So that's why I use it, but I also want to follow it up by talking personally with you. I want to tell you what I learned about you individually and with respect to the rest of your class, but most important, I want to get to know you better by hearing what you have to say about it all."

Some of the more astute students will wonder how you can measure something accurately if you let them answer emphatically, or if you let them opt out by circling a question mark. Yes, such students will often be those who cause you trouble. No, they are not trying to cause you more grief by asking such things. Curiosity will prompt these questions even as they take the test. Also, remember, you have invaded their territory. Some might even think you are taking advantage of them by using your authority to extract information from them they would not normally give you (for such, this is true of any test). If you are going to get to know them better, you need to let them know you are properly handling the information they have already given you and are doing so for their benefit.

In Ken's case, when you ask him why he answered so negatively, he could say "I don't remember." But he might say "I just don't like giving out that kind of information, and I just felt a little reluctant about it." Or he might say "My Momma made me eat mush for breakfast." Or it could be that this is just the way Ken's response pattern worked out because of where his is. I tend to think so, but it might be a combination of things, because when he did answer emphatically, it was always on the negative side, never the positive. Of one thing we can be sure, and we can use his teacher's word for it, Ken is "solid." Now let's look at a student whose responses include considerable uncertainty.

Name: Ann (fictitious name) **School:** **Grade:** 10

Ethnic Background: White **Gender:** Female **Age:** 15

No.	Misrepresentation Items	SD	D	?	A	SA
1.	I can remember "playing sick" to get out of something.	5 M-	4 M	3	2 R	1 R+
6.	I have never intensely disliked anyone.	1 R+	2 R	3	4 M	5 M-
11.	I sometimes try to get even, rather than forgive and forget.	5 M-	4 M	3	2 R	1 R+
16.	I never resent being asked to return a favor.	1 R+	2 R	3	4 M	5 M-
21.	I sometimes feel resentful when I don't get my way.	5 M-	4 M	3	2 R	1 R+
26.	I have almost never felt the urge to tell someone off.	1 R+	2 R	3	4 M	5 M-

No.	Virtue Items	SD	D	?	A	SA
23.	I rebel when someone talks to me about doing what I should.	5V+	4 V	3	2 U	1 U-
15.	I am tired of those in charge trying to show me a better way.	5V+	4 V	3	2 U	1 U-
20.	I get angry when those in authority insist I do things their way.	5V+	4 V	3	2 U	1 U-
18.	I have trouble telling right from wrong.	5V+	4 V	3	2 U	1 U-
3.	I often refuse to do what I know is right.	5V+	4 V	3	2 U	1 U-
10.	I feel unwilling to help even when I know I should.	5V+	4 V	3	2 U	1 U-
5.	I frequently insist on my own way even if I sense I might be wrong.	5V+	4 V	3	2 U	1 U-
8.	I find it hard to really enjoy myself when doing daily chores.	5V+	4 V	3	2 U	1 U-
13.	I resist establishing values in my life so I can be free to be who I am.	5V+	4 V	3	2 U	1 U-
25.	I am afraid of what others might think if I do as I ought.	5V+	4 V	3	2 U	1 U-
4.	I do what I should, even if friends reject me for it.	1 U-	2 U	3	4 V	5 V+
17.	I am fully committed to do what I know I should.	1 U-	2 U	3	4 V	5 V+
22.	I openly defend what is right.	1 U-	2 U	3	4 V	5 V+
19.	I can easily distinguish between good, better and best.	1 U-	2 U	3	4 V	5 V+
2.	I maintain my priorities so that I can do what is best.	1 U-	2 U	3	4 V	5 V+
12.	I consistently remain true to what is best.	1 U-	2 U	3	4 V	5 V+
14.	I gladly respond without hesitation when something is required of me.	1 U-	2 U	3	4 V	5 V+
9.	I am an example of whole-hearted dedication to duty.	1 U-	2 U	3	4 V	5 V+
24.	I immediately confess and make it right whenever I do something wrong.	1 U-	2 U	3	4 V	5 V+
7.	I am fully committed to change whatever keeps me from doing what I should.	1 U-	2 U	3	4 V	5 V+

	SD	D	?	A	SA
Norm Response Totals	3	7	3	9	4
Individual Response Totals	(0)	(4)	(13)	(9)	(0)

	Misrepresentation	Virtue
Uncertainty Count	(1) of 6	(12) of 20
Certainty Count	(2) of 6	(8) of 20
Raw Score	(17) of 30	(68) of 100
Norm Rank	(Possible)	(Average)

Misrepresentation		Virtue	
Ranking Description	Raw Score	Ranking Description	Raw Score
Extremely Unlikely	6 to 10	Very Low	20 to 50
Very Unlikely	11 to 13	Low	51 to 55
Unlikely	14 to 16	Moderately Low	56 to 60
Possible	17 to 19	Average	61 to 70
Likely	20 to 22	Moderately High	71 to 75
Very Likely	23 to 25	High	76 to 80
Extremely Likely	26 to 30	Very High	81 to 100

Virtue Response Analysis

Item Number	23	15	20	18	3	10	5	8	13	25	4	17	22	19	2	12	14	9	24	7
Item Rank	1	2	3	4	5	6	7	8	9	10	11	12	13	14	15	16	17	18	19	20
Item Direction	-	-	-	-	-	-	-	-	-	-	+	+	+	+	+	+	+	+	+	+
Item Basis	D	B	D	B	D	B	D	B	D	B	D	B	D	B	D	B	D	B	D	B
Character		?		?	V		?		?		V		V		?		?		?		V
Conduct	?		?		V		?		?		V		V		V		?		?	
Virtue Levels	Examining		Experimenting		Establishing		Evaluating		Embodying											

Virtue Balance	Character (Inner Being)	Conduct (Outward Doing)
Virtue Item Count	(4) of 10	(4) of 10

In most cases, making adjustments for students' uncertainty and emphasis does not amount to much of a difference (usually only a point or two), as with Ken, but in some cases, it really can, and students can sense that it can. Let's look at an example where uncertainty and emphasis made quite a difference. After testing Frost High School, I was discussing the results with Mr. Lockett, the principal. He would ask about someone and not tell me what he knew, and I would give a brief description of that student to him. He would say repeatedly, "Well, that's right! Tell me about this one." First, he asked about the troublesome students, and then after a few minutes, he asked about someone he believed to be highly virtuous, but he did not tell me that. So what follows is an example of a highly virtuous person whose score was greatly influenced by considerable uncertainty.

Three things immediately stand out when we consider Ann's scores: First, a full half of her answers were uncertain. This is over 4 times the norm for uncertain responses—highly unusual. Second, she never answered emphatically, and third, whenever she answered with certainty, it was always on the virtuous side. Intuitively this means, if we take out her uncertain responses and adjust for lack of emphasis, her virtue score will be considerably higher. Mr. Lockett knew this girl; I did not. After asking about a good many students and being pleased with the description I gave from the test results, when I gave Ann's initial scores to him, he frowned and said, "I would have expected a higher virtue score from her." Her unadjusted scores were average. Keep in mind that the unadjusted scores usually only vary a few points from the adjusted scores, but Ann's response pattern is highly unusual.

Adjusting her scores to norm (which can be done with precision using our computerized scoring), for uncertainty and emphasis, made an incredible difference. After making these adjustments, I told Mr. Lockett, "Ann's virtue score adjusts from 68 to 87, and her misrepresentation score went down a point from 17 to 16. She clearly represents a highly virtuous response." He said, "That's what I would have expected."

However, the lack of emphatic responses, the amazing number of uncertain responses, and the questions about which she was uncertain (comparing her answers with the analytic table below) breaks our heart for this girl. These things indicate a virtue structure shot full of holes (uncertainty) and without much strength of desire left (no emphasis)—or at least no capacity to be bold or at the very least, a carefully guarded response. Clearly, this is a wonderfully virtuous girl who is being shaken to the roots. Let's look at the analytic table to see how I formed these preliminary conclusions.

Surely, the teenage years are a time of adjustment, a time of reconsidering what students have grown up with and of personalizing their parent's values or at least beginning to develop their own personal ethical systems. Yet Ann's score reflects much more than that. For 8 of 10 items on the low side, she is uncertain. To have as many virtuous responses as Ann does from one end of the spectrum to the other, to the exclusion of the Examining Level (Level 1) is incredible. In addition, she is also having considerable trouble at Level 3, with establishing virtue. These things indicate that a marvelously virtuous young girl is reexamining things with a good deal of uncertainty, and things that were once established are now very weak indeed. When you discover these indicators, wouldn't you want to sit down and talk with her to find out what exactly is happening with her?

Here are her teacher's written responses to our follow-up (without knowing the test results): first, regarding her attitude in general, Mr. Logan (not his real name) said, "Her attitude is good. She seems to always have a smile;" regarding her behavior in class, he reported, "It's good. She participates, asks questions, etc."; and concerning her academic performance, he added, "She has an "A" average. Sometimes, she does falter on homework papers (below 80)." Our teacher could profit from seeing this assessment of her inner attitudes and from a discussion of these things with Ann or her parents or both. But from her attitude, behavior, and grades alone, a teacher might never be concerned about Ann. Now let's consider an example of a very positive response.

Name: Luke (fictitious name)   **School:**   **Grade:** 7
Ethnic Background: White   **Gender:** Male   **Age:** 12

No.	Misrepresentation Items	SD	D	?	A	SA
1.	I can remember "playing sick" to get out of something.	5 M-	4 M	3	2 R	1 R+
6.	I have never intensely disliked anyone.	1 R+	2 R	3	4 M	5 M-
11.	I sometimes try to get even, rather than forgive and forget.	5 M-	4 M	3	2 R	1 R+
16.	I never resent being asked to return a favor.	1 R+	2 R	3	4 M	5 M-
21.	I sometimes feel resentful when I don't get my way.	5 M-	4 M	3	2 R	1 R+
26.	I have almost never felt the urge to tell someone off.	1 R+	2 R	3	4 M	5 M-

No.	Virtue Items	SD	D	?	A	SA
23.	I rebel when someone talks to me about doing what I should.	5 V+	4 V	3	2 U	1 U-
15.	I am tired of those in charge trying to show me a better way.	5 V+	4 V	3	2 U	1 U-
20.	I get angry when those in authority insist I do things their way.	5 V+	4 V	3	2 U	1 U-
18.	I have trouble telling right from wrong.	5 V+	4 V	3	2 U	1 U-
3.	I often refuse to do what I know is right.	5 V+	4 V	3	2 U	1 U-
10.	I feel unwilling to help even when I know I should.	5 V+	4 V	3	2 U	1 U-
5.	I frequently insist on my own way even if I sense I might be wrong.	5 V+	4 V	3	2 U	1 U-
8.	I find it hard to really enjoy myself when doing daily chores.	5 V+	4 V	3	2 U	1 U-
13.	I resist establishing values in my life so I can be free to be who I am.	5 V+	4 V	3	2 U	1 U-
25.	I am afraid of what others might think if I do as I ought.	5 V+	4 V	3	2 U	1 U-
4.	I do what I should, even if friends reject me for it.	1 U-	2 U	3	4 V	5 V+
17.	I am fully committed to do what I know I should.	1 U-	2 U	3	4 V	5 V+
22.	I openly defend what is right.	1 U-	2 U	3	4 V	5 V+
19.	I can easily distinguish between good, better and best.	1 U-	2 U	3	4 V	5 V+
2.	I maintain my priorities so that I can do what is best.	1 U-	2 U	3	4 V	5 V+
12.	I consistently remain true to what is best.	1 U-	2 U	3	4 V	5 V+
14.	I gladly respond without hesitation when something is required of me.	1 U-	2 U	3	4 V	5 V+
9.	I am an example of whole-hearted dedication to duty.	1 U-	2 U	3	4 V	5 V+
24.	I immediately confess and make it right whenever I do something wrong.	1 U-	2 U	3	4 V	5 V+
7.	I am fully committed to change whatever keeps me from doing what I should.	1 U-	2 U	3	4 V	5 V+

	SD	D	?	A	SA
Norm Response Totals	3	7	3	9	4
Individual Response Totals	(0)	(0)	(8)	(18)	(0)

	Misrepresentation	Virtue
Uncertainty Count	(1) of 6	(7) of 20
Certainty Count	(3) of 6	(7) of 20
Raw Score	(19) of 30	(61) of 100
Norm Rank	(Possible)	(Average)

Misrepresentation		Virtue	
Ranking Description	Raw Score	Ranking Description	Raw Score
Extremely Unlikely	6 to 10	Very Low	20 to 50
Very Unlikely	11 to 13	Low	51 to 55
Unlikely	14 to 16	Moderately Low	56 to 60
Possible	17 to 19	Average	61 to 70
Likely	20 to 22	Moderately High	71 to 75
Very Likely	23 to 25	High	76 to 80
Extremely Likely	26 to 30	Very High	81 to 100

Virtue Response Analysis

Item Number	23	15	20	18	3	10	5	8	13	25	4	17	22	19	2	12	14	9	24	7
Item Rank	1	2	3	4	5	6	7	8	9	10	11	12	13	14	15	16	17	18	19	20
Item Direction	-	-	-	-	-	-	-	-	-	+	+	+	+	+	+	+	+	+	+	+
Item Basis	D	B	D	B	D	B	D	B	D	B	D	B	D	B	D	B	D	B	D	B
Character		U		?		U		?		U		V		V		V		V		V
Conduct	?		U		U		?		U		?		V		V		?		?	
Virtue Levels	Examining		Experimenting		Establishing		Evaluating		Embodying											

Virtue Balance	Character (Inner Being)	Conduct (Outward Doing)
Virtue Item Count	(5) of 10	(2) of 10

We have looked at a student who responded on the negative side and one who responded with considerable uncertainty. Let's examine a student who confined his answers on the positive side. Luke (not his name) is 12 years old and is in seventh grade. His teacher's name is Mrs. Parsons (also a fictitious name). Let's evaluate his response pattern. The most obvious thing from Luke's test is that he doesn't have a single "disagree" response. This, coupled with an unusually high number of uncertain responses, may indicate not so much that he was uncertain about a good many questions but that he could not find a positive way to answer them, so he circled question marks instead. He also had no emphatic responses.

Luke's responses are quite unusual, as we have seen, with every certain answer being positive, but to this point, we have no real idea what that might mean. There is nothing striking about Luke's uncertain responses, except that there are many (8), and that they range from one end of the spectrum to the other. You might tend to think that the younger the student, the more uncertainty there would be, but such is not the case. The data reveal that age has little to do with uncertainty. Three uncertain responses is about the average for all age groups. However, when you consider Luke's virtuous responses, you get a clue as to why he responded the way he did.

Every virtuous response he had was on the high end; not one was on the low end. This, along with his relatively high misrepresentation score, indicates his desire to present high virtue when such is not the case. Also, the fact that he had no emphatic responses may indicate that he is guarded about how he presents himself. His unvirtuous responses confirm these suspicions; every single one of them is on the low side. This is likely to mean that inside, he is unvirtuous but presents himself as virtuous when it is desirable to do so. Comparing character with conduct (Being = 5, Doing = 2), Luke is also wanting to misrepresent that he is more virtuous on the inside than on the outside. This tells us that, although he wants us to think he has inner character, he doesn't want to be held accountable for his conduct.

Being only 12 years old, it is likely that when adolescence comes, he will become openly defiant. Parents and former teachers will shake their heads in amazement and wonder what happened, because Luke was such a sweet kid. All of a sudden, he went bad. Only it wasn't all of a sudden, and it shouldn't have been a surprise. Yet listen to his teacher's response to our three follow-up questions.

First, Mrs. Parsons described his attitude in general this way: "Very good student in my class. He has a positive attitude toward others and is receptive to new ideas and concepts. He is willing to work hard." Here is how she depicted his behavior in class: "Very quiet; never a discipline problem; always cooperative and courteous when working with others. Superior behavior." And last, she said of his academic performance, "Luke is an average student who performs to his greatest potential. He desires to learn and always completes assignments on time. A terrific kid in or out of the classroom." But remember his imbalance between character and conduct.

I am very reluctant to dispute a teacher's remarks concerning a student, especially at the end of the school year, and I may well be wrong about Luke, but unless I miss my guess, he is headed for trouble. This is confirmed by reading the statements to which Luke answered unvirtuously. The sad thing about it is, his bad attitude will probably not become noticeable until he is in open rebellion. Right now, Luke is dutiful because he knows it doesn't pay to present a bad image. He probably also enjoys the praise he receives for acting like he is doing well. But as adolescence pressures him to change, as temptations become stronger, as peers influence him, such duty will become drudgery, and Luke will be lost. Next, I want you to look at the response of a Special Ed student.

Name: Norman (fictitious name) **School:** **Grade:** 11
Ethnic Background: White **Gender:** Male **Age:** 18

No.	Misrepresentation Items	SD	D	?	A	SA
1.	I can remember "playing sick" to get out of something.	5 M-	4 M	3	2 R	1 R+
6.	I have never intensely disliked anyone.	1 R+	2 R	3	4 M	5 M-
11.	I sometimes try to get even, rather than forgive and forget.	5 M-	4 M	3	2 R	1 R+
16.	I never resent being asked to return a favor.	1 R+	2 R	3	4 M	5 M-
21.	I sometimes feel resentful when I don't get my way.	5 M-	4 M	3	2 R	1 R+
26.	I have almost never felt the urge to tell someone off.	1 R+	2 R	3	4 M	5 M-

No.	Virtue Items	SD	D	?	A	SA
23.	I rebel when someone talks to me about doing what I should.	5 V+	4 V	3	2 U	1 U-
15.	I am tired of those in charge trying to show me a better way.	5 V+	4 V	3	2 U	1 U-
20.	I get angry when those in authority insist I do things their way.	5 V+	4 V	3	2 U	1 U-
18.	I have trouble telling right from wrong.	5 V+	4 V	3	2 U	1 U-
3.	I often refuse to do what I know is right.	5 V+	4 V	3	2 U	1 U-
10.	I feel unwilling to help even when I know I should.	5 V+	4 V	3	2 U	1 U-
5.	I frequently insist on my own way even if I sense I might be wrong.	5 V+	4 V	3	2 U	1 U-
8.	I find it hard to really enjoy myself when doing daily chores.	5 V+	4 V	3	2 U	1 U-
13.	I resist establishing values in my life so I can be free to be who I am.	5 V+	4 V	3	2 U	1 U-
25.	I am afraid of what others might think if I do as I ought.	5 V+	4 V	3	2 U	1 U-
4.	I do what I should, even if friends reject me for it.	1 U-	2 U	3	4 V	5 V+
17.	I am fully committed to do what I know I should.	1 U-	2 U	3	4 V	5 V+
22.	I openly defend what is right.	1 U-	2 U	3	4 V	5 V+
19.	I can easily distinguish between good, better and best.	1 U-	2 U	3	4 V	5 V+
2.	I maintain my priorities so that I can do what is best.	1 U-	2 U	3	4 V	5 V+
12.	I consistently remain true to what is best.	1 U-	2 U	3	4 V	5 V+
14.	I gladly respond without hesitation when something is required of me.	1 U-	2 U	3	4 V	5 V+
9.	I am an example of whole-hearted dedication to duty.	1 U-	2 U	3	4 V	5 V+
24.	I immediately confess and make it right whenever I do something wrong.	1 U-	2 U	3	4 V	5 V+
7.	I am fully committed to change whatever keeps me from doing what I should.	1 U-	2 U	3	4 V	5 V+

	SD	D	?	A	SA
Norm Response Totals	3	7	3	9	4
Individual Response Totals	(5)	(4)	(0)	(16)	(1)

	Misrepresentation	Virtue
Uncertainty Count	(0) of 6	(0) of 20
Certainty Count	(2) of 6	(18) of 20
Raw Score	(14) of 30	(80) of 100
Norm Rank	(Unlikely)	(High)

Misrepresentation		Virtue	
Ranking Description	Raw Score	Ranking Description	Raw Score
Extremely Unlikely	6 to 10	Very Low	20 to 50
Very Unlikely	11 to 13	Low	51 to 55
Unlikely	14 to 16	Moderately Low	56 to 60
Possible	17 to 19	Average	61 to 70
Likely	20 to 22	Moderately High	71 to 75
Very Likely	23 to 25	High	76 to 80
Extremely Likely	26 to 30	Very High	81 to 100

Virtue Response Analysis

Item Number	23	15	20	18	3	10	5	8	13	25	4	17	22	19	2	12	14	9	24	7
Item Rank	1	2	3	4	5	6	7	8	9	10	11	12	13	14	15	16	17	18	19	20
Item Direction	-	-	-	-	-	-	-	-	-	-	+	+	+	+	+	+	+	+	+	+
Item Basis	D	B	D	B	D	B	D	B	D	B	D	B	D	B	D	B	D	B	D	B
Character		V+		U		V+		U		V		V		V		V		V		V
Conduct	V		V		V+		V		V+		V		V		V		V		V	
Virtue Levels	Examining		Experimenting		Establishing		Evaluating		Embodying											

Virtue Balance	Character (Inner Being)	Conduct (Outward Doing)
Virtue Item Count	(8) of 10	(10) of 10

The first thing to notice about Norman's score is that it is a true representation of high virtue. Also, he is not troubled with uncertainty. Nor is his score inflated with emphatic responses. Neither does he restrict his responses. He is moderately emphatic, with a preference for the negative side when expressing emphasis. This is interesting because he generally prefers to answer on the positive side (twice as many as the negative side), where he almost never answers emphatically.

Two thirds of his misrepresentation responses point to a true representation, and he borders on being a very unlikely misrepresentation. He has a 90% virtue response and borders the Very High category. He shows strong development of virtue in all five levels. An interesting feature of his responses is that all the emphatic responses are on the lower side, and the only unvirtuous responses (2) are on the lower side. One indicates he is still experimenting, one indicates he is still examining, nothing unusual or alarming. This is clearly an exceptionally virtuous response. What makes it even more interesting is that Norman is mentally handicapped (third grade level). Mental deficiency apparently does not limit moral integrity.

Now that you have had a chance to see how I have interpreted my findings, I want you to make the attempt. The scoring forms for the next eight students will be followed by a series of assessment questions. For the next four students, the factual questions will be answered for you, and you can observe where the information comes from on the scoring form, but the interpretive questions will be left for you to fill in. The final four will be left for you to assess entirely on your own.

The actual examples you will observe, then interpret, consist of four boys and four girls. First, there will be a boy who truly represents a high level of virtue. Next, there will be a boy who misrepresents high virtue. Then, you will see a boy who represents low virtue. And, finally, you will look at a boy who misrepresents low virtue. Following these, there will be similar examples of girls; representing high, misrepresenting high, representing low, misrepresenting low. This is done to show you how the questionnaire handles a large range of responses.

All of the examples will have some background information to set context for your interpretation, except the last two. The reason these last two do not is to give you an opportunity to struggle with interpreting without any knowledge of the student. You will encounter this quite frequently, especially at the beginning of the school year. Hopefully, you will conclude that your interpretation is speculative at best and that any degree of certainty will have to wait for an interview with the student or until you get to know him or her after awhile.

Name: Roger (fictitious name) **School:** **Grade:** 12

Ethnic Background: White **Gender:** Male **Age:** 18

No.	Misrepresentation Items	SD	D	?	A	SA
1.	I can remember "playing sick" to get out of something.	5 M-	4 M	3	2 R	1 R+
6.	I have never intensely disliked anyone.	1 R+	2 R	3	4 M	5 M-
11.	I sometimes try to get even, rather than forgive and forget.	5 M-	4 M	3	2 R	1 R+
16.	I never resent being asked to return a favor.	1 R+	2 R	3	4 M	5 M-
21.	I sometimes feel resentful when I don't get my way.	5 M-	4 M	3	2 R	1 R+
26.	I have almost never felt the urge to tell someone off.	1 R+	2 R	3	4 M	5 M-

No.	Virtue Items	SD	D	?	A	SA
23.	I rebel when someone talks to me about doing what I should.	5 V+	4 V	3	2 U	1 U-
15.	I am tired of those in charge trying to show me a better way.	5 V+	4 V	3	2 U	1 U-
20.	I get angry when those in authority insist I do things their way.	5 V+	4 V	3	2 U	1 U-
18.	I have trouble telling right from wrong.	5 V+	4 V	3	2 U	1 U-
3.	I often refuse to do what I know is right.	5 V+	4 V	3	2 U	1 U-
10.	I feel unwilling to help even when I know I should.	5 V+	4 V	3	2 U	1 U-
5.	I frequently insist on my own way even if I sense I might be wrong.	5 V+	4 V	3	2 U	1 U-
8.	I find it hard to really enjoy myself when doing daily chores.	5 V+	4 V	3	2 U	1 U-
13.	I resist establishing values in my life so I can be free to be who I am.	5 V+	4 V	3	2 U	1 U-
25.	I am afraid of what others might think if I do as I ought.	5 V+	4 V	3	2 U	1 U-
4.	I do what I should, even if friends reject me for it.	1 U-	2 U	3	4 V	5 V+
17.	I am fully committed to do what I know I should.	1 U-	2 U	3	4 V	5 V+
22.	I openly defend what is right.	1 U-	2 U	3	4 V	5 V+
19.	I can easily distinguish between good, better and best.	1 U-	2 U	3	4 V	5 V+
2.	I maintain my priorities so that I can do what is best.	1 U-	2 U	3	4 V	5 V+
12.	I consistently remain true to what is best.	1 U-	2 U	3	4 V	5 V+
14.	I gladly respond without hesitation when something is required of me.	1 U-	2 U	3	4 V	5 V+
9.	I am an example of whole-hearted dedication to duty.	1 U-	2 U	3	4 V	5 V+
24.	I immediately confess and make it right whenever I do something wrong.	1 U-	2 U	3	4 V	5 V+
7.	I am fully committed to change whatever keeps me from doing what I should.	1 U-	2 U	3	4 V	5 V+

	SD	D	?	A	SA
Norm Response Totals	3	7	3	9	4
Individual Response Totals	(6)	(3)	(2)	(10)	(5)

	Misrepresentation	Virtue
Uncertainty Count	(0) of 6	(2) of 20
Certainty Count	(2) of 6	(17) of 20
Raw Score	(14) of 30	(85) of 100
Norm Rank	(Unlikely)	(Very High)

Misrepresentation		Virtue	
Ranking Description	Raw Score	Ranking Description	Raw Score
Extremely Unlikely	6 to 10	Very Low	20 to 50
Very Unlikely	11 to 13	Low	51 to 55
Unlikely	14 to 16	Moderately Low	56 to 60
Possible	17 to 19	Average	61 to 70
Likely	20 to 22	Moderately High	71 to 75
Very Likely	23 to 25	High	76 to 80
Extremely Likely	26 to 30	Very High	81 to 100

Virtue Response Analysis

Item Number	23	15	20	18	3	10	5	8	13	25	4	17	22	19	2	12	14	9	24	7
Item Rank	1	2	3	4	5	6	7	8	9	10	11	12	13	14	15	16	17	18	19	20
Item Direction	-	-	-	-	-	-	-	-	-	-	+	+	+	+	+	+	+	+	+	+
Item Basis	D	B	D	B	D	B	D	B	D	B	D	B	D	B	D	B	D	B	D	B
Character		V+		V+		V		V		V+		V		V+		V		?		V+
Conduct	V+		?		V		U		V+		V		V+		V		V+		V	
Virtue Levels	Examining		Experimenting		Establishing		Evaluating		Embodying											

Virtue Balance	Character (Inner Being)	Conduct (Outward Doing)
Virtue Item Count	(9) of 10	(8) of 10

Virtue Assessment

I. *Response Totals:*

Are there more than 5 uncertain (?) responses? *No.*

Are there more than 10 total emphatic (SD/SA) responses? *Yes.*

What could this signify?

Are there more than either 15 positive (A/SA) or 10 negative (D/SD) responses? *No.*

II. *Uncertainty:*

Is there more than 1 uncertain response among the 6 misrepresentation items? *No.*

Are there more than 3 uncertain responses among the 20 virtue items? *No.*

III. *Certainty:*

How does the proportion of answers that indicate misrepresentation compare with the total number of misrepresentation items? *Two thirds indicate true representation.*

How does the proportion of answers that indicate virtue compare with the total number of virtue items? *Almost 90% virtuous response.*

IV. *Raw Scores:*

Is the misrepresentation score borderline to the ranking description given in the table? *Yes, to the very unlikely side.*

Is the virtue score borderline to the ranking description provided in the table? *No.*

V. *Norm Rank: Fashion a statement reflecting your findings:*

It is *unlikely* that Roger is misrepresenting a *very high* virtue score.

VI. *Virtue Level Analysis:*

What levels are solid with virtue responses?

What levels are solid with unvirtuous responses?

What levels are solid with uncertain responses?

Is the whole structure riddled with uncertainty?

Does anything seem peculiar? If so, what could it indicate?

VII. *Virtue Balance:*

Is there a balance between character and conduct? *Yes.*

What does this mean?

Background information: This individual was an honor student and received numerous awards and scholarships. His parents were going through a painful divorce at the time.

Name: Carlyle (fictitious name) **School:** **Grade:** 7
Ethnic Background: Black **Gender:** Male **Age:** 14

No.	Misrepresentation Items	SD	D	?	A	SA
1.	I can remember "playing sick" to get out of something.	5 M-	4 M	3	2 R	1 R+
6.	I have never intensely disliked anyone.	1 R+	2 R	3	4 M	5 M-
11.	I sometimes try to get even, rather than forgive and forget.	5 M-	4 M	3	2 R	1 R+
16.	I never resent being asked to return a favor.	1 R+	2 R	3	4 M	5 M-
21.	I sometimes feel resentful when I don't get my way.	5 M-	4 M	3	2 R	1 R+
26.	I have almost never felt the urge to tell someone off.	1 R+	2 R	3	4 M	5 M-

No.	Virtue Items	SD	D	?	A	SA
23.	I rebel when someone talks to me about doing what I should.	5V+	4 V	3	2 U	1 U-
15.	I am tired of those in charge trying to show me a better way.	5V+	4 V	3	2 U	1 U-
20.	I get angry when those in authority insist I do things their way.	5V+	4 V	3	2 U	1 U-
18.	I have trouble telling right from wrong.	5V+	4 V	3	2 U	1 U-
3.	I often refuse to do what I know is right.	5V+	4 V	3	2 U	1 U-
10.	I feel unwilling to help even when I know I should.	5V+	4 V	3	2 U	1 U-
5.	I frequently insist on my own way even if I sense I might be wrong.	5V+	4 V	3	2 U	1 U-
8.	I find it hard to really enjoy myself when doing daily chores.	5V+	4 V	3	2 U	1 U-
13.	I resist establishing values in my life so I can be free to be who I am.	5V+	4 V	3	2 U	1 U-
25.	I am afraid of what others might think if I do as I ought.	5V+	4 V	3	2 U	1 U-
4.	I do what I should, even if friends reject me for it.	1 U-	2 U	3	4 V	5 V+
17.	I am fully committed to do what I know I should.	1 U-	2 U	3	4 V	5 V+
22.	I openly defend what is right.	1 U-	2 U	3	4 V	5 V+
19.	I can easily distinguish between good, better and best.	1 U-	2 U	3	4 V	5 V+
2.	I maintain my priorities so that I can do what is best.	1 U-	2 U	3	4 V	5 V+
12.	I consistently remain true to what is best.	1 U-	2 U	3	4 V	5 V+
14.	I gladly respond without hesitation when something is required of me.	1 U-	2 U	3	4 V	5 V+
9.	I am an example of whole-hearted dedication to duty.	1 U-	2 U	3	4 V	5 V+
24.	I immediately confess and make it right whenever I do something wrong.	1 U-	2 U	3	4 V	5 V+
7.	I am fully committed to change whatever keeps me from doing what I should.	1 U-	2 U	3	4 V	5 V+

	SD	D	?	A	SA
Norm Response Totals	3	7	3	9	4
Individual Response Totals	(7)	(2)	(1)	(6)	(10)

	Misrepresentation	Virtue
Uncertainty Count	(1) of 6	(0) of 20
Certainty Count	(4) of 6	(17) of 20
Raw Score	(23) of 30	(87) of 100
Norm Rank	(Very Likely)	(Very High)

Misrepresentation		Virtue	
Ranking Description	Raw Score	Ranking Description	Raw Score
Extremely Unlikely	6 to 10	Very Low	20 to 50
Very Unlikely	11 to 13	Low	51 to 55
Unlikely	14 to 16	Moderately Low	56 to 60
Possible	17 to 19	Average	61 to 70
Likely	20 to 22	Moderately High	71 to 75
Very Likely	23 to 25	High	76 to 80
Extremely Likely	26 to 30	Very High	81 to 100

Virtue Response Analysis

Item Number	23	15	20	18	3	10	5	8	13	25	4	17	22	19	2	12	14	9	24	7
Item Rank	1	2	3	4	5	6	7	8	9	10	11	12	13	14	15	16	17	18	19	20
Item Direction	-	-	-	-	-	-	-	-	-	-	+	+	+	+	+	+	+	+	+	+
Item Basis	D	B	D	B	D	B	D	B	D	B	D	B	D	B	D	B	D	B	D	B
Character		V+		V		V+		U		V+		V+		V+		V		V		V+
Conduct	V+		U-		V+		V+		U		V+		V+		V+		V+		V+	
Virtue Levels	Examining		Experimenting		Establishing		Evaluating		Embodying											

Virtue Balance	Character (Inner Being)		Conduct (Outward Doing)	
Virtue Item Count	(9) of 10		(8) of 10	

Virtue Assessment

I. *Response Totals:*

Are there more than 5 uncertain (?) responses? *No.*

Are there more than 10 total emphatic (SD/SA) responses? *Yes.*

What could this signify?

Are there more than either 15 positive (A/SA) or 10 negative (D/SD) responses? *Yes.*

What could this indicate?

II. *Uncertainty:*

Is there more than 1 uncertain response among the 6 misrepresentation items? *No.*

Are there more than 3 uncertain responses among the 20 virtue items? *No.*

III. *Certainty:*

How does the proportion of answers that indicate misrepresentation compare with the total number of misrepresentation items? *Two thirds indicate misrepresentation.*

How does the proportion of answers that indicate virtue compare with the total number of virtue items? *Almost 90% virtuous response.*

IV. *Raw Scores:*

Is the misrepresentation score borderline to the ranking description given in the table? *Yes, to the lower "likely" category.*

Is the virtue score borderline to the ranking description provided in the table? *No.*

V. *Norm Rank: Fashion a statement reflecting your findings:*

It is _____ that Carlyle is misrepresenting a _____ virtue score.

VI. *Virtue Level Analysis:*

What levels are solid with virtue responses?

What levels are solid with unvirtuous responses?

What levels are solid with uncertain responses?

Is the whole structure riddled with uncertainty?

Does anything seem peculiar? If so, what could it indicate?

VII. *Virtue Balance:*

Is there a balance between character and conduct? *Yes.*

Background information: This student was a talented athlete and very popular socially.

Name: Ross (fictitious name) **School:** **Grade:** 7
Ethnic Background: White **Gender:** Male **Age:** 14

No.	Misrepresentation Items	SD	D	?	A	SA
1.	I can remember "playing sick" to get out of something.	5 M-	4 M	3	2 R	1 R+
6.	I have never intensely disliked anyone.	1 R+	2 R	3	4 M	5 M-
11.	I sometimes try to get even, rather than forgive and forget.	5 M-	4 M	3	2 R	1 R+
16.	I never resent being asked to return a favor.	1 R+	2 R	3	4 M	5 M-
21.	I sometimes feel resentful when I don't get my way.	5 M-	4 M	3	2 R	1 R+
26.	I have almost never felt the urge to tell someone off.	1 R+	2 R	3	4 M	5 M-

No.	Virtue Items	SD	D	?	A	SA
23.	I rebel when someone talks to me about doing what I should.	5V+	4 V	3	2 U	1 U-
15.	I am tired of those in charge trying to show me a better way.	5V+	4 V	3	2 U	1 U-
20.	I get angry when those in authority insist I do things their way.	5V+	4 V	3	2 U	1 U-
18.	I have trouble telling right from wrong.	5V+	4 V	3	2 U	1 U-
3.	I often refuse to do what I know is right.	5V+	4 V	3	2 U	1 U-
10.	I feel unwilling to help even when I know I should.	5V+	4 V	3	2 U	1 U-
5.	I frequently insist on my own way even if I sense I might be wrong.	5V+	4 V	3	2 U	1 U-
8.	I find it hard to really enjoy myself when doing daily chores.	5V+	4 V	3	2 U	1 U-
13.	I resist establishing values in my life so I can be free to be who I am.	5V+	4 V	3	2 U	1 U-
25.	I am afraid of what others might think if I do as I ought.	5V+	4 V	3	2 U	1 U-
4.	I do what I should, even if friends reject me for it.	1 U-	2 U	3	4 V	5 V+
17.	I am fully committed to do what I know I should.	1 U-	2 U	3	4 V	5 V+
22.	I openly defend what is right.	1 U-	2 U	3	4 V	5 V+
19.	I can easily distinguish between good, better and best.	1 U-	2 U	3	4 V	5 V+
2.	I maintain my priorities so that I can do what is best.	1 U-	2 U	3	4 V	5 V+
12.	I consistently remain true to what is best.	1 U-	2 U	3	4 V	5 V+
14.	I gladly respond without hesitation when something is required of me.	1 U-	2 U	3	4 V	5 V+
9.	I am an example of whole-hearted dedication to duty.	1 U-	2 U	3	4 V	5 V+
24.	I immediately confess and make it right whenever I do something wrong.	1 U-	2 U	3	4 V	5 V+
7.	I am fully committed to change whatever keeps me from doing what I should.	1 U-	2 U	3	4 V	5 V+

	SD	D	?	A	SA
Norm Response Totals	3	7	3	9	4
Individual Response Totals	(7)	(5)	(0)	(4)	(10)

	Misrepresentation	Virtue
Uncertainty Count	(0) of 6	(0) of 20
Certainty Count	(1) of 6	(2) of 20
Raw Score	(10) of 30	(31) of 100
Norm Rank	(Extremely Unlikely)	(Very Low)

Misrepresentation		Virtue	
Ranking Description	Raw Score	Ranking Description	Raw Score
Extremely Unlikely	6 to 10	Very Low	20 to 50
Very Unlikely	11 to 13	Low	51 to 55
Unlikely	14 to 16	Moderately Low	56 to 60
Possible	17 to 19	Average	61 to 70
Likely	20 to 22	Moderately High	71 to 75
Very Likely	23 to 25	High	76 to 80
Extremely Likely	26 to 30	Very High	81 to 100

Virtue Response Analysis

Item Number	23	15	20	18	3	10	5	8	13	25	4	17	22	19	2	12	14	9	24	7
Item Rank	1	2	3	4	5	6	7	8	9	10	11	12	13	14	15	16	17	18	19	20
Item Direction	-	-	-	-	-	-	-	-	-	-	+	+	+	+	+	+	+	+	+	+
Item Basis	D	B	D	B	D	B	D	B	D	B	D	B	D	B	D	B	D	B	D	B
Character		U-		V		U-		U-		U		U		U		U-		U-		V
Conduct	U-		U-		U-		U-		U-		U-		U		U		U-		
Virtue Levels	Examining		Experimenting		Establishing		Evaluating		Embodying											

Virtue Balance	Character (Inner Being)	Conduct (Outward Doing)
Virtue Item Count	(2) of 10	(0) of 10

Virtue Assessment

I. *Response Totals:*

Are there more than 5 uncertain (?) responses? *No.*

Are there more than 10 total emphatic (SD/SA) responses? *Yes.*

What could this signify?

Are there more than either 15 positive (A/SA) or 10 negative (D/SD) responses? *Yes.*

If so, what could this indicate?

II. *Uncertainty:*

Is there more than 1 uncertain response among the 6 misrepresentation items? *No.*

Are there more than 3 uncertain responses among the 20 virtue items? *No.*

III. *Certainty:*

How does the proportion of answers that indicate misrepresentation compare with the total number of misrepresentation items? *Only 17% misrepresentation.*

How does the proportion of answers that indicate virtue compare with the total number of virtue items? *Only 10% virtue.*

IV. *Raw Scores:*

Is the misrepresentation score borderline to the ranking description given in the table? *Yes, to the very unlikely side.*

Is the virtue score borderline to the ranking description provided in the table? *No.*

V. *Norm Rank: Fashion a statement reflecting your findings:*

It is _____ that Ross is misrepresenting a _____ virtue score.

VI. *Virtue Level Analysis:*

What levels are solid with virtue responses?

What levels are solid with unvirtuous responses?

What levels are solid with uncertain responses?

Is the whole structure riddled with uncertainty?

Does anything seem peculiar? If so, what could it indicate?

VII. *Virtue Balance:*

Is there a balance between character and conduct? *No.*

If not, what could this mean?

Background information: This student was in an alternative school for his lawlessness. He allegedly broke into a convenience store, sold some of the goods to his friends, and burned it down.

Name: Thomas (fictitious name)   **School:**   **Grade:** 12
Ethnic Background: Black   **Gender:** Male   **Age:** 17

No.	Misrepresentation Items	SD	D	?	A	SA
1.	I can remember "playing sick" to get out of something.	5 M-	4 M	3	2 R	1 R+
6.	I have never intensely disliked anyone.	1 R+	2 R	3	4 M	5 M-
11.	I sometimes try to get even, rather than forgive and forget.	5 M-	4 M	3	2 R	1 R+
16.	I never resent being asked to return a favor.	1 R+	2 R	3	4 M	5 M-
21.	I sometimes feel resentful when I don't get my way.	5 M-	4 M	3	2 R	1 R+
26.	I have almost never felt the urge to tell someone off.	1 R+	2 R	3	4 M	5 M-

No.	Virtue Items	SD	D	?	A	SA
23.	I rebel when someone talks to me about doing what I should.	5 V+	4 V	3	2 U	1 U-
15.	I am tired of those in charge trying to show me a better way.	5 V+	4 V	3	2 U	1 U-
20.	I get angry when those in authority insist I do things their way.	5 V+	4 V	3	2 U	1 U-
18.	I have trouble telling right from wrong.	5 V+	4 V	3	2 U	1 U-
3.	I often refuse to do what I know is right.	5 V+	4 V	3	2 U	1 U-
10.	I feel unwilling to help even when I know I should.	5 V+	4 V	3	2 U	1 U-
5.	I frequently insist on my own way even if I sense I might be wrong.	5 V+	4 V	3	2 U	1 U-
8.	I find it hard to really enjoy myself when doing daily chores.	5 V+	4 V	3	2 U	1 U-
13.	I resist establishing values in my life so I can be free to be who I am.	5 V+	4 V	3	2 U	1 U-
25.	I am afraid of what others might think if I do as I ought.	5 V+	4 V	3	2 U	1 U-
4.	I do what I should, even if friends reject me for it.	1 U-	2 U	3	4 V	5 V+
17.	I am fully committed to do what I know I should.	1 U-	2 U	3	4 V	5 V+
22.	I openly defend what is right.	1 U-	2 U	3	4 V	5 V+
19.	I can easily distinguish between good, better and best.	1 U-	2 U	3	4 V	5 V+
2.	I maintain my priorities so that I can do what is best.	1 U-	2 U	3	4 V	5 V+
12.	I consistently remain true to what is best.	1 U-	2 U	3	4 V	5 V+
14.	I gladly respond without hesitation when something is required of me.	1 U-	2 U	3	4 V	5 V+
9.	I am an example of whole-hearted dedication to duty.	1 U-	2 U	3	4 V	5 V+
24.	I immediately confess and make it right whenever I do something wrong.	1 U-	2 U	3	4 V	5 V+
7.	I am fully committed to change whatever keeps me from doing what I should.	1 U-	2 U	3	4 V	5 V+

	SD	D	?	A	SA
Norm Response Totals	3	7	3	9	4
Individual Response Totals	(6)	(6)	(0)	(8)	(6)

	Misrepresentation	Virtue
Uncertainty Count	(0) of 6	(0) of 20
Certainty Count	(5) of 6	(8) of 20
Raw Score	(25) of 30	(55) of 100
Norm Rank	(Very Likely)	(Low)

Misrepresentation		Virtue	
Ranking Description	Raw Score	Ranking Description	Raw Score
Extremely Unlikely	6 to 10	Very Low	20 to 50
Very Unlikely	11 to 13	Low	51 to 55
Unlikely	14 to 16	Moderately Low	56 to 60
Possible	17 to 19	Average	61 to 70
Likely	20 to 22	Moderately High	71 to 75
Very Likely	23 to 25	High	76 to 80
Extremely Likely	26 to 30	Very High	81 to 100

Virtue Response Analysis

Item Number	23	15	20	18	3	10	5	8	13	25	4	17	22	19	2	12	14	9	24	7
Item Rank	1	2	3	4	5	6	7	8	9	10	11	12	13	14	15	16	17	18	19	20
Item Direction	-	-	-	-	-	-	-	-	-	-	+	+	+	+	+	+	+	+	+	+
Item Basis	D	B	D	B	D	B	D	B	D	B	D	B	D	B	D	B	D	B	D	B
Character		U-		V+		U-		U		V+		V		V+		U		U		U-
Conduct	U		U		U-		V		U		V		U-		U		V+		V	
Virtue Levels	Examining		Experimenting		Establishing		Evaluating		Embodying											

Virtue Balance	Character (Inner Being)	Conduct (Outward Doing)
Virtue Item Count	(4) of 10	(4) of 10

Virtue Assessment

I. *Response Totals:*

Are there more than 5 uncertain (?) responses? *No.*

Are there more than 10 total emphatic (SD/SA) responses? *Yes.*

What could this signify?

Are there more than either 15 positive (A/SA) or 10 negative (D/SD) responses? *Yes.*

What could this indicate?

II. *Uncertainty:*

Is there more than 1 uncertain response among the 6 misrepresentation items? *No.*

Are there more than 3 uncertain responses among the 20 virtue items? *No.*

III. *Certainty:*

How does the proportion of answers that indicate misrepresentation compare with the total number of misrepresentation items? *80% misrepresentation.*

How does the proportion of answers that indicate virtue compare with the total number of virtue items? *40% virtue.*

IV. *Raw Scores:*

Is the misrepresentation score borderline to the ranking description given in the table? *Yes, to extremely likely.*

Is the virtue score borderline to the ranking description provided in the table? *Yes, to moderately low*

V. *Norm Rank: Fashion a statement reflecting your findings:*

It is that _____ Thomas is misrepresenting a _____ virtue score.

VI. *Virtue Level Analysis:*

What levels show virtue?

What levels do not?

Does uncertainly figure in?

Does anything seem peculiar?

If so, what could it indicate?

VII. *Virtue Balance:*

Is there a balance between character and conduct? *Yes.*

Background information: Sent to alternative school for career training. Mentally retarded. When his nonretarded friend was sent for a bad attitude, teachers said he assumed his friend's attitude.

Name: Terrie (fictitious name) **School:** **Grade:** 10
Ethnic Background: White **Gender:** Female **Age:** 16

No.	Misrepresentation Items	SD	D	?	A	SA
1.	I can remember "playing sick" to get out of something.	5 M-	4 M	3	2 R	1 R+
6.	I have never intensely disliked anyone.	1 R+	2 R	3	4 M	5 M-
11.	I sometimes try to get even, rather than forgive and forget.	5 M-	4 M	3	2 R	1 R+
16.	I never resent being asked to return a favor.	1 R+	2 R	3	4 M	5 M-
21.	I sometimes feel resentful when I don't get my way.	5 M-	4 M	3	2 R	1 R+
26.	I have almost never felt the urge to tell someone off.	1 R+	2 R	3	4 M	5 M-

No.	Virtue Items	SD	D	?	A	SA
23.	I rebel when someone talks to me about doing what I should.	5 V+	4 V	3	2 U	1 U-
15.	I am tired of those in charge trying to show me a better way.	5 V+	4 V	3	2 U	1 U-
20.	I get angry when those in authority insist I do things their way.	5 V+	4 V	3	2 U	1 U-
18.	I have trouble telling right from wrong.	5 V+	4 V	3	2 U	1 U-
3.	I often refuse to do what I know is right.	5 V+	4 V	3	2 U	1 U-
10.	I feel unwilling to help even when I know I should.	5 V+	4 V	3	2 U	1 U-
5.	I frequently insist on my own way even if I sense I might be wrong.	5 V+	4 V	3	2 U	1 U-
8.	I find it hard to really enjoy myself when doing daily chores.	5 V+	4 V	3	2 U	1 U-
13.	I resist establishing values in my life so I can be free to be who I am.	5 V+	4 V	3	2 U	1 U-
25.	I am afraid of what others might think if I do as I ought.	5 V+	4 V	3	2 U	1 U-
4.	I do what I should, even if friends reject me for it.	1 U-	2 U	3	4 V	5 V+
17.	I am fully committed to do what I know I should.	1 U-	2 U	3	4 V	5 V+
22.	I openly defend what is right.	1 U-	2 U	3	4 V	5 V+
19.	I can easily distinguish between good, better and best.	1 U-	2 U	3	4 V	5 V+
2.	I maintain my priorities so that I can do what is best.	1 U-	2 U	3	4 V	5 V+
12.	I consistently remain true to what is best.	1 U-	2 U	3	4 V	5 V+
14.	I gladly respond without hesitation when something is required of me.	1 U-	2 U	3	4 V	5 V+
9.	I am an example of whole-hearted dedication to duty.	1 U-	2 U	3	4 V	5 V+
24.	I immediately confess and make it right whenever I do something wrong.	1 U-	2 U	3	4 V	5 V+
7.	I am fully committed to change whatever keeps me from doing what I should.	1 U-	2 U	3	4 V	5 V+

	SD	D	?	A	SA
Norm Response Totals	3	7	3	9	4
Individual Response Totals	(8)	(3)	(3)	(7)	(5)

	Misrepresentation	Virtue
Uncertainty Count	(0) of 6	(3) of 20
Certainty Count	(1) of 6	(17) of 20
Raw Score	(13) of 30	(89) of 100
Norm Rank	(Very Unlikely)	(Very High)

Misrepresentation		Virtue	
Ranking Description	Raw Score	Ranking Description	Raw Score
Extremely Unlikely	6 to 10	Very Low	20 to 50
Very Unlikely	11 to 13	Low	51 to 55
Unlikely	14 to 16	Moderately Low	56 to 60
Possible	17 to 19	Average	61 to 70
Likely	20 to 22	Moderately High	71 to 75
Very Likely	23 to 25	High	76 to 80
Extremely Likely	26 to 30	Very High	81 to 100

Virtue Response Analysis

Item Number	23	15	20	18	3	10	5	8	13	25	4	17	22	19	2	12	14	9	24	7
Item Rank	1	2	3	4	5	6	7	8	9	10	11	12	13	14	15	16	17	18	19	20
Item Direction	-	-	-	-	-	-	-	-	-	-	+	+	+	+	+	+	+	+	+	+
Item Basis	D	B	D	B	D	B	D	B	D	B	D	B	D	B	D	B	D	B	D	B
Character		V+		?		V+		V		V+		V+		V		?		V		V
Conduct	V+		V+		V+		V		V+		V+		V+		?		V+		V+	
Virtue Levels	Examining				Experimenting				Establishing				Evaluating				Embodying			

Virtue Balance	Character (Inner Being)	Conduct (Outward Doing)
Virtue Item Count	(8) of 10	(9) of 10

Virtue Assessment

I. Response Totals:

Are there more than 5 uncertain (?) responses?

If so, why is this important?

Are there more than 10 total emphatic (SD/SA) responses?

If so, what does this signify?

Are there more than either 15 positive (A/SA) or 10 negative (D/SD) responses?

If so, what can this indicate?

II. Uncertainty:

Is there more than 1 uncertain response among the 6 misrepresentation items?

Why would this be important?

Are there more than 3 uncertain responses among the 20 virtue items?

Why would this be important?

III. Certainty:

How does the proportion of answers that indicate misrepresentation compare with the total number of misrepresentation items?

How does the proportion of answers that indicate virtue compare with the total number of virtue items?

IV. Raw Scores:

Is the misrepresentation score borderline to the ranking description given in the table?

Is the virtue score borderline to the ranking description provided in the table?

V. Norm Rank: Fashion a statement reflecting your findings:

It is _____ that Terrie is misrepresenting a _____ virtue score.

VI. Virtue Level Analysis:

What levels are solid with virtue responses?

What levels are solid with unvirtuous responses?

What levels are solid with uncertain responses

Is the whole structure riddled with uncertainty?

Does anything seem peculiar?

If so, what could it indicate?

VII. Virtue Balance:

Is there a balance between character and conduct?

If not, what could this mean?

Background information: This student went largely unnoticed.

Name: Lupe (fictitious name) **School:** **Grade:** 11
Ethnic Background: Hispanic **Gender:** Female **Age:** 15

No.	Misrepresentation Items	SD	D	?	A	SA
1.	I can remember "playing sick" to get out of something.	5 M-	4 M	3	2 R	1 R+
6.	I have never intensely disliked anyone.	1 R+	2 R	3	4 M	5 M-
11.	I sometimes try to get even, rather than forgive and forget.	5 M-	4 M	3	2 R	1 R+
16.	I never resent being asked to return a favor.	1 R+	2 R	3	4 M	5 M-
21.	I sometimes feel resentful when I don't get my way.	5 M-	4 M	3	2 R	1 R+
26.	I have almost never felt the urge to tell someone off.	1 R+	2 R	3	4 M	5 M-

No.	Virtue Items	SD	D	?	A	SA
23.	I rebel when someone talks to me about doing what I should.	5V+	4 V	3	2 U	1 U-
15.	I am tired of those in charge trying to show me a better way.	5V+	4 V	3	2 U	1 U-
20.	I get angry when those in authority insist I do things their way.	5V+	4 V	3	2 U	1 U-
18.	I have trouble telling right from wrong.	5V+	4 V	3	2 U	1 U-
3.	I often refuse to do what I know is right.	5V+	4 V	3	2 U	1 U-
10.	I feel unwilling to help even when I know I should.	5V+	4 V	3	2 U	1 U-
5.	I frequently insist on my own way even if I sense I might be wrong.	5V+	4 V	3	2 U	1 U-
8.	I find it hard to really enjoy myself when doing daily chores.	5V+	4 V	3	2 U	1 U-
13.	I resist establishing values in my life so I can be free to be who I am.	5V+	4 V	3	2 U	1 U-
25.	I am afraid of what others might think if I do as I ought.	5V+	4 V	3	2 U	1 U-
4.	I do what I should, even if friends reject me for it.	1 U-	2 U	3	4 V	5 V+
17.	I am fully committed to do what I know I should.	1 U-	2 U	3	4 V	5 V+
22.	I openly defend what is right.	1 U-	2 U	3	4 V	5 V+
19.	I can easily distinguish between good, better and best.	1 U-	2 U	3	4 V	5 V+
2.	I maintain my priorities so that I can do what is best.	1 U-	2 U	3	4 V	5 V+
12.	I consistently remain true to what is best.	1 U-	2 U	3	4 V	5 V+
14.	I gladly respond without hesitation when something is required of me.	1 U-	2 U	3	4 V	5 V+
9.	I am an example of whole-hearted dedication to duty.	1 U-	2 U	3	4 V	5 V+
24.	I immediately confess and make it right whenever I do something wrong.	1 U-	2 U	3	4 V	5 V+
7.	I am fully committed to change whatever keeps me from doing what I should.	1 U-	2 U	3	4 V	5 V+

	SD	D	?	A	SA
Norm Response Totals	3	7	3	9	4
Individual Response Totals	(9)	(1)	(3)	(5)	(8)

	Misrepresentation	Virtue
Uncertainty Count	(1) of 6	(2) of 20
Certainty Count	(4) of 6	(18) of 20
Raw Score	(24) of 30	(92) of 100
Norm Rank	(Very Likely)	(Very High)

Misrepresentation		Virtue	
Ranking Description	Raw Score	Ranking Description	Raw Score
Extremely Unlikely	6 to 10	Very Low	20 to 50
Very Unlikely	11 to 13	Low	51 to 55
Unlikely	14 to 16	Moderately Low	56 to 60
Possible	17 to 19	Average	61 to 70
Likely	20 to 22	Moderately High	71 to 75
Very Likely	23 to 25	High	76 to 80
Extremely Likely	26 to 30	Very High	81 to 100

Virtue Response Analysis

Item Number	23	15	20	18	3	10	5	8	13	25	4	17	22	19	2	12	14	9	24	7
Item Rank	1	2	3	4	5	6	7	8	9	10	11	12	13	14	15	16	17	18	19	20
Item Direction	-	-	-	-	-	-	-	-	-	-	+	+	+	+	+	+	+	+	+	+
Item Basis	D	B	D	B	D	B	D	B	D	B	D	B	D	B	D	B	D	B	D	B
Character		V		V		V+		V+		V+		V+		V+		V+		?		V+
Conduct	V+		V+		V+		?		V+		V		V		V+		V+		V	
Virtue Levels	Examining		Experimenting		Establishing		Evaluating		Embodying											

Virtue Balance	Character (Inner Being)	Conduct (Outward Doing)
Virtue Item Count	(9) of 10	(9) of 10

Virtue Assessment

I. *Response Totals:*

Are there more than 5 uncertain (?) responses?

If so, why is this important?

Are there more than 10 total emphatic (SD/SA) responses?

If so, what does this signify?

Are there more than either 15 positive (A/SA) or 10 negative (D/SD) responses?

If so, what can this indicate?

II. *Uncertainty:*

Is there more than 1 uncertain response among the 6 misrepresentation items?
Why would this be important?

Are there more than 3 uncertain responses among the 20 virtue items?
Why would this be important?

III. *Certainty:*

How does the proportion of answers that indicate misrepresentation compare with the total number of misrepresentation items?

How does the proportion of answers that indicate virtue compare with the total number of virtue items?

IV. *Raw Scores:*

Is the misrepresentation score borderline to the ranking description given in the table?

Is the virtue score borderline to the ranking description provided in the table?

V. *Norm Rank: Fashion a statement reflecting your findings:*

It is _____ that Lupe is misrepresenting a _____ virtue score.

VI. *Virtue Level Analysis:*

What levels are solid?

Does anything seem peculiar?

If so, what could it indicate?

VII. *Virtue Balance:*

Is there a balance between character and conduct?

If not, what could this mean?

Background information: This student usually worked hard and was helpful. Other students found her irritating and avoided her. Sometimes, she became critical of other students.

Name: Donna (fictitious name) **School:** **Grade:** 9
Ethnic Background: White **Gender:** Female **Age:** 16

No.	Misrepresentation Items	SD	D	?	A	SA
1.	I can remember "playing sick" to get out of something.	5 M-	4 M	3	2 R	1 R+
6.	I have never intensely disliked anyone.	1 R+	2 R	3	4 M	5 M-
11.	I sometimes try to get even, rather than forgive and forget.	5 M-	4 M	3	2 R	1 R+
16.	I never resent being asked to return a favor.	1 R+	2 R	3	4 M	5 M-
21.	I sometimes feel resentful when I don't get my way.	5 M-	4 M	3	2 R	1 R+
26.	I have almost never felt the urge to tell someone off.	1 R+	2 R	3	4 M	5 M-

No.	Virtue Items	SD	D	?	A	SA
23.	I rebel when someone talks to me about doing what I should.	5V+	4 V	3	2 U	1 U-
15.	I am tired of those in charge trying to show me a better way.	5V+	4 V	3	2 U	1 U-
20.	I get angry when those in authority insist I do things their way.	5V+	4 V	3	2 U	1 U-
18.	I have trouble telling right from wrong.	5V+	4 V	3	2 U	1 U-
3.	I often refuse to do what I know is right.	5V+	4 V	3	2 U	1 U-
10.	I feel unwilling to help even when I know I should.	5V+	4 V	3	2 U	1 U-
5.	I frequently insist on my own way even if I sense I might be wrong.	5V+	4 V	3	2 U	1 U-
8.	I find it hard to really enjoy myself when doing daily chores.	5V+	4 V	3	2 U	1 U-
13.	I resist establishing values in my life so I can be free to be who I am.	5V+	4 V	3	2 U	1 U-
25.	I am afraid of what others might think if I do as I ought.	5V+	4 V	3	2 U	1 U-
4.	I do what I should, even if friends reject me for it.	1 U-	2 U	3	4 V	5 V+
17.	I am fully committed to do what I know I should.	1 U-	2 U	3	4 V	5 V+
22.	I openly defend what is right.	1 U-	2 U	3	4 V	5 V+
19.	I can easily distinguish between good, better and best.	1 U-	2 U	3	4 V	5 V+
2.	I maintain my priorities so that I can do what is best.	1 U-	2 U	3	4 V	5 V+
12.	I consistently remain true to what is best.	1 U-	2 U	3	4 V	5 V+
14.	I gladly respond without hesitation when something is required of me.	1 U-	2 U	3	4 V	5 V+
9.	I am an example of whole-hearted dedication to duty.	1 U-	2 U	3	4 V	5 V+
24.	I immediately confess and make it right whenever I do something wrong.	1 U-	2 U	3	4 V	5 V+
7.	I am fully committed to change whatever keeps me from doing what I should.	1 U-	2 U	3	4 V	5 V+

	SD	D	?	A	SA
Norm Response Totals	3	7	3	9	4
Individual Response Totals	(2)	(7)	(0)	(14)	(3)

	Misrepresentation	Virtue
Uncertainty Count	(0) of 6	(0) of 20
Certainty Count	(1) of 6	(7) of 20
Raw Score	(12) of 30	(51) of 100
Norm Rank	(Very Unlikely)	(Low)

Misrepresentation		Virtue	
Ranking Description	Raw Score	Ranking Description	Raw Score
Extremely Unlikely	6 to 10	Very Low	20 to 50
Very Unlikely	11 to 13	Low	51 to 55
Unlikely	14 to 16	Moderately Low	56 to 60
Possible	17 to 19	Average	61 to 70
Likely	20 to 22	Moderately High	71 to 75
Very Likely	23 to 25	High	76 to 80
Extremely Likely	26 to 30	Very High	81 to 100

Virtue Response Analysis

Item Number	23	15	20	18	3	10	5	8	13	25	4	17	22	19	2	12	14	9	24	7
Item Rank	1	2	3	4	5	6	7	8	9	10	11	12	13	14	15	16	17	18	19	20
Item Direction	-	-	-	-	-	-	-	-	-	+	+	+	+	+	+	+	+	+	+	+
Item Basis	D	B	D	B	D	B	D	B	D	B	D	B	D	B	D	B	D	B	D	B
Character		U		U		V		U		U-		U		U		V		U-		V
Conduct	U		U		V		U		U		V		V		V		U		U	
Virtue Levels	Examining		Experimenting		Establishing		Evaluating		Embodying											

Virtue Balance	Character (Inner Being)	Conduct (Outward Doing)
Virtue Item Count	(3) of 10	(4) of 10

Virtue Assessment

I. *Response Totals:*

Are there more than 5 uncertain (?) responses?

If so, why is this important?

Are there more than 10 total emphatic (SD/SA) responses?

If so, what does this signify?

Are there more than either 15 positive (A/SA) or 10 negative (D/SD) responses?

If so, what can this indicate?

II. *Uncertainty:*

Is there more than 1 uncertain response among the 6 misrepresentation items?

Why would this be important?

Are there more than 3 uncertain responses among the 20 virtue items?

Why would this be important?

III. *Certainty:*

How does the proportion of answers that indicate misrepresentation compare with the total number of misrepresentation items?

How does the proportion of answers that indicate virtue compare with the total number of virtue items?

IV. *Raw Scores:*

Is the misrepresentation score borderline to the ranking description given in the table?

Is the virtue score borderline to the ranking description provided in the table?

V. *Norm Rank: Fashion a statement reflecting your findings:*

It is _____ that Donna is misrepresenting a _____ virtue score.

VI. *Virtue Level Analysis:*

What levels are solid with virtue responses?

What levels are solid with unvirtuous responses?

What levels are solid with uncertain responses?

Is the whole structure riddled with uncertainty?

Does anything seem peculiar? If so, what could it indicate?

VII. *Virtue Balance:*

Is there a balance between character and conduct?

If not, what could this mean?

Name: Lola (fictitious name) **School:** **Grade:** 9
Ethnic Background: White **Gender:** Female **Age:** 15

No.	Misrepresentation Items	SD	D	?	A	SA
1.	I can remember "playing sick" to get out of something.	5 M-	4 M	3	2 R	1 R+
6.	I have never intensely disliked anyone.	1 R+	2 R	3	4 M	5 M-
11.	I sometimes try to get even, rather than forgive and forget.	5 M-	4 M	3	2 R	1 R+
16.	I never resent being asked to return a favor.	1 R+	2 R	3	4 M	5 M-
21.	I sometimes feel resentful when I don't get my way.	5 M-	4 M	3	2 R	1 R+
26.	I have almost never felt the urge to tell someone off.	1 R+	2 R	3	4 M	5 M-

No.	Virtue Items	SD	D	?	A	SA
23.	I rebel when someone talks to me about doing what I should.	5V+	4 V	3	2 U	1 U-
15.	I am tired of those in charge trying to show me a better way.	5V+	4 V	3	2 U	1 U-
20.	I get angry when those in authority insist I do things their way.	5V+	4 V	3	2 U	1 U-
18.	I have trouble telling right from wrong.	5V+	4 V	3	2 U	1 U-
3.	I often refuse to do what I know is right.	5V+	4 V	3	2 U	1 U-
10.	I feel unwilling to help even when I know I should.	5V+	4 V	3	2 U	1 U-
5.	I frequently insist on my own way even if I sense I might be wrong.	5V+	4 V	3	2 U	1 U-
8.	I find it hard to really enjoy myself when doing daily chores.	5V+	4 V	3	2 U	1 U-
13.	I resist establishing values in my life so I can be free to be who I am.	5V+	4 V	3	2 U	1 U-
25.	I am afraid of what others might think if I do as I ought.	5V+	4 V	3	2 U	1 U-
4.	I do what I should, even if friends reject me for it.	1 U-	2 U	3	4 V	5 V+
17.	I am fully committed to do what I know I should.	1 U-	2 U	3	4 V	5 V+
22.	I openly defend what is right.	1 U-	2 U	3	4 V	5 V+
19.	I can easily distinguish between good, better and best.	1 U-	2 U	3	4 V	5 V+
2.	I maintain my priorities so that I can do what is best.	1 U-	2 U	3	4 V	5 V+
12.	I consistently remain true to what is best.	1 U-	2 U	3	4 V	5 V+
14.	I gladly respond without hesitation when something is required of me.	1 U-	2 U	3	4 V	5 V+
9.	I am an example of whole-hearted dedication to duty.	1 U-	2 U	3	4 V	5 V+
24.	I immediately confess and make it right whenever I do something wrong.	1 U-	2 U	3	4 V	5 V+
7.	I am fully committed to change whatever keeps me from doing what I should.	1 U-	2 U	3	4 V	5 V+

	SD	D	?	A	SA
Norm Response Totals	3	7	3	9	4
Individual Response Totals	(6)	(4)	(3)	(3)	(10)

	Misrepresentation	Virtue
Uncertainty Count	(0) of 6	(3) of 20
Certainty Count	(4) of 6	(10) of 20
Raw Score	(23) of 30	(68) of 100
Norm Rank	(Likely)	(Average)

Misrepresentation		Virtue	
Ranking Description	Raw Score	Ranking Description	Raw Score
Extremely Unlikely	6 to 10	Very Low	20 to 50
Very Unlikely	11 to 13	Low	51 to 55
Unlikely	14 to 16	Moderately Low	56 to 60
Possible	17 to 19	Average	61 to 70
Likely	20 to 22	Moderately High	71 to 75
Very Likely	23 to 25	High	76 to 80
Extremely Likely	26 to 30	Very High	81 to 100

Virtue Response Analysis

Item Number	23	15	20	18	3	10	5	8	13	25	4	17	22	19	2	12	14	9	24	7
Item Rank	1	2	3	4	5	6	7	8	9	10	11	12	13	14	15	16	17	18	19	20
Item Direction	-	-	-	-	-	-	-	-	-	-	+	+	+	+	+	+	+	+	+	+
Item Basis	D	B	D	B	D	B	D	B	D	B	D	B	D	B	D	B	D	B	D	B
Character		V+		?		U-		U-		?		V+		U-		V+		U		V+
Conduct	V+		V		V+		U		U		?		V+		V+		V+		U-	
Virtue Levels	Examining		Experimenting		Establishing		Evaluating		Embodying											

Virtue Balance	Character (Inner Being)	Conduct (Outward Doing)
Virtue Item Count	(4) of 10	(6) of 10

Virtue Assessment

I. *Response Totals:*

Are there more than 5 uncertain (?) responses?

If so, why is this important?

Are there more than 10 total emphatic (SD/SA) responses?

If so, what does this signify?

Are there more than either 15 positive (A/SA) or 10 negative (D/SD) responses?

If so, what can this indicate?

II. *Uncertainty:*

Is there more than 1 uncertain response among the 6 misrepresentation items?

Why would this be important?

Are there more than 3 uncertain responses among the 20 virtue items?

Why would this be important?

III. *Certainty:*

How does the proportion of answers that indicate misrepresentation compare with the total number of misrepresentation items?

How does the proportion of answers that indicate virtue compare with the total number of virtue items?

IV. *Raw Scores:*

Is the misrepresentation score borderline to the ranking description given in the table?

Is the virtue score borderline to the ranking description provided in the table?

V. *Norm Rank: Fashion a statement reflecting your findings:*

It is _____ that Lola is misrepresenting a _____ virtue score.

VI. *Virtue Level Analysis:*

What levels are solid with virtue responses?

What levels are solid with unvirtuous responses?

What levels are solid with uncertain responses?

Is the whole structure riddled with uncertainty?

Does anything seem peculiar? If so, what could it indicate?

VII. *Virtue Balance:*

Is there a balance between character and conduct?

If not, what could this mean?

Summary

Please keep in mind when performing these rather mechanical procedures that this information is giving you a basis for forming opinions about students who have feelings and usually care about how you assess them. Not only that, they have parents who care about how you assess their children. Furthermore, there are administrators over you who very seriously consider how you deal with your students. And you are measuring whether or not they are really representing themselves and that with regard to how they like doing what they are supposed to do. These can be very personal and delicate matters. Strict confidentiality and acute sensitivity are imperative.

In this chapter, you have had a chance to use the evaluation tools provided, to judge their effectiveness, and to consider how you will use them to measure your own students. In the next chapter, I hope to impress you with the importance of virtue as it relates to knowledge. The principle of proportion between these two elements in education is vital to understand. Also, it is essential to understand the need to establish virtue before knowledge so that knowledge can be properly assimilated. Please stay tuned.

Things to Review and Remember From Chapter 6

1. A thorough evaluation from the LVAQ includes three things:
   a. First, it includes taking into account a student's individual score, without reference to others. This is the raw, unadjusted score.
   b. Second, it includes a consideration of how the student's score relates to others, adjusting for emphasis and uncertainty, and norm ranking.
   c. Third, this means going beyond the results of the test and interviewing students for clarification and communication and a deeper understanding of who they are and the nature of their responses.

2. An objective consideration of students' general attitudes in class, their specific behaviors, and their academic performances also provide balanced evaluations. Positive as well as negative assessments ensure balance. An all-positive or all-negative assessment may indicate a lack of objectivity on your part.

7

The Dynamics of Knowledge and Virtue

Virtue is to knowledge as oil is to machinery. It's what keeps it working. You can have all the right parts in all the right places, but machinery will fail to function without oil. In the same way, removing virtue from education produces problems in the classroom. Big ones. In U.S. schools, we have beautiful facilities, tremendous teachers, and excellent resources. But these days, students bring little virtue to the classroom, are usually taught even less, and our whole educational machine is freezing up. Removing virtue from education neuters knowledge. You can teach students what is true, how it's good, and when it's appropriate, but without virtue, they will not want to make such knowledge work for themselves. Here's why.

The Principle of Proportion

The principle of proportion applies to virtue and knowledge like elements in chemistry: A little imbalance will produce a significant reaction. People can't handle knowledge without virtue because they are moral creatures. They must be willing to do what is right as soon as they discover what it is. They cannot merely operate on instinct, like animals. It is not automatic for human beings to do what is right. We must learn what is true and then how to make it work to be successful in life. When students accumulate knowledge without a desire to put it into practice, they become arrogant and offensive. Virtue enables people to assimilate the knowledge they learn because virtue makes knowledge practical. One of the major sources of conflict in your classroom is between students whose knowledge and virtue levels are disproportionate.

Let's graph Amanda's and Scotty's virtue and knowledge. Let's suppose that you could measure their knowledge and virtue, and that on a scale of 100, Amanda's knowledge reached 85 and her virtue only 60. And let's say that Scotty's knowledge approached 30 and his virtue 50. There are problems associated with each of these students, and the problems with Amanda are more significant and elusive than with Scotty. That's not to minimize Scotty's problems. What's more, teachers tend to react to Amanda and Scotty differently than students do.

Amanda loves to learn. You think she's terrific. She's not. She's just easy. She does what you tell her. She's interested in what you have to say. She doesn't cause problems. She even stands up for you. It seems so wonderful to you to have a student like that, but the other students hate her. You may not realize it, but she is a source of conflict between you and the rest of your learners. She will try to gain special favor from you and turn you against the rest of your students. She can spoil the atmosphere of the classroom and ruin your attitude toward the other students, if you let her. Scotty hates to learn. You think he is hopeless. He's not. He's just difficult. He won't do what you tell him. He doesn't care what you have to say. He causes trouble. He even undermines your authority as a teacher. But a lot of students like Scotty. Nonetheless, he is a source of irritation to you. He will openly defy you and turn the rest of your students away from you.

Scotty and Amanda are problem students. Amanda does not seem like it, Scotty does. Scotty may realize the damage he is doing, it's likely Amanda will not. She will be harder to approach, harder to correct than he will. Moreover, the problems with Scotty are obvious; those with Amanda are not. You will be tempted to favor her and react to him. The rest of your students will be tempted to favor him and react to her. They have watched this dynamic unfold many times and will be very sensitive to the way you handle it. They will evaluate and react to you as a teacher by how you handle this situation. If you are inexperienced or insecure, not discerning or uncaring, Scotty and Amanda will play you to their advantage, and the rest of your students will suffer for it.

Why do the other students tend to like Scotty and dislike Amanda? Why is this issue so important to them? Why is it so fuzzy and elusive to teachers? The problem is peculiar to the proportion of their virtue to their knowledge. When knowledge outstrips virtue, as with Amanda, she becomes proud and offensive, which students dislike. But when virtue outstrips knowledge, as with Scotty, even though he has little of either, he handles what knowledge he has properly. He knows that he doesn't know very much, but he doesn't play any games about it either. He's down to earth. Everyone can relate to his struggles, his directness, his simplicity. Students like him. Teachers tend to dislike him because he reacts to their support of Amanda's arrogance and because he takes little interest in their subject matter. In his mind, Amanda's arrogance is reason enough to stay dumb.

Scotty finds the way people use knowledge to make something of themselves very offensive. He is not a quick learner. School has never come easy for him, but he has found reason enough not to accumulate knowledge he can't use. He sees no sense to it. He observes what people do with it. He disdains it and perceives that other people do, too. By the time you get to know him, he has pretty much determined that it's better to remain dumb than become arrogant.

This is what causes some students who have little knowledge and little virtue to have more practical sense about things than those with a lot of knowledge and proportionately little virtue. Sure, it's better to have a lot of knowledge and a lot of virtue at the same time, but where can students find people who combine both today? Most of the people they observe in everyday life have little virtue and little

Students who have little virtue and less knowledge have more practical sense about things than those with a lot of knowledge and proportionately less virtue.

When knowledge outstrips virtue, a student becomes proud and offensive, which other students dislike.

When virtue outstrips knowledge, students handle their knowledge properly. Even if they have little knowledge, it's attractive.

Virtue begins as a willingness to do as you should before you even know what it is you have to do.

knowledge in a relatively proportionate amount. They seem sensible and down to earth. Most of those with considerable knowledge often have a disproportionate amount of virtue. They often relate in concepts and theory but have no practical sense of how their knowledge relates to everyday living, or they simply do not take the time to present it in that manner. Is it any wonder that many students choose to remain ignorant rather than accumulate knowledge when this is all they see?

Besides all this, there is a certain amount of hypocrisy obvious in all who have knowledge without virtue. Here's why. Virtue begins as a willingness to do as you should before you even know what it is you have to do. Without a proportionate amount of virtue, people question the implications of the knowledge they receive and twist it so that they do not have to do it. Knowledge and truth have a compelling feature to them. If something is true and you know it, you are obliged to live it. Consequently, an imbalance between virtue and knowledge causes an equal amount of corruption in a student. Let's consider how knowledge without virtue corrupts what a student learns.

The Principle of Priority

You first come to know Ricky because of his curiosity. He always asks, "Why?" Initially, you like that, but you find that it isn't mere curiosity that prompts his inquisitiveness. No doubt about it, he is intelligent. He scores high in scholastic aptitude, and his grades confirm it. But, oddly enough, he is reluctant to follow the implications of what he is learning. You discover that he will often second guess the plain implications of what is true. You test his virtue and discover that it is not unusually low, but it occurs to you that it is proportionately lower than his knowledge. This imbalance brings considerable confusion to Ricky's life.

When knowledge exceeds virtue, it obscures what is true.

Ricky has just learned from a lesson on Nazi Germany that the notion of racial superiority is a killer. He begins asking questions about why some people dislike other people. You do not know that his grandfather has told him that black people are a lower form of human being. He suggests that there must be legitimate reasons why people feel the way they do about others. His questions continue until he says he can see reasons why people maintain white supremacy. He insists that he does not hold such a viewpoint but understands how some can. He concedes that in some cases, the notion of racial superiority may have led to killing but is unwilling to conclude that it is wrong.

The way students choose affects the way they think. The way they think determines how much they understand.

The fact that Ricky's knowledge exceeds his virtue causes confusion about what is true. He feels justified in doing nothing about much of what he learns because he has confused himself about what he should do. It works like this: Ricky has not determined beforehand that he will live as he should. When he first encounters what is true, he reserves judgment about whether or not it is true until he can examine the implications of it. If it is something he likes to do, he will decide it is true. But if it is not, he will question it until he cannot come to any conclusion about it at all. Last, he will rationalize to himself that he cannot be held responsible for doing something about which he is uncertain, and so he does nothing.

The result is that Ricky determines what is truth, instead of letting truth instruct him about what he should do. It's a rebellion problem. It is not a discernment problem, as he would like to believe. If he were to determine ahead of time to live the truth whenever he encountered it, it would become self-evident and compelling to him. He would have no problem with it. But he thinks that to do such would leave him naively doing whatever comes along. In actuality, those who determine to do as they should, before they even know what it is, perceive truth quite readily and find little to cloud their discernment.

Those who do not develop this inclination remain suspicious of most everything that comes along because their discernment is clouded by their unwillingness to commit to doing what is true before they know what it is. Ricky needs to learn the difference between critical thinking and a critical attitude. The way students choose affects the way they think. If they decide to do whatever is right and true before knowing what it is, then they will be able to discern whether or not it is right and true, and then, they will be able to see how it applies to their lives.

The Principle of Processing

Life provides new knowledge to people most every day. But it does so in a living context that can be readily assimilated. Concentrated doses, such as come from the classroom or book learning, quickly accumulate to weaken virtue by violating the law of proportion. Virtue helps students assimilate knowledge. If they sustain the attitude of a willingness to comply with the truth, they will spend the time they have figuring out how to make the truth work. If they do not cultivate this attitude, they will spend their time trying to discern if what they have learned is true. They will cultivate confusion and a critical attitude, and will not assimilate what they have learned. They will merely accumulate it and become arrogant and offensive.

Willingness to comply with the truth leaves the mind free to ponder practical uses for knowledge.

The ratio of knowledge to virtue in such students will be disproportionate. They will exhibit problems peculiar to this imbalance, and they will be a challenge to the effectiveness of your teaching. You can fight it and insist that your job is to just teach subject matter, or you can use the occasion as an opportunity to teach virtue so that your students can more readily assimilate the knowledge you have for them. You will be tempted to neglect virtue for subject matter, because such problems will take away your time and make what time you do have less effective. Yet more knowledge will not be assimilated without virtue. It is time well spent, teaching virtue to help your students assimilate knowledge.

You are teaching Health Science. Your subject matter presently is the physical senses and how to take care of them. Intuitively, you know that taking proper care of the eyes and ears, for instance, comes from an appreciation of the functions they perform and that people usually don't appreciate them until they lose them through abuse or neglect. You also know they usually don't appreciate them because they take them for granted. You wonder how you can approach your students to make what is so familiar, fresh and exciting. You have already done the senses of taste and smell. It was easy—expensive, but easy—and the kids really enjoyed tasting the delicacies from foreign countries. Great discussion afterward, too. And the fact that Jason didn't have a sense of smell helped. But now you have to do touch, sight, and hearing.

Your students have lived with their senses all their lives. All those who have not are in the Special Ed classes. Too bad. You could use their experiences and perspectives to cultivate an appreciation for what everyone takes for granted. Hmmm, wonder if Mr. Schmidt would be open to combine Special Ed with Health Sci for a couple of days. The next day, you ask him, "Leonard, I'm teaching on the physical senses and was wondering if you might be interested in doing something together with our classes?" He's leery because he's protective of his disabled students. "Like what?" he says cautiously. You admire his defensiveness for his kids. "Well, I have an idea that your students could teach mine an appreciation for their senses, specifically hearing, sight, and touch."

Leonard is open; he says, "I'm interested. Tell me more." You're thinking out loud now. "The blind girl, what's her name?" "Helen," he says. "Right, Helen, she could show a group how to use her stick and dog. Then, blindfolded, my kids could try it." Leonard, somewhat enthusiastic, adds, "And one of your students could be assigned to be Helen's eyes and give a play-by-play account while it's happening, and the rest could change places as they take turns." You're relieved that Mr. Schmidt is responsive. You continue, "Right, and another group could work with Eddie, the quadriplegic, on touch." Leonard interjects, "Don't forget Helen and her Braille for touch." You say "Terrific, and Lisa on signing for the deaf, for the sense of hearing. No one could talk, they would have to sign." You spend 2 hours after school working up lesson plans for the following Monday.

As the class begins, there is a lot of interest and curiosity among the students as the Special Ed students come in. You, Mr. Schmidt, and a couple of teacher's aides each take a group and explain the purpose of what you are doing. Before long, it is complete pandemonium, semiorganized chaos, but everyone is loving it. The class period ends quickly, and there is no time for discussion. Afterward, you and Mr. Schmidt decide to give the entire class period the next day for discussion. The students are buzzing with hilarious stories of their experiences, and you can't wait to give them opportunity to share their new perspectives.

You open the discussion by suggesting that there is a connection between appreciation of their senses and the way people take care of them. Max opens up and says, "Until Helen explained to me what it is like to live without eyesight, I never thought much about my eyesight, and until I had to walk blindfolded, I did not appreciate what it meant to see; now I'm careful to keep my contact lenses clean. Besides that, I used to make fun of blind people; not any more."

Mr. Schmidt sits just in front of Lisa, signing for her; a few students practice some of the signs they see him do for Lisa. Frank sits next to Helen and describes what is happening. You rejoice over how effective teaching can be, when being and doing work together, when students desire to do what is required, when virtue and knowledge embrace.

Harry, the star running back on the football team, protectively hovers over Eddie, the quadriplegic, in the back of the room. He speaks out, "I have always taken the sense of touch for granted. Eddie can't touch or feel touch . . . except on his head." He affectionately rubs Eddie's head and continues, "Just about every year, you hear about athletes doing something careless and getting paralyzed, like diving or hitting wrong in football." Susan enters the discussion: "I've never thought a lot about hearing. I've always taken it for granted until Lisa told me how hard it is to talk so you can be understood when you can't hear and showed me how to sign. I know loud music hurts our ears, but I've never cared before. Also, I'm glad to have learned how to clean them properly."

Some might wonder about giving so much time to teach a few simple concepts. It might seem like an awful waste. Certainly, not every subject can be taught this way nor any subject all the time, but a lot more subject matter could, and it is so effective. It's especially great for the first week of school, when students have a lot of extra energy and have difficulty settling into the classroom routine. Another good time is when . . . well, there is that certain distancing that occurs between you and your students—that falls like a deathly pallor on your classroom from time to time—the kind you can't explain and for which you have no solution. Also, the last few weeks of the school year are ideal for something like this, when students can't stand to stay in their seats any longer.

As the class winds to a close, you begin to wonder how you can work with Lewis, the retarded boy, when it comes time to study the mind in a few months. As you continue to listen, you marvel at the tolerance and understanding the events of the past week have given your students. By giving 2 days to virtue, you will probably get about 2 weeks of improved attitudes. You and Leonard have brought virtue and knowledge together in the lives of your students. They will never be the same because of it. You have made a difference in their lives, one they will never forget.

If virtue is taught at home, in the community, in places of worship, like "the good old days," then teachers can devote most of their time to subject matter and get away with it. This is why teachers did not use to have the problems you face today. However, virtue is not being taught in homes, communities, and even many places of worship any longer. You may think it is not your job to teach virtue, but it is the key to effectiveness in today's classrooms. Those who analyze education are focusing today on how to better teach knowledge when teachers are teaching subject matter better than they ever have. Instead, the focus should be on how students assimilate knowledge through a virtuous attitude.

> Life provides knowledge in small practical doses that can be readily assimilated. Concentrated academic doses cannot be easily processed.

Vindicating Virtue

Let's be honest, now, and bring truth to the forefront of our thinking. You are well aware of the problems we have in our educational system in the good old U.S. of A., but let's be straightforward about what is *good* in our system. We tend to minimize what is good and emphasize what is bad. When we do, we confuse the issues and complicate the solutions. Instead, if we would look at what's good and then at what's lacking, solutions would become more obvious. Let's face it, for the most part, we have good-hearted teachers who have had good training. We have fine

We tend to think virtue is bad because people who seem virtuous often present an austere, inflexible, mean-spirited, judgmental attitude.

Counterfeit virtue forces itself to control conduct with harshness, because it does not have the calm confidence that comes from strength of character.

facilities and excellent equipment. We're spending plenty of money ($7.5 billion for 1995). Overall, we have wonderful faculty and capable administrators. We have well-reasoned plans and outstanding programs. In fact, these things are not just *good* around the United States, in most cases, they are *very good.*

If these things are true, and they are, then why are we having such problems? No question about it: awful attitudes! Then why are we pressuring the teachers and administrators to perform better? Why are we throwing excessive money at facilities and equipment? Why are we nit-picking the plans and programs? Why don't we just do something about those bad attitudes? Simply because we either don't think we can, or we just don't know how. The solution is simple: Vindicate virtue. Then, we can stop hassling teachers and administrators and pay them what they are worth. We can quit picking them apart and encourage them in a very difficult job. But why should virtue need to be vindicated?

We tend to think virtue is bad because people who *seem* virtuous often present an austere, inflexible, mean-spirited, judgmental attitude. Such things do not represent true virtue. They indicate counterfeit virtue. This has given genuine virtue a bad name. We need to correct that. Phony virtue is usually second-generation virtue. It's copied from first-generation virtue, which is flexible and free, compassionate and committed, right and appropriate all at the same time. Fake virtue is the external shell without internal substance. Counterfeit virtue forces itself to control conduct with harshness, because it does not have the calm confidence that comes from strength of character. Phony virtue feels compelled to control everyone else the way it does itself, with harshness. It's dead inside, and it kills outside. It just has the appearance of something good, but it is very, very bad. It is worse than the defiantly bad attitudes so obvious in your classrooms today. It just doesn't appear to be what it really is.

Mrs. Wilson is influential in the community. Her husband is a judge, but you'd think she was. She is on the school board, but that does not keep her busy enough. It seems as if she monitors everything going on in town. How she keeps up with it, you'll never know, or why she even bothers is beyond reason. She's the kind of person you wonder about: *Has she ever made a mistake in her life? Is she as perfect at home as she appears in the community? It seems like she doesn't even breathe wrong.* She is a scary person to be around. You always feel like you have to walk on egg shells when you see her. She is like law and order personified. When she is on the school grounds, the faculty immediately hope they are doing everything right and feel great relief when she is gone.

What a contrast Mrs. Liebchen is. She's taught for over 30 years and seems unruffled when Mrs. Wilson comes around. She seems curiously calm and confident about who she is and what she is about. Yet she is unassuming, gracious, and pleasant to be around. She is understanding and patient, if you wrong her, and quick to forgive. She is also readily available to help if you need her, especially to young and inexperienced teachers. She is everyone's delight, but a lot of times, she is taken for granted and left unnoticed. Yet that never seems to bother her. You secretly hope you will someday be like her.

One day, Mrs. Liebchen has trouble with one of her students. Wendy, one of her favorites, reports that Mrs. Liebchen has stolen money from her purse. Apparently, Wendy left her purse in Mrs. Liebchen's classroom the last period of the day. She came back the first thing the next morning to find the purse where she left it but without the $100 she had been saving. Everyone knew these were hard times for Mrs. Liebchen. Her husband had died years ago, and she did not have much, but everyone found it impossible to believe she would have taken the money. Yet Wendy was an honest girl, and everyone knew how much she liked Mrs. Liebchen as a teacher. She had no reason to lie.

Well, the matter was referred to the school board, and that's where Mrs. Wilson came into the picture. The incident was fully investigated but without further evidence forthcoming. Mrs. Wilson pressed the board to request the resignation of Mrs. Liebchen, to the protests of all the teachers. The administration was strangely silent on the matter. Students didn't know what to think. Friends stood back and watched. Under the influence of Mrs. Wilson, Mrs. Liebchen was asked to resign. She quietly refused, without explanation. Mrs. Wilson demanded she be dismissed with a public rebuke. After all, justice must be served for Wendy's sake. She also insisted the school's reputation was at stake. And, of course, the board must be vindicated. The debate over these things continued.

Then one day, Mr. Foster, the principal, reported to the board that the janitor, Cecil Little, had come forward, confessing that he had taken the money. It seems he felt badly for Mrs. Liebchen and wanted to come forward sooner but had immediately spent the money and wanted to be able to give it back when he confessed. It had taken him a couple of weeks to save it up. Mrs. Wilson immediately had the janitor fired, and the matter was over. A public word was never spoken against Mrs. Wilson. A public word was never spoken for Mrs. Liebchen.

Consequently, virtue was blemished in the minds of many people. Why? No one thought of Mrs. Liebchen as a virtuous woman. She was just a sweet old lady who was the victim of circumstance. Many thought of Mrs. Wilson as a virtuous person, but they subconsciously decided soon thereafter that they wanted nothing to do with virtue. Why wasn't virtue vindicated in the life of Mrs. Liebchen? Virtue does not demand, it does not strut, it is calm, and confident, and quiet. It is gentle and unassuming. It is not self-vindicating, but it is self-validating. Nevertheless, Mrs. Wilson held the title of "virtuous," and virtue got a bum rap.

Knowledge and virtue work great together in education, if one is kept in proportion to the other, if virtue is given priority, if knowledge is assimilated by virtue, and if it's *real* virtue. But virtue must be vindicated in the classroom, and it is up to teachers to do it. However, typical classroom conditions are centered around knowledge. Virtue has not been given its place. Students struggle, teachers are tormented, and the situation worsens year by year. Consider typical classroom conditions from the student's perspective.

Typical Classroom Conditions

The problem is not with how you communicate knowledge, it's that your students don't desire to do what is required, so they resent you, and they reject your information.

Please keep in mind that you are not the problem. Yet there are some aggravating factors, and they involve you in a big way. These factors make it seem as if you are the problem to students. This is the age of information. Just you, all by yourself, are passing on incredible amounts of knowledge to your students. Not only that, there are five or six other key people in your students' lives who are doing the same thing. On the receiving side of things, your students' minds are being stuffed with information like Thanksgiving turkeys. And consider this, by the time these students come to your classroom in high school, this has been going on for years. All of this is fine, if the principle of proportion has not been violated, if their virtue has been increasing along with their knowledge. It is fine, if priority has been given to virtue in their lives, if there has been sufficient virtue to process all of that knowledge, and if we are talking about genuine virtue, not its counterfeit.

Another complicating factor is the number of assignments your students receive. Many teachers compulsively feel the need to exact their pound of flesh in work required, whether reading or written, in order to satisfy themselves that they are doing their job. This is not to say it is bad to give assignments or require hard work. I just want you to stop and think about how that makes your students feel, when they cannot offset the feeling of *have to* with equal intensity of *want to*. As assignments mount up for them, the intensity of the feeling of obligation increases. If there is not a corresponding intensity of desire to do all that is required, they become overwhelmed, frustrated, and resentful . . . of you. This causes them to perceive the knowledge you give them in a different way than you intend. The problem is not the assignments or even the number of them. The problem is not with how you communicate knowledge, it is that they don't have enough desire to do what is required, so they resent you, and they reject your information.

In addition, there is not near enough practical doing of the thing being learned. Just about every teacher senses this, but theoreticians, and administrators who listen to them, are pressuring you to make your students perform better. Consequently, it's much easier to use the dump-truck approach. You just fill up with content, back into position, and unload. Never mind if your students feel buried. You endured it, now it's their turn. You paid your dues going through this educational system and lived to tell about it. You may even slightly feel that it gives you the right to do unto others. But more likely, you have forgotten the feeling of being hopelessly buried, the panic of fighting to the top of the pile just to get a breath of air. Trouble is, many students never make it out from under the pile; they suffocate.

Besides all that, think of what this does to being and doing. Think of the kind of being you develop by stuffing other people's knowledge into your students, often without the real-life context, often without involving personal choice or the joy of discovery. Think of the kind of doing you sponsor by not assisting your students to put into practice what they have conceptualized. Think of what it means to receive truth void of real-life situations. It's like vaccination time, and we have yet to figure out how to get students to stand in line to receive shots without forcing them. Do they care if the needle is sterile, if the nurse is nice, if it's good for them? They have to be forced. This procedure is fine for inoculating students against deadly diseases, but there are better ways of teaching, and you know what they are. It's just a lot more work, and it takes more time than you think you have, what with all the pressure for student scores to improve.

Even if students survive these typical classroom conditions, handling knowledge without a proportionate amount of virtue produces arrogance; intolerance; contempt for others; and a forced, rigid application of other people's knowledge into a life that is unique, with circumstances that require appropriate adjustment. These things produce tremendous tensions between students and teachers, students and parents, and students among themselves as well. Let's follow Kyle through the first few weeks of the school year and watch what increasing duty does to diminishing desire. Keep in mind, this is not your fault. We are not blaming you for this imbalance in your students' lives. But also keep in mind, there is something you can do about it, if you want to.

Kyle has had an outstanding summer. He played Little League baseball, went to camp for a week, spent some time on the farm with his grandparents, and is really pumped up about coming back to school and seeing his friends. He has a lot of desire, but it is not directed toward education. It has been years since he has been excited about learning. This does not mean he does not get interested in some of the things he is being taught, once he gets into them. But school is something you go and do, just because. If some lesson is exciting or challenging, then good for the teacher. Kyle will engage himself, but he does not carry a sense of anticipation to class. This does not disappoint you. This is the way it is with most kids. You expect it and accept it. It's the air you breathe, part of teaching, goes with the territory.

But Kyle, and the rest of the kids for the most part, carry considerable excitement into the first couple of weeks of school. They come to first period laughing and happy. They find their seats, and the teacher begins to give an overview of what will be covered and then what will be expected of them. Kyle groans inwardly, some do outwardly, but still, it's not so bad. Then the next period comes, and it's the same thing. This goes on throughout the first few days. On top of this, there are the endless lectures, senseless assignments, and sterile classrooms, void of any reality. After a couple of weeks, Kyle is subdued by a low-level despondency. Changing teaching techniques helps to infuse a little of your desire into your students, but you realize it needs to be a deepening of their own desire, and you wonder what you can do to help them.

> **Handling knowledge without a proportionate amount of virtue produces a forced, rigid application of someone else's knowledge on a life that is unique.**

Summary

Now that you know what virtue is, now that you have the capacity to measure it and can appreciate its relationship to knowledge, you probably want to know how you can cultivate it in the lives of your students and maybe in your own life. There are eight principles of instilling virtue in your students, but before we look at them, we need to first consider how virtue breaks apart in human lives. Then, we will want to look at a few things that prepare people to cultivate virtue. After considering the breakdown of virtue, after pondering how to prepare hearts to cultivate virtue, only then will the eight principles mean something. So let's first consider how virtue breaks apart in the human soul, specifically in the human will.

Things to Review and Remember From Chapter 7

1. The principle of *proportion:* When a balance is maintained between virtue and knowledge, students assimilate knowledge and handle it properly.

    a. When knowledge exceeds virtue in students, they become arrogant and offensive.

    b. Virtue enables students to assimilate the knowledge they learn because it makes knowledge personally practical.

        • When knowledge exceeds virtue, theory is given preference over practice.

        • When students receive knowledge without cultivating a desire to live it, they rationalize away the implications of what they have learned.

2. The principle of *priority:* Virtue begins as a willingness to do what should be done, even before knowing what it is. In this sense, virtue has priority over knowledge.

    a. Because humans are social beings and do not act on instinct, they are morally obligated to do what is right.

    b. If virtue is not given priority in education, knowledge will be of little practical benefit, because the way students choose affects the way they think. And the way they think determines how much they understand.

    c. When students have settled the issue of whether they will do whatever is right, the practical implications of knowledge seem intuitive.

3. The principle of *processing:* Life provides knowledge in small, practical doses that can be readily assimilated. Concentrated doses that come in academic form cannot be easily processed and quickly accumulate to bring an imbalance between knowledge and virtue.

4. The vindication of virtue: Virtue is best vindicated by a calm demonstration of inner character in the face of opposition.

    a. Counterfeit virtue forces itself to control conduct with harshness because it lacks the calm confidence that comes from strength of character.

    b. Virtue gets vilified by counterfeits who often present an austere, inflexible, mean-spirited, judgmental attitude in the name of virtue.

8

The Self Cycles

The lack of virtue in your students does not simply mean they have difficulty learning. It means their lives are breaking apart. It's a matter of degree for most, of course, but there are a lot of extreme examples around. You see them, and they clearly expose the tragedy of an unvirtuous life. Ted's life has been shattered by a lack of virtue. He wants to give up on life . . . at 16! The events of life make no sense to him. Habits shackle him. Grief over guilt gnaws at his guts. The pressure to perform makes him want to scream. The fear of failure constantly nags him. He is so inwardly angry he doesn't dare express it. He is so filled with anxiety he doesn't know which way to turn. And he is so tired and frustrated that he just wants to die! How did things get this way for him?

Ted was a happy-go-lucky boy, bouncing from one event to the next as he grew up. He always had a twinkle in his eye, a kind word, always ready to help; a really decent kid. When he turned 13, things changed. His father received a promotion, and the family moved from the country to the Metroplex. His school was big, and nice, and new, bustling with activity, but he felt lonely and didn't know how to fit in at first. People seemed to stare at him as if he was from some other planet. When he did get to know a few of the other students, they criticized the way he dressed and the way he talked. But he quickly adjusted to their comments and began to conform, and before long, they accepted him.

He also began to experience changes in his body. New and different desires surprised him, and they were not unpleasant, either. The boys talked about things he never heard before. He was shown pictures of things he had never seen before. He started thinking about things he never thought about before, even doing things he had never done before. This prompted a lot of mixed feelings in Ted. He would feel wonderfully exhilarated one moment and guilty and ashamed the next. Curiosity, bad company, and selfish desires changed the way Ted looked at girls, the way he treated them, the way he felt about them, and . . . the way he felt about himself.

Ted also discovered that his chores in the country had left him strong and agile. He excelled in physical education. One day, another boy challenged him to a fight just to prove himself. He shouldn't have. The basketball coach watched Ted play sports and invited him to try out for the team. He did surprisingly well and became a school favorite. Sometimes, he found himself thinking he could do just about whatever he wanted. At the same time, he suppressed fears he would not be able to keep doing as well as he had.

In the classroom, Ted also did better than average. His teachers liked him and looked for ways to help him any way they could. He did not have top grades, but they weren't mediocre, either. He was pleasant in class. Students liked him, and he got along well with them. But he wanted to perform better, to be liked better. He worked hard, and he loved the exhilaration of success and the admiration it brought. He made a special effort to get to know everyone in his classes. He freely participated and volunteered whenever he had opportunity. Yet he felt driven and often spent.

Ted's social life picked up. He went to parties and afterward drove around with some of the older boys. They told him about doing drugs and offered him some. For a long time, he refused. But one evening, he decided to give them a try. He did not know it would become the turning point in his life. He had been sort of despondent and half hoping something would happen that would give him a lift. It did, but after that evening, he felt bad inside. So he tried harder to be better but was soon stressed out. He sought out drugs again. Only this time, he kept doing them. Before long, he felt like he couldn't help himself.

Eventually, he quit playing sports. His grades dropped. He quit socializing. Last, he was caught with drugs at school. His father came to the principal's office and took him home. After a week's suspension, Ted returned to the principal's office with his father. They made an agreement whereby Ted could return to classes if he promised that he would give up drugs. He promised, and things went well for awhile, but then he fell back into his old ways. Back and forth he went from bad to good to bad, until he despaired of life. He was 16, and he wanted to die. That's how it looked from the outside. Let's take a look inside of Ted.

Instead of doing good from his heart and enjoying the results of it, Ted put himself under intense pressure to perform. This led to a selfish striving for success. Initially, he did well, but this brought pride of performance. But instead of producing self-acceptance, it led to a fear of failure because of the expectations that accompanied success. Not only did Ted hold high expectations for himself, he found that other people did, too. As these expectations increased, so did the pressure to perform to meet them. This pressure led to an even greater striving for success, and Ted began to think he could do anything he decided to do. But it wasn't long before the pressure to perform, fed by the fear of failure, became overwhelming. Duty once enjoyed soon became drudgery. We call this the cycle of *willfulness*; doing your duty without nurturing the inner desire to continue. Figure 8.1 shows how it looks.

The Cycle of Willfulness

This cycle promotes pride in people for doing their duty. It shows how a duty-dominated life increasingly becomes isolated from desire. It leads people to falsely believe that they can do anything they determine to do. It engenders false expectations, it builds false hope, and ultimately, leads to a lifestyle few people can sustain, and those that do are secretly miserable. But this was only half of Ted's problem. The other half involved pursuing desires to the neglect of duty.

Willfulness

**Pressure
to Perform**

**Selfish
Striving**

**Promoting
Pride**

**Fear of
Failure**

**Pride of
Performance**

Figure 8.1. Duty Without Desire

By stimulating selfish desires, Ted's will to resist the desire to do it again decreased, then his weakened will gave way to increasing indulgence. The more that Ted did what he believed he should not do, the more his guilty conscience condemned him. The more his conscience condemned him, the more tantalizing became the temptation to do what he felt he shouldn't. Consequently, he became more inclined to pursue pleasure. He also felt a greater need to appease his guilty conscience. He felt bad enough to start searching for something to make him feel better. Repeating this cycle increasingly convinced him that he was not able to do anything at all about his problems. We call this the cycle of *will-less-ness*; pursuing selfish desires to the neglect of duty (see Figure 8.2).

The Cycle of Will-less-ness

Figure 8.2 shows how a desire-dominated lifestyle increasingly becomes isolated from duty. Guilt from feeding selfish appetites actually inflames indulgence. A guilty conscience prompts people not to do selfish things. Rebellion reacting to guilt rejects the notion of wrongdoing. When people experience guilt from having done something wrong, in rebellion, they won't admit that it was wrong or do anything to change. When guilt attempts to check selfishness, selfishness seems that much more alluring and appealing. The more people selfishly stimulate their bodies, the less able they are to resist. Consequently, they find themselves caught in a curious ambivalence, torn by what they hate and love at the same time.

The literature on virtue through the ages discusses duty and desire, but it often does so as if they are at odds with one another. For instance, *will* and *wish* are explained in opposition to each other. Will is expressed as determination, wish is

Will-less-ness

Figure 8.2. Desire Without Duty

expressed as desire, and both as mutually exclusive. But I am convinced that virtue properly involves both duty and desire, and not one to the exclusion of the other, in case you haven't caught my drift by now. A third pattern of behavior shows how peace is produced in the life when duty and desire come together. This peace-producing pattern is different from the first two cycles in that it is not self-centered. Desire and duty must work in harmony instead of in isolation from the other. To accomplish this, people need to sacrifice both the selfish appetites of the body and the selfish ambitions of the soul and willingly live their lives the way they should.

Living the way you should cannot mean merely doing required duties. It must also include actively conforming individual desires to what is required. This means learning to desire what is required of you. When selfish appetites and selfish ambitions are sacrificed, when duty is done with desire, then the life is no longer fragmented by pursuing pleasure or promoting pride. The end product is peace, and the life is characterized neither by will-less-ness nor willfulness but by a *willingness* to do what should be done, hence the name of the third cycle (see Figure 8.3). It prevents desire from degenerating into a search for the fulfillment of selfish appetites and duty from degenerating into striving for the fulfillment of selfish ambitions. The soul is restored to wholeness.

The Cycle of Willingness

To prevent a return to willfulness, people must remain at rest. This means they must not yield to selfish ambitions and selfish appetites; they must be content with who they are, their position in life, and what they have. To prevent rest from degenerating into will-less-ness, they must become other oriented. This means that

Figure 8.3. Conforming Desires to Duties

the focus of their attention is on the needs of others instead of seeking the fulfill-ment of selfish appetites and selfish ambitions. If they are not content with who they are and what they have, if they are not other oriented, they will return to the lifestyles of will-less-ness and willfulness. Self-sacrifice and remaining at rest are not passive activities. Neither are conforming desires to duties and being other oriented anxious activities. All four steps on cycle three run harmoniously and coterminously. Hence, remaining at rest and being other oriented promote self-sacrifice and strengthen a willingness to do what is required.

The complaint of the cycle of will-less-ness is, "I can't." The boast of the cycle of willfulness is, "I can." In both cases, the focus is wrong. One denies capability, the other overestimates ability. The funny thing about these very different lifestyles is that people react to willfulness and will-less-ness the same way, with indifference. People perceive that the person who says they can't, no matter how much someone tries to help, is really saying they won't, so people become indifferent to their cries for help. Also, people are perfectly happy to watch those who boast fall on their faces without the slightest interest in helping them. However, those who say they are willing easily find others ready to help them, even if they need a lot of help, even if they stumble and fall. This is not a game of words. Teachers will be strongly tempted to treat both willful and will-less students with indifference.

> Will-less-ness complains, "I can't." Willfulness boasts, "I can." People react to both with indifference!

Desire-Dominant Lifestyle

Let's suppose you have taught music for 15 years. One student, Danielle, is a very quiet girl, not very responsive. She struggles with the music assignments you give her. She customarily carries a semi-sad countenance, kind of a forlorn look. At first, it was a little annoying, nothing you couldn't endure but mildly irritating. You had long since determined to help every student you could, regardless of how you felt about them, and there had certainly been those who were less endearing than Danielle, some a lot less. She needed help, you could easily see that, and there was always someplace in the school band for those who were less capable.

Therefore, you decide to offer a little time to Danielle. One day after practice, you ask her if she would like to come to school early for some help. She says, "Sure." You thought you saw a light come on in her eyes for just a moment. So you respond, "Great! 7:30," and smile kindly toward her. And sure enough, the next morning she is there promptly. As you work with her, you can see she is trying, but with almost every attempt, she fails and says, "I can't do it. I just can't." As the days pass, your frustration prompts you to ponder her response pattern. You feel helpless some days with Danielle, and she is often on the verge of tears. You sense she is capable but doesn't really want to improve, and you are becoming indifferent to her need for help.

However, you determine over the weekend that on Monday morning you will get to the bottom of this. Instead of going over assignments with Danielle when she comes in, you ask her if she would be willing to talk for a few moments. Reluctantly, she agrees. You decide to risk a probing question right from the start. "Danielle, do you really want to play in the school band?" Very quietly she responds, "Not really." You ask, "Do you enjoy playing the clarinet?" Almost tearfully, she says, "I haven't in the past, but I am now a little bit." You think you get the picture now and ask, "Are you here because your parents want you to be here?" With tears, she nods. You decide to ask one final question. "Have your parents ever insisted you do something you didn't want to do before?" She shakes her head no.

Danielle has a desire-dominant lifestyle that she initiated and that her parents had allowed. Recently, they came to realize this, and they are now rightly challenging her in this area of her life. You have observed that when she says she can't, she is really saying she won't. She needs to realize that if she becomes willing, she will become able, and if she becomes willing and able, she will actually come to enjoy what is required of her. The desire-dominant lifestyle is not just represented by the drug addict dropout. It takes many forms. In this instance, Danielle has been spoiled. She has always had whatever she wanted. She has always had her own way. She has inadvertently learned that she can't really enjoy something unless it's what she wants to do. This is untrue. She has also taught herself that if she doesn't want to do something, she can't perform. This is also not true. She needs help and with more than music.

Danielle looks up at you with her sad face. You explain to her what you have been thinking. Then, you look into her mournful eyes and say, "I can help you master your instrument. I can help you enjoy playing in the school band. But you have to overcome your resistance to do what is required of you and be willing to perform what your parents ask of you. Are you willing to commit yourself to that?" She looks you right in the eye and smiles. "Of course." After a few weeks, Danielle stops by after band practice one day and says, "Thank you for helping me realize how I was keeping myself from doing what I could and for helping me enjoy what I could not." You smile and think to yourself, *"Virtue is its own reward."*

Duty-Dominant Lifestyle

Jack is very insecure. Most would never guess it, and he would argue with you about it if you confronted him with it, but he is. He is often loud and boastful, and although his fellow students openly admire his accomplishments, you guess that they also secretly wince at his arrogance, and you can tell some intensely dislike him. He's good at whatever he does, but he knows it and wants everyone else to know it too. In your keyboarding class, things are different. Although he has relatively good hand-eye coordination, his fingers are big and clumsy. You find yourself secretly smirking at his inability and hope it will help him become more sensitive to those less capable. You determine he is one person to whom you will offer no extra help—no way, no how. But Jack needs help in a special way, and he needs it desperately.

Jack boasts to those around him that he will be typing 60 words a minute without mistakes by the end of the school year. Knowing Jack, you conclude that he just might, but it will be without your help. Yet you wonder about your reluctance to help him. You tell yourself, *The kind of help he needs, I can't give him.* You think he needs someone to rattle his cage, but he really doesn't. He needs someone soft and understanding, patient and kind—someone who is not irked with what he's like, who will overlook his bragging. Yet Jack repels any direct approach for help. You are stymied.

Then one day, you get an idea. Jack needs a different approach demonstrated to him. He wouldn't accept it otherwise. The direct approach won't work. You have listened to him talk about sports many times. All of a sudden, it dawns on you: He needs to see capable people who are quiet and unassuming. So far, his role models have been sports figures who command large salaries and are used to getting whatever they want. He has determined that success is measured by fame and fortune. It's not something he spends time thinking about, he just absorbs this attitude as he studies the sports world. Because the loud and proud sports heroes are the ones who get media attention, he assumes all professional players are that way. He does not realize that only a few of the dozens of people that make up a professional team are that way or that in times past, most of the great players did not act that way. It's something he has just grown up with.

You realize that Jack needs to observe success in its quiet, calm, unassuming form. Jack is struggling with typing, and you sense that he is getting ready to drop your class in spite of his boasts. There is a very quiet girl sitting on the other side of the room you would like for him to observe. You inwardly hope Jack will fail because he is such a braggart, but you overcome your natural feelings by finding a way of helping him, a way that will help his typing and his attitude. You tell him, "Jack, I am going to relocate your seat next to Audrey; she might have some ideas about how you can reach your goal of 60 words per minute. The only problem is, she is kind of quiet and shy. If you want her help, you'll have to ask her for some tips and techniques. She probably won't voluntarily help you, but she is very good. In fact, she is already typing 70 words per minute."

Jack is stunned. His jaw drops as he responds, "I never would have guessed she was that good. She is so quiet!" As the days pass, you observe that Jack is learning more from Audrey than typing. She has become his hope for reaching his goal. What he doesn't realize is that she is influencing his demeanor as well. Her short, calm answers surely provide helpful techniques, but her quiet success shows him another approach toward achievement. Although he will never be who Audrey is because of his flamboyant personality, he is learning that achievement need not find its motivation in anxiety. It's also funny to watch him mimic Audrey. You laugh to yourself, *"They would make a good couple."*

Virtue-Dominant Lifestyle

Martin is retarded, and he is in your physical education class. There isn't much he can do. He knows it, yet he never says he can't. At the same time, you never hear him boast. It's strange, he suffers no illusions about himself. He could get out of taking PE if he wanted to, no question about it, but he wants to try everything. He's got guts. You admire him and so do most students, not for what he can accomplish but for what he is willing to attempt. Not only that, students fall all over themselves trying to help him. It's the craziest thing you have ever seen. You know all too well how blunt teenagers can be about anyone who is different, but nobody hassles this kid. It is a very curious thing to watch.

It is testing week, and the boys are at the pull-up bars. A couple of boys are lifting Martin's wizened little body up so he can grasp the bar with his one good hand. You stifle the urge to laugh and then the urge to cry as you observe him wiggle there in space for a few frantic moments before they take him down to time his sit-ups. You ponder why it is that people are so willing to help this helpless young man. You call one of his helpers over and probe him, "Hey Todd, why is everyone so willing to help Martin?" He cocks his head and stares at you kind of half disgusted, half curious, and says, "We're willing because he's willing." And he runs off.

You contemplate, "If I could bottle his willingness and give regular doses of it to about a dozen kids, life would sure be simpler." Well, coach, it's called virtue and it's taught, but not like other subjects. Someone has to live it right in front of them; they have to see it, and it only becomes comprehensible to teens in real-life situations. A crisis in the classroom or a confrontation on the ball field provide workable circumstances, but the teacher who would teach virtue must be ready when the opportunity presents itself. First, this means you must discern it for what it is, as a situation unfolds. The three cycles described in this chapter give you an idea of how virtuous and unvirtuous lifestyles look. To teach it, you need to develop a mental library of different students and situations from which to draw when those treasured, teachable moments arise.

Things to Review and Remember From Chapter 8

1. *The cycle of willfulness* demonstrates how a duty-dominated life increasingly becomes isolated from desire through promoting pride. The focus is on doing.

   a. Selfish ambitions lead to pride of performance, presuming a measure of success for the initial efforts invested.

   b. But instead of producing self-acceptance, pride of performance actually leads to the fear of failure, because of the expectations that accompany it.

   c. As expectations increase, so does the pressure to perform to meet them.

   d. This leads to a greater striving for success, until the pressure to perform becomes so great, it is thrown off for the pursuit of pleasure and the cycle of will-less-ness.

   - Willfulness leads people to falsely believe that they can do anything they determine to do.
   - Willfulness engenders false expectations and builds false hope.
   - Willfulness ultimately leads to a lifestyle few people can sustain, and those that do are secretly miserable.

2. *The cycle of will-less-ness* demonstrates how a desire-dominated lifestyle becomes increasingly isolated from duty through the pursuit of pleasure. The focus is on being.

   a. Selfish appetites lead to an inability to resist the temptations of self-indulgence.

   b. The inability to resist causes students to do what they know they should not do.

   c. The more they do what they know they should not do, the more guilt they feel.

   d. The more guilt they feel, the more they pursue pleasure to make themselves feel better, until the guilt becomes so great they decide to try harder to reform and return to the cycle of willfulness.

   - Will-less-ness leads people to falsely believe that they are helpless to do anything to change their hopeless condition.
   - Will-less-ness promotes discouragement and despair.
   - Will-less-ness ultimately leads to addictions, from which relatively few people recover.

3. *The cycle of willingness* demonstrates how desire and duty come together in life to produce peace. The focus is on being and doing, good character and good conduct.

   a. Willingness begins when selfish appetites and selfish ambitions are sacrificed.

   b. Willingness then actively conforms individual desires to what is required.

   c. Such willingness produces peace, which governs future choices.

d. Peace brings the freedom to become concerned with the needs of others, which in turn promotes a further willingness to sacrifice selfish ambitions and appetites.

- Willingness prevents the life from being fragmented by pursuing pleasure or promoting pride.
- Willingness prevents desire from degenerating into the search for the fulfillment of selfish appetites.
- Willingness prevents duty from degenerating into striving to fulfill selfish ambitions.

9

Preparing the Heart for Instilling Virtue

Willfulness and will-less-ness shatter virtue in the human heart, leaving the dutiful just going through the motions without joy and those pursuing pleasure with little sense of responsibility. Those who flip-flop between the two find fleeting happiness only in passing pleasures and also find their sense of responsibility cannot be sustained. To experience wholeness, the broken-hearted need to instill virtue in their fractured lives. But before they can learn principles for instilling virtue, their hearts must be prepared to cultivate virtue. It's like preparing soil for planting. Hard ground must be broken up. Weeds must be rooted out. Fertilizer and mulch must be added in proper measure. Water must be supplied. Above all, timing is everything. Virtue in the human heart is much the same. The heart must be prepared for the principles of virtue to take root, flourish, and bloom.

There are at least four things that prepare the heart to instill virtue. First, students can prepare their hearts by assessing negative feelings. Second, they can prepare their hearts for instilling virtue by changing perspective. Third, they can prepare their hearts by convincing their minds that something is right, good, and appropriate. And fourth, they can prepare their hearts for instilling virtue by deepening their desire. Basically, this merely means that students must see how their negative feelings intensify their sense of obligation, they must shift their focus, they must convince themselves of the worthiness of what is required, and they must be willing to deepen their desire to do what they should. These things are very intangible to students generally, and it is almost impossible for them to understand and perform them without guidance. Parents usually do this with successful students, but problem students often have problem parents who are not able to help them. That leaves it up to you.

> **Problem students often have problem parents who are not able to help them. That leaves it up to you!**

Assessing Negative Feelings

It's hard enough to assess your own feelings, let alone someone else's, but when you have to help students assess *their* feelings, it is next to impossible. It's like trying to

Students must learn to distinguish the actual weight of obligation from the intensity they feel.

explain how to work a Rubik's cube without being able to hold it and say, "Like this." Words will fail you, and the words you find will seem trite to you and to your students. This is why it is so important to treasure the circumstances surrounding classroom crises. They provide all you need to assess and express how negative feelings work. If you trash these circumstances, hurriedly purge them from your classroom, get rid of troublesome students to preserve order, you throw away their prescription for healing.

The first thing students need to be able to do is sort out the confusion. They have to be able to distinguish the actual weight of obligation from the intensity they feel. Then, they need to discern where the additional weight is coming from. Last, they must be able to detect why they feel the additional intensity. To talk about these things with your students in a clinical way is death to them: "Boring." "Who cares?" Not only that, if you try to become one of them in order to relate, it is nauseating, and they will resent it: "Disgusting!" "Repulsive!" In addition, if you try to get too personal with them, most can't handle the intimacy: "Don't touch me!" "Lemme outta here." In other words, it's next to impossible.

You just can't do it . . . alone. But you can accomplish all of these things by helping your students talk it through with each other. They will need leading and guiding questions. They will need a referee at times. And they will need space and freedom to work things out. But most of all, they will need to be in charge, or they won't open up and they won't do it. If you do the doing of it, you may have a few who tag along, but if you want them to get involved, let them do it.

It's the first week of school, and you are laying out the way things will happen in your classroom between you and your students. You state from the start how discipline problems will be handled. You tell them that when conflict happens in the classroom, it will be handled in the classroom, by the students in the classroom. You tell them that you will guide the discussion to work things out, but that they will work it out. They will have the freedom to form conclusions, make decisions, and—so long as someone does not suffer injustice—their decisions will stand. You establish the guidelines you wish, and the school year begins.

That night as you are falling asleep, several things are going through your mind. The kids seemed somewhat excited about handling trouble in the classroom them-selves. They also seemed kind of like it was their due; as if they should be involved in working things out; as if it was about time adults were respecting them and treating them as capable. Of course, not all of them *are* capable. What if some kids hatch plots and contrive fake situations to use up class time and make things excit-ing? What if some kind of violence occurs? What if there is trouble *every day* or if problems drag on and on? You drift off into a troubled sleep.

After a fitful night's rest, you arrive at school somewhat bleary-eyed but ready to face the coming week. Sure enough, trouble begins the first week after instituting your new approach, but it originates with the administration instead of the stu-dents. It has been decided that students will begin wearing uniforms or "prescribed wardrobes" to school. You must make the announcement to your students. You were aware that there had been talk about this through the summer but did not expect it would be approved. As you announce this new requirement to your stu-dents, there is stunned silence, then an outbreak of objections and complaints. You ask them to weigh the intensity of the obligation they feel on a scale of 1 to 10. Most answer, "10."

Your class is American history. You explain that when the wagon trains faced trouble as they crossed the frontier, they circled the wagons. You call out to the class to "Circle the wagons!", explaining this is their cue to form a circle with their chairs around the perimeter of the room. You lead the discussion by asking, "Why does the idea of uniforms bother you?" Their answers return, rapid fire: "They're treating us like babies." "They are taking away our freedom." "It stifles self-expression." "There's no individuality." "We feel manipulated." "It's ridiculous." Next you ask, "Why do people universally around the world use uniforms for various things, anyway? Where does the idea come from? Diana, go get the dictionary. Mark, get the Thesaurus. Patty, get on-line to the library on the computer and see what you can find."

There is a flurry of activity. Diana reports back, "Hmmm. 'Dress of a distinctive design or fashion worn by members of a particular group and serving as a means of identification.' " Mark adds, "Under *uniform,* it doesn't give much, but under *uniformity,* it gives a lot!" You suggest, "Pick some of the words out that seem important, Mark." He adds, "Okay, *stability, monotony, harmony, consistent, inflexible.*" By now, Patty has linked up to the on-line encyclopedia. She adds, "Hey, listen to this: When it talks about officially designated clothing for the military and police, it says, 'As a system of communication, the uniform enables these organizations to maintain control and to foster the attainment of organizational goals. It also encourages the wearer to fulfill organizational requirements.' "

You sense the importance of this situation and realize that the problem will not vanish. You also know that solving it will consume considerable time. You suggest to the class, "We need time to think about these things and to talk them over. How about if we devote a little time each class period to this until we work it through?" They seem to understand the need to give time to subject matter, even if it is history, and appreciate the fact that you gave time to help them with their problem. You breathe a sigh of relief because you had no idea what to do next, and this will allow you time to consider how to guide them, but you have accomplished one thing to this point. You have begun to help them sort out the confusion.

Imperceptibly, the attitude of the class has changed from frustration and complaining to excitement, interest, and problem solving, all in a matter of minutes. You ask them once again to weigh the intensity of the obligation they feel on a scale of 1 to 10. This time, they come in at about 8. You ask them to consider, for tomorrow, why the change, after only a couple of minutes. "Did the obligation itself change, or was the sense of obligation influenced by something else?"

That evening, as you ponder their predicament, you try to distinguish the intensity of obligation they feel from the actual weight of it. You begin by putting yourself in their position. At first, you think, dress is really a minor matter. If the administration required the faculty to wear uniforms, in one way, it would be a relief from having to dress differently and attractively on your meager salary. It would probably be a relief to parents for the same reasons. Why is it so bothersome to students? Then it dawns on you. Your situation is not the same as theirs is.

> The feeling of helplessness intensifies the feeling of obligation and diminishes the desire to do something constructive.

They are at a point in their lives when dress and identity are very closely tied together. They can express and experiment, adjust and alter individually, and that is being taken away. Almost every other aspect of their lives is regulated and has been as far back as they care to remember. That's why this seems so important to them. Hmmm. We want them to make adult decisions, but we limit opportunities for them to experiment. As you consider these things, you get an idea of how you can help them distinguish the actual weight of obligation from the intensity they feel. Their feeling of helplessness intensifies the feeling of obligation and diminishes their desire to do something constructive. It just promotes a negative attitude.

The next day in class, you ask your students to ponder two things: First, if they were allowed to design the uniforms, how would they feel about the obligation, then second, if that were their responsibility, what would they come up with. As they begin thinking about these things, you designate five task groups, and let the students choose which they would like to be in. Group 1 considers the option of different uniforms for each grade. Group 2 considers color combinations and variations. Group 3 considers styles. Group 4 considers costs. Group 5 considers dress problems. Over the next few days, you have the students shift from group to group. They only have 10 minutes each time.

At the end of the week, you ask them to rate the intensity of the obligation of school uniforms. It has dropped to 4s and 5s. You then ask them to rate their desire to do something positive about the situation. They rate their desire on an average of between 6 and 7. This explains their change in attitude. The intensity of the obligation was magnified by their feeling of helplessness. As soon as there was something they could constructively do about it, the intensity of obligation began to drop and the desire to comply increased. A simple executive order left them with a feeling of helplessness that produced a bad attitude, whereas involvement in the process quickly restored their virtue.

The intensity of the obligation was especially significant because of the extensive limitations on young people to experiment with self-expression. Experimentation can be threatening to those trying to maintain order, but canceling experimentation to bring order is no solution, either. Can dress be harmful? Of course, it can. Take for instance gang dress, or immodest dress, or unclean dress, or distracting dress. Are there other ways to experiment, to express individuality? Why, certainly.

It is absolutely crucial to treasure the circumstances surrounding classroom crises.

What students think, choose, and feel are all expressions of their individuality. Even what students do in groups—their activities, the associations they make—all express their individuality. Uniforms actually can enhance that. Take for instance sports uniforms, PE uniforms, and band uniforms. Students do not object to them because they gain special identity from them. Identity is directly related to individual choice and special activities accomplished together. Can uniform dress be helpful? Surely it can, to the poor, for modesty, against gangs, against making a spectacle.

Do I favor or oppose uniform dress? Neither one. I just want to suggest that when faced with a difficult situation, the problems that arise from that situation can provide incredible teachable moments. After such, your class can begin to discern where the additional weight is coming from and detect why they felt the additional intensity. As a teacher, you can help them and the administration with a problem, but much more than that. Your students can begin to develop the ability to detect the origin of their negative feelings. It is absolutely crucial to treasure the circumstances surrounding classroom crises.

Changing Perspective

A second thing that helps prepare the heart to instill virtue, besides assessing the origin of negative feelings, is viewing things from a variety of perspectives. This means students must shift focus from themselves to those around them. Both the problem of a heightened sense of obligation and the problem of diminished desire are favorably changed by viewing problem situations from various perspectives. With a change in perspective comes an imaginary change in position, giving students a break from the intensity of emotions they feel, because they are assuming someone else's position.

Stacy turns quickly around and says rather loudly to Gene, "Leave me alone!" There is immediate silence as the entire class stares at Gene. Somewhat bewildered, Gene says, "I didn't do anything." There is some laughter and snide remarks, such as, "Sure, Gene," and "Yeah, right." Rather than just resume class, you stop things right where they are and have the students form a circle with their chairs. There's muttering, and murmuring, and laughing while everyone rearranges the room. But there is also a low level of excitement, and anticipation, and even a sense of significance.

In your mind, you are a little frantic because you don't yet know how things will develop, but you feel confident that the problem is small enough to be handled in this way. What takes place, however, is astounding. Instantly, both Stacy and Gene are somewhat embarrassed, and you feel the need to be especially sensitive to them. But by immediately getting them to move the chairs around helps breaks the embarrassment they feel. You begin by asking Gene what happened. He is still non-plussed. After sputtering around for a moment, he says, "I don't have any idea what's going on, but I didn't do anything. Period." He is starting to get a little angry because of the attention and because of the earlier heckling. So you ask Stacy what happened. Looking down, with a pout, she quietly says, "He pulled my hair." Gene immediately breaks in and says, "That's not true!" There is a murmur of voices as you decide to bring the class into it.

You begin, "Okay students, what's the problem here?" Sam says, "She's trying to get him into trouble." Cheryl adds defensively, "He's harassing her, and he can't get away with it." Someone else asks, "Did anyone see Gene pull Stacy's hair?" Everyone is quiet for a long time, then Sarah says, "I did." Gene shakes his head and says, "This is incredible." Evelyn says, "I don't think Gene did it." You interject, "But what is the problem here, class?" Louis adds, "The problem is that one of them has disrupted the class." You say, "Okay, but why is that a problem?" Sherry offers, "Because that keeps the whole class from continuing on with what we were doing."

You pose the question, "Well, class, what should be done about it?" After a brief discussion, the class agrees that the offending party should report to the principal's

The desire to learn is greatly enhanced by relieving classroom tensions.

A change in perspective gives students a break from the intensity of the emotions they feel.

office. The class votes 22 to 3 that Gene is guilty and sends him off to the principal's office. As he leaves, Stacy begins quietly crying. Her friend Sarah, who said she saw Gene do it, says sheepishly, "Gene didn't do anything. Stacy and I planned this whole thing, but we didn't think it would turn out like this." Sam asks indignantly, "Why?" You immediately send someone off to bring Gene back before he reaches the principal's office. Sarah continues, "She likes Gene, but he never pays any attention to her." Your first thought is, What a mess! I should never have allowed this to take this turn. But then you tell yourself, Somehow this can be instructive and positive, if I can guide it properly.

You tell the class to remain silent for the next few moments out of fairness to Gene until he returns. As Gene comes in and sits down, you apologize for the class and explain to him why you sent someone after him and what had transpired. Before you allow Gene to respond, you ask the class to put themselves in Gene's position and imagine how he must feel right now. Sam says, "Well, if I were in his spot, I would be hot!" Evelyn adds, "He's probably embarrassed." Another volunteers, "I don't know, but I would be confused." Now, you let Gene speak. He says, "I feel all of those things, and I'm also hurt and humiliated. But I want to know how Stacy and Sarah feel."

There is a long silence. You break in. "Class, let's help them. Put yourselves in their place. Cheryl speaks up, "It's hard when you like someone and they don't even know you exist. It's like you're dead inside." Louis follows by offering, "I imagine right now they both want to crawl in a hole. Matter of fact, I feel sorry for all three of them." Sam, getting over his indignation, continues the discussion by saying, "Yeah, I think we as a class were pretty quick to get rid of Gene and pretty quick to be angry with Stacy and Sarah." You conclude, "Class, you have been very sympathetic with Gene and Stacy and Sarah. I'm really pleased."

However, you don't want to leave this incident dangling with everyone feeling badly for everyone else, so you ask, "What has *changing perspective* brought to you personally through all of this? How has it affected you inside?" Doreen begins, "I found myself move from being put out, to being angry, to feeling guilty, to sympathizing, to being peaceful once again." Bill adds, "Well, at first I was defensive for Stacy, then grieved for Gene, then angry at Sarah and Stacy, and now I'm strangely . . . well, happy, but I'm not sure why." "Yeah," others ask, "Why do we feel this way?" You conclude for them, "Well, hidden feelings are out in the open. You have felt what each other has felt and you have brought resolution to the problem. Good work, class."

What you don't say, but immediately notice, is that their desire to learn together has just been greatly enhanced by relieving classroom tensions. It would have been far different if the problem were ignored or if you had dictated a quick fix. Either could have been done a whole lot easier, with less grief, but without the results that were achieved. Helping your students change perspective has prepared them to instill virtue in their hearts, and it has kept other people's problems from sidetracking them.

Convincing the Mind

A third thing that can help your students get past the *have to* of what is required of them, is for them to list reasons why it would be right, and good, and appropriate to do what is required of them. In other words, they have to consider the rightness of what is prescribed, the benefits, and when it would be appropriate, to convince their minds that what is required is also agreeable or acceptable. They will probably need help here. It will be hard for them to readily think of positive things, because requirements often conjure themselves up in a negative way. Besides this, there's a problem with listing reasons for doing what is required. Each reason may seem like an intensification of the requirement. This is because reasons act like persuaders.

Listing reasons for doing what is required may seem like an intensification of the requirement, rather than an encouragement.

Rebekah's parents had already helped her realize that, when asked to do something, her inner desire to do it needed to be especially strong whenever she felt obligated. Miss Eland, her math teacher, had given an assignment earlier that day that seemed ridiculous to her. She had to write out multiplication tables up to 12, 10 times. Rebekah sensed that she lacked desire, because she really didn't want to do this assignment. She complained to her mother, "We have calculators these days. I haven't done multiplication by hand since third grade! Besides, I'm in seventh grade now."

Later, she sat in the living room discussing the matter with her parents. Her mother said, "How about making a list of reasons to help you feel more like doing what you've been asked to do? I'll help you." But as her mother started listing reasons, Rebekah felt her mother had just become a traitor. She said, "Now, it seems like you're on Miss Eland's side." Her father quickly realized what had taken place. He interjected, "Becky, if listing reasons is going to help increase your desire, they will need to be your reasons. If they are ours, you will feel put upon by us, for the same reason you felt obligated by Miss Eland."

Rebekah thought about that for a moment, then said, "Okay, but I'm having trouble thinking of reasons because I don't want to do this dumb assignment in the first place." Her mother intuitively responded, "How about if we ask you questions like, "What good things might come out of doing this assignment?" "Can I be of any help to others by doing this?" "How am I going to benefit from doing this?"

Rebekah went to her room and began thinking. *"I suppose there are some people in the class who still need to know the basics of how multiplication works. And Miss Eland always says, "Repetition is the best teacher." I guess doing this will help them see patterns as numbers are multiplied, that multiplication is nothing more than a fast form of addition, and also how division is the reverse of multiplication. And maybe it will help me to think creatively about other math problems, if these things become second nature to me. Hmmm. And maybe we won't make so many dumb mistakes on our assignments. Okay, I'll do it."*

Rebekah completed her assignment, but she still carried a little resentment about it. There is one more thing she could have done to help herself.

Character should drive conduct, but desire should conform to duty.

The internal aspects of virtue should drive the external. Inner desire should motivate people to accomplish what is externally required by others. But the internal aspects of virtue should also conform to the external. Inclinations should be adjusted to obligations. Students will frequently refuse to do right because it was forced on them. But occasionally, they will not even want to do what is right, whether they have to or not. This is because they have, for the most part, nurtured inclinations without regard for obligations. Either or both of two things have happened to them. They were never corrected or disciplined when wrong or they always got what they wanted.

Percy grew up in the ghetto, the Watts district of south central Los Angeles. He could never remember his father being home. There were men around from time to time, but never a father figure. There was a lot of arguing and fighting at home. Percy spent most of his waking moments in school or at the park. Early in life, no one cared to discipline him. Later, they did not dare. No one told Percy what to do. The police would not come into his neighborhood at night, and during the day, it didn't matter. When Percy heard people talking about doing what was right, he had no real idea what they were talking about. He had never consistently received discipline or correction when wrong.

Mary was an only child, living in a small Midwest town. Her parents didn't have much, but what they had they spent on her. They would often sacrifice to ensure she always had what her friends had. They considered it a disgrace to be without, like they had during the Depression. When they received Mary's grades, they would argue with the school administration for higher marks. If they were informed of some wrongdoing, it couldn't possibly have been Mary's fault. Mary was used to getting what she wanted without having to give account for what she did. In fact, she learned to measure what was right by what she did.

Andre grew up in a cultured home on the Riviera in Santa Barbara. He had everything he could ever want and more. His parents were high society. They traveled extensively and, when home, were often attending social functions. They were pleasant toward their son but aloof and distant. Andre never lacked anything, and he never knew correction. He was rarely *compelled* to do what was right nor did he feel driven to do what was wrong. In reality, he felt no strong desires at all.

Occasionally, you will encounter people who have either been spoiled or lacked discipline. Even though they have not been compelled to do what is right, they will not have any real desire to do so, either. Desire for what is right is difficult for them. These must gain insight by observing that desire in someone else. And they must be disciplined.

I must attach a disclaimer to my point about convincing the mind that something is right in order to deepen the inner desire to do it. If students have a problem with obedience or laziness, they might use the lack of *substantive* reasons to keep them from doing what they should. In other words, they will not want to find reasons for doing what they are supposed to do. However, in this case, we are talking about those who want to overcome complacency, not those who wish to become more complacent. This is a subtle but important distinction.

Nurturing Dutiful Desire

My oldest son was asking how many digits to carry out on his first tax form. I said, "It doesn't matter, just two past the decimal because you can't pay more than that anyway, and even the government just tells you to round it off to the nearest dollar." But I told him, "When I round, if it's something to be paid to the government, I always round up. If it's in my favor, I always round down. Same way at the gas pump. Same way with time worked for an employer." It's not wrong if you simply round down if less than half and round up if over half. That's a great way to do it. It is all really insignificant. Nor is it necessarily *always* better to give to the advantage of another and to the neglect of yourself. In fact, some will round to the advantage of others on pennies so they can feel good and then use an accumulation of such feelings to justify robbery or embezzlement on a grand scale. Happens with considerable frequency.

On the other hand, if you want to enhance your desire, you can use little things like that to encourage yourself, so that when extra is required, you are willing to step forward and do beyond what is expected. Here's how it works. Virtue is wanting to do what you have to do. How can your students get past the *have to*, and on to the *want to*? By recognizing that, when required to do something, the internal intensity of their desire to do it must exceed the intensity of the obligation, as they perceive it.

Jeremy is a free-spirited boy. He has just discovered that the student body has been confined to the campus during school hours. Recesses and lunch hours must be spent on the school grounds. This obligation stifles him. He has almost no desire to stay, and he perceives the obligation as oppressive.

Julie is a reader. She is not going anywhere anyway, except maybe to the library. This obligation means nothing to her. She forgot about it almost as soon as she learned of it. It was just not a problem for her. The intensity of her desire to remain on campus already far exceeded any sense of obligation imposed by the prohibition. She needed no assistance getting over the restriction, but Jeremy is different, and he is a leader in his class.

Realizing the difference in his students, Mr. Cauldwell gets a football at lunch time, and without saying a word, tosses it toward Jeremy. Jeremy flashes a big grin, and after playing catch for a minute, others gather around. Soon, the kids are consumed with a game of football. Cauldwell is referee of the game and champion in the hearts of his students. What happened to the feeling of oppression? Why did Julie not feel it? After lunch, Mr. Cauldwell asked such questions to his class and helped them recognize that when required to do something, the internal intensity of their desire to do it must exceed the intensity of the obligation as they perceive it.

You might think, "Cauldwell's just messed up. He's going to be behind. He wasted valuable class time. He probably had to scrap his whole lesson plan, probably lost continuity with what he had been doing." You're probably right . . . for

It is not necessarily better to give to the advantage of another and to the neglect of yourself.

Doing something that is not required of you is a cheap price to pay for gaining your students attention.

that lesson. But for many to follow, his students will be with him. And they won't be likely to forget him—for the lesson that day and for the subject matter they learned afterward because of renewed interest, because of the lack of discipline problems, because of commitment to him and his class.

You might still think, "What does any of this have to do with teaching my subject?" Well, in one sense, absolutely nothing. And your students will know that! But doing something that is not required of you is a cheap price to pay for getting their attention. So in one sense, it has nothing to do with teaching. Yet in another sense, earning the right to gain a hearing from your students has a lot to do with teaching. And it really doesn't take much time and effort, all things considered.

Your students can get past the *have to*, and on to the *want to* by *desiring to intensify their desire.* From a different perspective, all this means is that they want to overcome their complacency. It means they desire to deepen their desire. It means wanting to want to more than they already want to. This comes from recognizing exactly what an oppressive obligation does to them and wanting to do something about it.

David didn't like to read, so he wouldn't read. Simple as that. He was not as quick as some to catch on when he was younger. Before long, he gave up trying. When he was required to read aloud in class, the pressure to perform brought the fear of failure. Soon, he had no desire at all to read. Years later, when assignments came that required reading, he just refused to do them. He began failing classes.

Mr. Schmidt, the school counselor, asked why he did not do his assignments, and he just responded, "I hate to read!" When the counselor found out why, he asked, "Do you want to learn how?" David said, "I'm not sure I even want to, anymore." The counselor told him, "Well, if you don't really want to, I can use my time doing other things. But if you truly want to, I'll do everything I can to help." David thought for a minute, and responded, "I think I want to want to more than I really want to." The counselor wisely said, "That's good enough for me." David desired to intensify his desire.

However, Mr. Schmidt knew that *deep* desire does not usually come without repeated failure. So he asked David to come to school a half hour early every day for the next month for a reading lesson. David now wanted to learn to read. The more that he struggled, the more he wanted to learn. When the month was over, David was reading everything he could get his hands on. A whole new world was open to him. He never again had trouble doing his assignments, and he never lacked desire.

Things to Review and Remember From Chapter 9

There are four things that prepare hearts for instilling virtue:

1. First, students can prepare their hearts for instilling virtue by *assessing negative feelings* to see how they intensify the sense of obligation they feel.

2. Second, students can prepare their hearts for instilling virtue by *changing perspective* to shift their focus from themselves to those around them. This gives them a break from the intensity of emotions they feel by assuming someone else's perspective.

3. Third, students can prepare their hearts for instilling virtue by *convincing their minds* that something is right, and good, and appropriate. Looking at the worthiness of what is required makes it more desirable.

4. Fourth, students can prepare their hearts for instilling virtue by recognizing that when required to do something, *the internal intensity of their desire to do it must exceed the intensity of the obligation,* as they perceive it.

10

Principles for Instilling Virtue

You have learned from the previous chapters in this final section how vice shatters virtue in the human heart by divorcing desire from duty. This happens through cyclical patterns of behavior. You remember . . . the enslaving cycles of pursuing pleasure and promoting pride. This means that if people are to become virtuous, they must certainly sacrifice selfish appetites and selfish ambitions. But imposing negatives is a poor substitute for positive action and surely no solution for the problem of how to deepen dutiful desires. And though virtue is certainly the solution to overcoming vice, we are left with the problem of how virtue can be taught, struggling with the notion that if virtue hinges on willingness to do what we know we should do, how can we actually increase that willingness?

So we next looked at how we can prepare the heart for instilling virtue, and we likened it to preparing ground for planting. We saw how negative feelings intensify the sense of obligation, how looking at things from other perspectives can break that emotional intensity, and how training the mind to value what is right, and good, and appropriate can actually offset those negative feelings. And we saw how crucial it was to recognize that, when facing responsibilities or requirements, the internal intensity of desire must exceed the intensity of the obligation as it is perceived. But this still leaves the question, How can we deepen our desire to do what we should?

Athletes and salesmen will tell you to just "Get psyched up!"—by which they mean for you to use the power of positive thinking. This can work for those who are mentally disciplined and who already have a lot of desire to begin with. And their lives actually demonstrate how the little jolt they get from it gives them an edge in a highly competitive setting. But for students with attitude problems, who are neither mentally disciplined nor even ankle deep in desire, getting psyched up just does not last very long. So how can teachers deepen dutiful desires in students, when there just isn't very much? Before I tell you about it, I want you to get a glimpse of that kind of desire in its common, everyday, garden-variety form.

The other day, a young gal at a checkout stand in a local grocery store took over a station so that a new clerk could take an unscheduled break. When the checker next to her asked why she did this, she said, "I just wanted to. I know what it's like to stand here hour after hour." I happened to be standing there as all this took place, so I decided to ask how long she had been a checker, and she replied, "7 years." I thought to myself, Hmmm, that's a pretty good attitude after standing on your feet all those years! I was impressed, so I followed up with, "What if your boss said you *had* to do it?" She said with a smile, "I guess I'd get a little rebellious, but I'd probably still do it."

See how her sense of dutiful desire was stronger than her sense of feeling forced? That's growing, developing virtue! How does it happen? Students in primary grades can be led to dutiful desire by their teachers' enthusiasm, but this diminishes as they get older. Adults and teens can develop dutiful desires by putting certain principles into practice. I've come across eight of them. I'm sure there are more, but these will get you started plowing straight rows. And please notice that they are all activities that are either intensified or inspiring. It is the combination of the intensity, or inspiration, and the activity that stirs slumbering passions toward dutiful desire. Here's what it amounts to: When you feel forced into doing something you know you should do, you force yourself to become more actively involved than you would be if you were forced. That way, you override lesser negative feelings with greater positive actions, which ultimately stirs greater positive feelings. So here are eight principles for instilling virtue:

1. Exceeding expectations
2. Giving generously
3. Forgiving freely
4. Empowering enemies
5. Serving secretly
6. Judging justly
7. Suffering silently
8. Persisting patiently

Now, recall that virtue is good conduct growing out of good character. It is an inner desire to do what you know is right. Being and doing, along with desire and duty, are the basic elements of virtue, but virtue itself is that intangible aggregate that binds the conglomerate together, the concrete that grips the stones and the reinforcing steel. So when internal desire is low, not absent—that's an entirely different problem—when the desire to do your duty is not what you want it to be, external actions can be used to strengthen internal desires.

Generally, the ingredient that increases the desire to do what should be done is to go beyond what is expected; doing more, not less, exceeding expectations. We tend to think otherwise. When we feel like we have to, and at the same time we feel like we don't want to, and at the same time we wish we had more desire, we think the solution is to ease off, do less, rest up, and then to go at it again. Wrong! After lifting hay bales through harvest, cleaning the shed seems easy. But cleaning the shed seems overwhelming after a Saturday afternoon nap.

The Principle of Exceeding Expectations

If students are careful to do only what they are required to do, inside, they will nurture a selfish, begrudging spirit. They will begin telling themselves that they have done what they could, when they have only done what they should. It leaves them feeling overworked because they didn't really want to do it in the first place. They will also feel reluctant about doing anything else, even when some situations clearly call for them to do more than just their share. The principle of exceeding expectations is the determination to do more than what is required, and it drives away a begrudging spirit.

A long time ago, my best friend demonstrated this for me with his life. His name was Karl McMackins, but everyone knew him as "Mac." We were Marines, serving together in Vietnam at Khe Sanh Combat Base during the siege. At the end of the siege, as the Army was beginning to sweep through the valley and we were beginning to move out from the base, I was wounded by an enemy rocket and medevac'd out. I was told that Mac took it pretty hard when he found out what happened to me. But because I wasn't there, the story that follows is pieced together from those who were with him and from his citation for a Bronze Star, which he received posthumously for his heroism on Easter Sunday, April 14, 1968.

During the siege, we took a lot of rockets from a hill northwest of our position. It was later reported to me that the azimuth taken from the crater of the rocket that blew up in front of me indicated it came from this location. I consider it poetic justice that my buddy was instrumental in taking this hill from the enemy. The hill, known as 881 North—named after its height in meters and after its twin to the South—was an enemy stronghold. It was a strategic position that we had tried and failed to take at the onset of the siege. To route the enemy from their Khe Sanh Valley infiltration route, it was necessary to destroy this stronghold. Because it happened on Easter Sunday, the Marines called it their "Easter Egg Hunt."

Mac, serving with the Third Battalion, 26th Marines, went out from Hill 881 South under cover of darkness in the early morning hours. At 05:45 hours, just before sunup, they made initial contact with the enemy. Before long, Mac's unit began receiving heavy machine gun and rifle fire. The enemy was waiting for them in strongly fortified positions, and the Marines were initially turned back as they tried to advance up the slope of the hill. They also came under a shower of enemy grenades. Their position was tenuous. For other attack elements to move forward, Mac's unit had to take their objective. The Marines used mortars to work over the bunkers and trenches, but the lead element was pinned down.

The situation required initiative and action beyond the call of duty. What Mac did next is taken from his citation for the Bronze Star, which he received with the combat "V" for valor:

> Corporal McMackins was a member of the lead platoon as his company assaulted the crest of Hill 881 North, defended by an estimated North Vietnamese Army battalion utilizing automatic weapons and small arms fire from well-entrenched positions. Unable to employ his rocket launcher due to the proximity of friendly troops, Corporal McMackins completely disregarded his own safety as he armed himself with hand grenades and daringly maneuvered forward to assault the enemy positions. Unhesitatingly exposing himself to the intense enemy fire, Corporal McMackins repeatedly threw grenades into the enemy positions until he was mortally

wounded. His heroic actions and aggressive fighting spirit inspired all who observed him and contributed significantly to the accomplishment of his unit's mission.

Corporal McMackins's extraordinary courage, exceptional professionalism and *selfless devotion to duty* [italics added] were in keeping with the highest traditions of the Marine Corps and of the United States Naval Service. He gallantly gave his life in the service of his country.

Mac died on the battlefield from a gunshot wound to the chest. The day before, he wrote a letter to me that boldly stated that he was going to take that hill for me or die trying. Though I never saw him again, his virtue inspired fellow Marines to accomplish their mission, and his virtue still inspires me to live differently more than 25 years later. No one would have faulted Mac if he had lain low and waited for air support, but he knew that many more would have died, and they might have failed to take their objective. Teachers who exceed expectations inspire students to exceed expectations, like Mac inspires me. Virtue is very powerful. There are situations that arise occasionally that require service beyond what is expected. And what is true for students is more so for teachers. The solution to the most significant problems you face in the classroom will only be found when you extend your efforts beyond mere requirements. Besides, doing more than you have to do undermines a begrudging attitude.

Take Steve, for instance. He does not carry a begrudging attitude because, before he is even asked to do something, he has already determined that he will do more than what is required of him. In fact, he has found that this brings him a lot of satisfaction. Steve looks forward to obligations. They become opportunities for him to develop strong inclinations to do what is good. Not only does he do more than others expect of him when he is involved in something, he goes beyond what he even expects of himself; just a little extra for good measure. And then he takes joy from a job well done and encourages himself.

Let's watch Steve's indomitable spirit in action. It is recess time. He is out on the ball field, playing shortstop. Mrs. Harding comes running from her classroom, crying "Help! Please, somebody help!" Steve is off running, while others are saying "What's *her* problem?" He dashes into the classroom and finds a classmate convulsing from a seizure on the floor. She has begun turning a pale blue color. Steve has been a life guard, and immediately recognizes she is not getting oxygen. He resuscitates her quickly and efficiently. Panic's over, but Steve stays and helps the girl recover her composure and her dignity. Other students are standing around gaping. Some are making fun of the situation. Steve approaches the mockers and says, "Leave her alone." They know he means it and walk away.

Your students can get over the problem of feeling forced by going beyond the limits of what is required of them. Because actions affect attitudes, going beyond what is expected changes the way students feel about what they have done. This means they actually experience increased inner strength when they overextend themselves. The next principle has a different twist, with a different emphasis than the principle of exceeding expectations, but it is otherwise very similar.

Virtuous people willingly do what is right, and good, and appropriate because they want to.

The Principle of Giving Generously

Operating under a high level of stress can make routine responsibilities seem overwhelming.

You may be wondering, "What does generosity have to do with education?" Well, only this: it draws students to teachers like glitter to glue. Why? Because it indicates to those who receive, that the giver likes them, cares about them, and thinks they are special, and this forms a bond between them. Think about it. What constitutes good teaching? Right, an exchange between teacher and student that improves the life of the student. What usually blocks that exchange? Right again, the fact that teachers and students do not bond. Without that bonding, the transfer does not take place.

Teachers almost intuitively know this, and many are willing to give candy or small awards of recognition. And students respond in kind with momentary interest and minimal involvement, because students sense that a mouthful of candy or a moment's recognition is not a fair exchange for a long-term change in lifestyle. So they proportionately return to the teacher what they received. However, when they sense that teachers are willing to make a change in their own lifestyles, then they become willing to *consider* making a change in theirs, too. And what means the most to teenagers is individual time and attention.

We're talking about giving individual time and attention to them beyond their learning needs. I realize you attend to their learning needs all day long. But I want to make a double distinction: first, between what is required of you and what goes beyond that and second, between approaching them as a group and approaching them individually. If you effectively get it across to them that they individually mean something to you personally, they will give themselves to you. You will teach effectively. They will learn readily. Conflict and stress will be minimized, and you will be crowned with success.

You may think, "I'm already pressed to the max." I know many teachers share those feelings today, and I'm not going to minimize those feelings at all, but I would like to help you interpret them differently. Operating under a high level of stress can make performing routine responsibilities seem overwhelming. It will keep you feeling maxed out when you aren't, and it will turn your students away from you. However, if they sense you are intensely interested in them personally—to the point you generously give your time, your attention, your energy—they will love you for it. They will want to be around you. They might even want to be like you, and that's how virtue is best taught. And, believe it or not, this will reduce your stress to the point where routine responsibilities will become fulfilling, even invigorating. Hard to believe, hmmm?

Stuart is a smart aleck. He's sassy. He loves attention and knows how to get it. He's smart about all the wrong things, but he's young. The sap in the tree is just starting to rise. Though he cares little for learning, he doesn't have a foul attitude . . . yet. You know it's coming, but it's not here yet. You know you still have a shot at recovering him. Why? Because he still loves attention. Later, it won't matter. He will be dead inside. All the attention in the world won't make a difference then. But for now, there is hope. You know that if he craves attention, you can give it to him: not the kind he seeks, the kind he needs. Don't worry, he'll still accept it, he's desperate. Anything close will work.

Your art class is working with clay, and Stuart is keeping the class laughing with the blobs he creates, complete with sound effects. As the rest of the students become engaged, each with their own project, you sit down at Stuart's table and begin to work with him and his clay. Knowing he likes skiing, you quickly begin fashioning a skier on a downhill slope. You then invite him to help. Instead of getting him started and leaving, you spend time with him. Others come up with questions and ask for help. You tell them they will have to wait a few minutes. They seem to understand, but before long, there is a low level of commotion throughout the room. You ignore it, but Stuart is strangely unsettled by it. It's like, all of a sudden, he catches a glimpse of his own behavior as he watches others operate like he has.

As the days pass, it starts to become obvious to the rest of the class that you are giving special attention to Stuart, so you back off a little bit, but you still spend a little individual time with him every class period, and things begin to change, not significantly but noticeably. Stuart comes by occasionally after school to talk for a few minutes. And one evening, he drops in at your home with a neighborhood friend. They stay, and visit, and laugh, and hang out for a couple of hours. You wonder what this will mean to your private life if it catches on with other students but quickly decide it's worth it, even if it does.

Generous giving, like extra effort, is going farther than you have to so that it makes what you have to do seem less burdensome than it does if that's all you do. Strange concept, but it works. Stranger yet, if kids get a grip on this, the effect is stunning. Back in class, Stuart now goes around to each table observing the other students' work, encouraging them to ask you to come help if they need it. Where he can, he gives help and asks some if they want to come with him to visit you some evening. Some of your private life is gone, but overall, your life is more exciting and fulfilling, your teaching is more effective, and—incredibly—you're not as tired. It's a curious trade-off. You can give more so you have more to give, or you can carefully try to measure out what you have and never seem to have quite enough. It's your choice. Why not chance it? The next principle is related to giving generously, because forgiving freely only comes out of a generous spirit.

> Spending yourself reduces your stress, making routine responsibilities fulfilling, even invigorating.

The Principle of Forgiving Freely

Not every student will do something wrong in your classroom, but every single one of them will notice how you handle it once someone does. Some teachers become begrudging, suspicious, and mean-spirited when the general attitude of the class turns against them. It's a natural reaction. No one is surprised, but what is surprising is when a teacher does not react when wronged. If you remain positive, confident, and keep your sense of humor, your students will be secretly amazed and irresistibly drawn to you. But you can't do it if you don't freely forgive those who wrong you. What's worse, students usually won't help you by admitting they were wrong and by asking your forgiveness. This is something that must remain secretly inside of you.

You will be tempted to think, If they don't ask for forgiveness, why should I have to forgive them. You don't . . . but if not, you will forfeit your freedom. You

> The hidden issue behind forgiveness is freedom; freedom from grief and guilt, self-pity and bitterness.

will enslave yourself to petty thoughts of anger and revenge that your students will be quick to perceive and that will leave you sullen and ineffective. There are two sides to forgiveness: your side and their side. You must understand that each can be handled independently. Rarely will students come and admit they were wrong and ask you to forgive them.

The hidden issue behind forgiveness is getting free, for both offenders and offended. Offenders are enslaved to guilt from wrongdoing, which makes them emotional slaves of the people they have offended besides being morally obligated to correct whatever they have done wrong. Offenders get free from obligation, and from feeling badly, when they admit they were wrong, ask to be forgiven, and correct whatever they did wrong. Offended people get free when they let go of being offended. Self-pity and bitterness can give way to outbursts of anger and vengeful overreaction to little things students do. Teachers must learn to secretly release their offenders, without requiring students to admit they were wrong, without students seeking forgiveness, and without students even knowing their teachers have forgiven them. Students may not even realize they have offended their teachers. That's what I mean by *freely* forgiving. It is strictly a *your side* kind of thing. Forget about their side. Leave that with them.

Candy is a girl who really gets on your nerves. It's a personality thing, but it's often more than that. She knows you don't like her, and she doesn't like you either. What's more, the whole class senses it. She sits next to her best friend in your Spanish class. You have intercepted notes that depicted you as *El Tigre,* with expressions less than kind. Some notes have made it to the other side of the room, with improvements, and the general attitude of the class has become negative toward you. This is a new experience for you. You have not had to deal with this before. You have generally been well received by students. But you have taught for 10 years, and you have grown weary. Things that you once shrugged off now bother you, and you don't know why. You were hoping that a change to a new school would help, but it's been like starting over without the enthusiasm and vigor you once had. So what do you do?

You realize you are letting your students get to you. You know most students will not dramatically change in the short space of time you have with them, and you know you shouldn't let them set you off the way they do. You also know that even though they are offending you, they will not be likely to come and ask forgiveness. So you decide inwardly that, with each offense, you will try to imagine what is hurting them—what makes them want to hurt you—and then you will forgive them, secretly. You begin with Candy.

It readily comes to mind that she is putting you down. You consider how cruel teenagers can be in putting each other down and imagine that maybe Candy has been put down a lot. You ponder how much it hurts when people are put down and how young people have no way to sort all that out. You observe how naturally they put others down, once they have been put down, and realize their need to feel bigger and better. You begin to feel compassion for Candy and the tough life teenagers face. You decide you will secretly forgive her, and directly, you feel the load lift as you sigh with relief. Startled, you consider how you can reach Candy; what it is that you can do for her. And you realize that the old love for teaching has been rekindled.

With each offense, try to imagine what is hurting those who offend you. Then, you will be able to freely forgive them.

Students need to freely forgive, too. They hold bad attitudes against teachers and students that greatly affect their ability to learn. But they also feel so much pain they are often too protective to admit their own wrongdoing. In other words, you can't directly approach the subject with them. But if they see you being offended, observe that you *know* you have been offended, and then watch you respond with compassion and understanding, they can learn this lesson without a word. But you can also help them learn to freely forgive when you willingly admit you were wrong and ask their forgiveness.

One day in language lab, you realize that Candy has turned down the volume on her headset and is talking with her friend Jill instead of doing her verbal drills. You detect this as you are walking around the room because she keeps glancing up at you, and then as you draw near, she quickly reaches down to turn up the sound. For some reason, this infuriates you, and you give her a verbal thrashing. Later, you realize that you had a lot of pent-up anger and that you had done real damage to Candy and the rest of the class by your outburst. You know you should do something but resist the notion, hoping the kids will forgive and forget about it. And some will, but not those struggling with forgiveness.

So you determine you will face up to the fact that you blew it, admit it to the class, and ask if they will forgive you, especially Candy. You wisely decide to approach Candy first, individually. You offer, "Candy, I overreacted yesterday. I had a bad attitude, and I was wrong to humiliate you that way. I don't deserve your forgiveness, but I sure need it. Will you forgive me for my lack of self-control, for mistreating you, and for embarrassing you in front of the class?" Candy is clearly stunned. With tearful eyes and tightness in her throat, she responds, "Uh, sure. No problem." And you thank her as she walks away. You're left reflecting how much easier it was than you thought it would be. This bolsters your courage to approach the whole class the following day. To your surprise, they sympathize with you and Candy, and you realize that forgiving—just like giving—forms a bond between you and your students. The next principle is a logical extension of freely forgiving, though it sounds very illogical indeed.

The Principle of Empowering Enemies

Once you are free from either the guilt of offending someone or the self-pity of being offended, you are free to empower your enemies. This sounds ridiculous, but it actually makes you more effective. First, it keeps you from being corrupted by petty battles. Second, it strengthens your position by winning students to your side. And, third, it keeps you free from compulsive thoughts of anger and revenge. Besides all of that, empowering your enemies is a great virtue enhancer. It really increases your desire to do your duty. To empower your enemies, there are two things you must do: disarm them of their weapons and then enlist them to use yours.

This is accomplished simply by refusing to react when wronged, which can only be done if you have freely forgiven all your offenders (not just the person immediately before you) and then, empowering them to do what they should be doing. This can best be done through genuine praise and positive encouragement.

Refusing to react disarms classroom enemies. Offering encouragement empowers them to fight with you.

But this is not easy to do if your students are already alienated. Refusing to react disarms your enemies in the classroom. Offering genuine praise, support, and encouragement empowers them to fight with you instead of against you, and teachers need all the allies they can get these days.

Though some students feel a real bond with you now that you admitted you were wrong and asked forgiveness, others are still watching to see what you will do when pushed. So they push your button a few times and watch with smiles on their faces, waiting for a reaction. After the trouble you have had up to this point in the school year, you sense that to praise and encourage them would seem ingratiating or patronizing to them, especially right after an incident in class. So you decide to take a long-term approach and begin by refusing to react to them. You also decide to offer praise and encouragement at times other than when problems occur.

Time goes on. Students tease and taunt, disrupt, and are in general disorder. It's all you can do to get through each class period. You learn to briefly pause with each incident, empathize with each offender, secretly forgive them, collect your thoughts, regain your composure, and continue. You are surprised at how little time and effort it takes and how invigorating it is. You have released them from your anger, so you are able to keep going, and later, at appropriate times, you find it easier to offer positive encouragement. "Marsha, you have very good pronunciation." "Cal, with a little more time in the language lab, you could become fluent in your conversational Spanish." "Tom, I sense you're trying harder. Keep it up." "Kelly, would you help Penny with her parsing? You seem to have a good handle on things."

A couple of months pass, and you see little change in your students. You are tempted to become discouraged, but then you notice that *you* have changed. As you have forgiven them and refused to react to their offenses, your composure and confidence have returned, and you are beginning to enjoy teaching again. You tell yourself, Even if my students never change, getting free from my anger and being positive toward them has helped my attitude. I feel so much better.

Then a couple of weeks later, you overhear Candy say to her friend, "You know, El Tigre isn't so touchy anymore." You turn and say, "Thanks for being positive, Candy. I appreciate that. Sometimes, I get worn out from teaching. It's not always easy." She flushes because you heard her comment but smiles at your praise and your positive attitude. She says, "Oh, you're welcome, we've been pretty hard on you, but you've taken it pretty good. You're not so bad after all . . . I mean, we think you're going to be okay." You're over the hump. The first few months of school have really been rough, but you are back in the groove now.

The Principle of Serving Secretly

There is something internally gratifying about doing good things secretly, and they don't have to be as big as a barn, either. There is also something surprisingly motivating about serving someone without them knowing about it. But it's not easy for teachers to do things secretly on behalf of their students, because they usually watch you like frogs at the fishing hole; get too close or make a false move and they jump. Also it's not easy because, in a sense, you have become a performer. Working in a fishbowl can make what you do feel forced and deplete your desire to do it.

In case you haven't noticed, I am focusing more on you now and less on your students, trusting you won't become broody, like a sitting hen on a clutch of eggs. I haven't forgotten that students are the problem. I'm just hoping you adopt the perspective of becoming the solution. You are the one who is teaching them virtue, and virtue is better caught than taught. If virtue is in full flower in your life, they will be more likely to linger and pick a bouquet, rather than merely stop for a moment and sniff.

Now, let's suppose Bentley is in your homeroom class. He, like the proverbial egg, is spoiled rotten. He has always had more than he could want. It may be a case of too little, too late, but Bentley's parents recently decided to quit pampering him. So they dismissed his tutors and decided against a private school, hoping that public school would change in him what they could not. You don't teach subject matter in homeroom, you just kind of maintain order. You get the students to start thinking about school. You give them an opportunity to finish up homework assignments, make announcements—that kind of thing—and you get some of your grading done.

You could pass over Bentley. In fact, in homeroom, you could just preside, and everyone would be happy. But you like the boy and want to see if you can help him. It's a challenge, a game, no expectations from anyone. And to keep it that way, you decide that whatever you do for him must be kept secret, as much as you are able. Now that you have laid out the guidelines for your special project, you consider how you can help him. He certainly doesn't have any tangible needs. And in this class, you are not really teaching subject matter. And remember, you have limited yourself to secrecy. That really narrows the playing field. But it makes it seem more exciting, too. Yes, this will be a lot of fun.

The weeks pass, and nothing comes to mind about how you can help Bentley, but you arrive each day with anticipation. Maybe today will be the day that you hit on an idea that will get your special project rolling. Yet you begin wondering, too, if anything will happen for lack of ideas. But then one day it dawns on you, his biggest need is your best opportunity. More than anything else, he needs to realize that the world does not exist to serve him. Phase one: When you need help in class, you will ask Bentley. Yes, you will include others, but mostly him. "Bentley, please pass out these Cafeteria Menus." "Would you take roll for me, Bentley?" "Bentley, I would like you to take this message over to Miss Burns in the office."

After a few days of this, Bentley approaches you after class. "Do you have some thing against me?" he asks. "Why, no, Bentley; not at all!" you respond. He pauses to reflect, "Then, why are you picking on me all of the time?" You offer, "For two reasons, Bentley: I have so much to do, and I like you and trust you." He counters, "Don't you like anybody else?" You sidestep, "Bentley, would you rather not help?" "No, I'm glad to help, I guess." You conclude "Oh, good, I figured I could count on you." He walks away puzzled.

However, other students quickly ferret out the arrangement. When you next ask Bentley to help, Wayne smirks and exaggerates a "Thank you, Bentley." You decide to ease off before he becomes humiliated, and you hope you aren't too late.

Your students' greatest needs can become your best opportunity to help them.

Now, what to do for Phase 2? Days turn into weeks, but there is no pressure because no one knows what you are doing or why, and you still randomly though regularly give tasks to Bentley. The sense of anticipation is still there for you, so is the motivation, and you feel gratified that if nothing else happens, you have accomplished even this little bit. Besides, you have carried the positive attitude of this experience into your other classes.

Will there be a Phase 2? Yes, if time permits, but so far, it's been a very different school year because of your little secret. One day, as you are correcting papers from yesterday's classes, a student comes up asking for help with a homework assignment, and then another. You begin to feel a little irritated because you are getting behind. Then it comes to you. Bentley has been helping you; now, he can learn to help others. *Hmmm. Phase 2.* "Bentley? Would you come here, please? . . . Would you help Chuck with his homework? Thanks, I'm getting swamped."

Before long, you begin to appreciate how precious are the inner benefits of serving secretly: a renewed sense of anticipation for the day's events (realizing they hold exciting surprises), increased motivation to sustain daily routines (realizing that they form the cloak that hides your secrets), and relief from the pressure of petty expectations (realizing with confidence you are doing more than is required of you). In fact, it is so beneficial, you begin wondering how you could encourage students to do things secretly without giving away your secret. Then you realize, that would destroy the compelling feature of secrecy.

Only when serving secretly is accidentally discovered by others does it compel them to want to do the same thing. So you put it out of your mind lest you corrupt your motives, and you secretly hope no one will ever know. Years pass, and you have long forgotten about most of your little secrets and the compelling feature of secrecy. Then one evening, you are reminded when, some 18 years later, you receive a phone call, and it's Bentley. He is calling to say thank you. It finally dawned on him, after being bothered by it all these years, what you were doing and why. Some seeds require a long time before they return fruit.

The Principle of Judging Justly

Some of the most frustrated teenagers you will find will be those with a heightened sense of injustice. You will often discern who they are by their demand, "That's not fair!" Indignantly, they will accuse you of taking sides, showing favoritism, and being inconsistent. Equality, fair play, and consistency are extremely important to them. In fact, if you judge justly, they will become your cheerleaders. They will make you their role model and parrot your virtues. But judging justly requires wisdom, and wisdom requires experience. And if you lack these things, careful confrontation with such students can bring you both.

There is a dynamic at work in any group of teenage students with respect to judging justly. This dynamic involves two elements: those with a heightened sense of injustice, the smaller element within the group, and those who are idealistic, the larger element within the group. In addition, when those who have a heightened sense of injustice are also idealistic—and they usually are—it magnifies the problem. This dynamic has the potential to suddenly change your model learning center into a morgue.

When injustice occurs in the classroom and is not dealt with, it has two visible features to it: first, an explosion—outrage—then, an implosion—deathly silence. If teens sense that things are not going as they should, they will, first, loudly complain, and then, if it doesn't do any good, they will quickly become discouraged and withdraw into themselves. If this happens, they are no longer teachable, at least by you. They figure, "If teachers don't care about doing as they should, why should I?" Many students will not have the maturity or internal fortitude to conclude, "Even if those in charge are wrong, I still have the responsibility to do what is right."

Randy is an extremely quick-witted boy, very sharp, eyes like a hawk. He is exceptionally observant, and he has an uncanny sense for what ought to be. It's kind of scary when he's around, because you fear he'll see something you'll miss. But you quickly find that, if he does, he'll tell you about it, so you quit worrying. Nevertheless, you feel somewhat threatened by him. It's kind of maddening, in a way, that an adult should be put on the defensive by a teenager, but teaching is full of such surprises, right?

One day, Jeff, a friend of Randy's, comes into class 10 minutes late. You are time oriented, Jeff is event oriented. It's hard for him to think in terms of minutes and seconds, especially if something is happening. It's hard for you to overlook 10 minutes. It's an irritating disruption when Jeff saunters in late, and a waste of valuable class time. "Jeff, do you have an excuse for being late?" "Yeah." He laughs, "I got hit by the school bus." You think, Here we go again. "So what happened?" He looks shocked. "I died, of course." The class erupts in laughter.

You are tired of playing his straight man. You are tired of his tardiness. And you are tired of the interruptions. "Jeff, 3 hours detention." He moans good-naturedly, but Randy calls out, "That's not fair, Helen came in late, and she didn't get detention." You remind Randy, "Helen was only a half a minute late. That's quite a bit different from 10 minutes." Randy sours, and the class becomes very quiet. You wonder whether others feel uneasy, if they think you are playing favorites or if you have something out for Jeff. There is a low-level tension, and you hate to just leave things like that.

So you decide to air this out with the class. And you determine to give Randy a hearing. But before you do, you just level with them: "Look, I'm getting bent out of shape. I shouldn't, but I am. I want to back up. My attitude was bad. I had a fixed idea about what should happen in class, and Jeff and Randy just helped me face my inflexibility. Sorry, class, I was locked in. Okay, Randy, you have a good sense of justice. Tell us what you are thinking."

He starts slowly, "Well, I was just thinking that you let Helen off, and that was pretty decent, but Jeff got no slack." Picking up momentum, he adds, "If Jeff gets detention, it seems like Helen should get detention; maybe not as much, but some. If Helen doesn't get detention, Jeff shouldn't, either. It just seems strange that you let Helen off, but you slam Jeff."

You pace slowly as you quickly ponder what Randy said. "You've sorted that out pretty well for us, Randy. Thank you! Okay, Helen gets 10 minutes; Jeff gets an

Failure to face injustice can turn your model learning center into a morgue.

hour. But it seems to me that Helen is never late, and Jeff is often late, and that ought to be taken into consideration. What do you think, Randy?"

He looks off for a moment, "Well, something bothers me about that. I think once something has been punished, it's done. It shouldn't keep coming back to that person. It's like Jeff gets double punishment because you're angry."

You sense he has a point, but you feel you do, too. You retort, "Yes, I agree, but I want to feel the freedom to let someone off for a minor infraction to reward them for being prompt all the rest of the time. And at the same time I want to be tougher on those who don't seem to respond to correction, and repeatedly are late."

Randy follows up, "I see what you mean, but maybe you could say ahead of time, "If it happens again, it will double the punishment." It just seems like all of a sudden, you get put out and overpunish, and we feel like you don't care about us. And maybe if someone is always on time, they should get a reward for being on time instead of rewarding them by excusing their failure."

Randy has made some good points. You have to admit he has really helped to balance things out in your thinking, and he has helped give the class a well-rounded picture of the whole event. You tell him so, in front of the class. You also tell him you will ask for his help again, if he doesn't mind. He says, "Sure thing." The class is happy. You are happy. Everyone is ready to move on. You have left them with the sense in their hearts that even if things get all fouled up, they can be straightened out, and everything will be all right. This leaves them positive toward you and toward learning.

The Principle of Suffering Silently

There will be times when you think you are doing everything right, yet it seems like everything goes wrong. Fortunately, such times aren't frequent, and they usually don't last very long. How you handle these times not only affects your desire to continue teaching but also how you are perceived by your students. The key to overcoming unjust adversity is sustained silence. At times like this, your enemies may come forward to try to ruin you, and your friends may shrink back from you to watch how you will react. The temptation is to complain and try to justify yourself, but, surprisingly, the solution is silence.

If you complain, people will observe that you are sour and will pull away from you. If you try to justify yourself, people will try to weigh what you say against what others have said. Those who are for you will try to remain objective, whereas those who are against you will use your own words to intensify their assault. If you remain silent through the struggle, your friends may rally to your defense, win over some of your enemies, and put to shame those who still oppose you. What's more, inner silence will bring continual healing to you, so that when it is all over, the ordeal will seem relatively minor.

It's Friday, and you're glad. Dr. Johnson, the principal, wants to see you. It has been a grueling week. You have been struggling this week to communicate well with your students. But the harder you tried, the more they misunderstood you and, at times, senselessly argued with you. They became frustrated, and you are now on edge. Unwittingly, you carry your irritation into Dr. Johnson's office with you. Your principal takes note of your expression and motions you to a seat as you enter his office. He stares at an empty desk for a long minute before looking up. You sense this is not going to be a positive meeting. Your suspicions are confirmed as he informs you that Mrs. Reed, another faculty member, has apparently charged you with unprofessional conduct in class. Quickly sifting through recent events brings nothing to mind, so you ask him for some time to think things over before you respond. He'll be glad to see you first thing Monday morning.

Half puzzled, half stunned, you find your way to your car and proceed home. Preoccupied with your thoughts, you pass a stop sign and a policeman. You begin asking yourself what is going on, as he fills out your ticket. You try to convince yourself you don't mind getting a ticket for doing something wrong but find Mrs. Reed's accusations are beginning to anger you. You decide you are not going to let this day end on a down note. You consider going out for dinner, but when you arrive home, you find your spouse in a stupor from a bad head cold, sniveling and sneezing. You timidly suggest having dinner out. Your spouse, feeling poorly, resents your suggestion and tears into you for your lack of sensitivity, recalling numerous examples of how you care about nobody but yourself. While stirring the chicken noodle soup, you sigh. You were hoping you would be able to discuss the events of the day with your partner. Now, instead, you are confined to silence.

However, as the evening wears on, you find the quietness strangely comforting. As you ponder the events of the past couple of weeks, you discover you are amazingly calm, knowing the accusations against you are false. You also realize that some weeks are better than others with the students. And you reflect that there's nothing uncommon about people getting sick and feeling grouchy when they do. Yet it seems strange that all of these things should happen at the same time. You determine that you are not going to let these things build up and bother you. But wonder how you can handle it if things keep building up? Hmmm. Peaceful silence. You decide that you will see this series of events through in silence and simply watch what happens.

The next week begins with more of the same. You tell the principal there is nothing to the accusations against you but that you have nothing further to say. Your students seem a little hyper to you, some a little more goofy than usual, but as you enter the faculty lounge, you refuse to complain about these things to your colleagues. Instead, you listen in silence as a friend pours out her problems. Another teacher breaks into the conversation and asks about the accusations Mrs. Reed has leveled against you. Surprised that others know, you state that there is nothing to them and that you would prefer not to talk about it. At other times, remaining silent would seem stifling. Today, it's refreshing. When you return home, your spouse is still carrying a grudge against you, apparently for your insensitivity, and wonders why you can't do anything right. You smile silently and feel tears fill your eyes. Things continue this way over the next couple of days.

You are sorely tempted to complain about everything going wrong and to try to explain your position but decide against it, confident that the truth will come

The key to overcoming unjust adversity is sustained silence.

Standing firm in the face of opposition strengthens inner character.

out. You enter the faculty lunchroom and immediately everyone stops talking. You decide to sit silently and watch those in the room. There is a long silence. Then Mrs. Reed opens things up by running you down. You do not respond. To your surprise, your colleagues defend you, and Mrs. Reed leaves the room chagrined. Your friends could detect your calm confidence and explain that that's why they came to your defense. You suddenly realize that standing firm in the face of opposition strengthens inner character.

At the end of the week, the principal dismisses the charges against you for lack of substantive evidence. Your spouse finally asks forgiveness for putting you down, praises you for your restraint through the ordeal, and invites you out to supper. You think, "How different things would have been had I complained and tried to defend myself!" and with amazement, you begin to explain to your spouse what you learned through suffering silently.

Complaining is like bumping into everyone with a skinned-up elbow. You holler, and everyone wonders why you are making such a fuss. Self-justification is like picking the scab; it takes forever to heal, and people get tired of seeing the bloody mess. Silence is like rubbing salve on the wound; it brings quick healing and improves the appearance. Listening and smiling (even through tears) is like a miracle healing that removes even the scar. But listening and smiling only grow out of sustained silence. Silent suffering keeps your heart right through difficult times and helps you continue fulfilling your duties, when others give up. Those of you who are very verbal need not worry; this kind of suffering does not come very often nor does it last very long. Sustained silence is not a way of life, but the principle of suffering silently can be very effective in the midst of trying times.

The Principle of Persisting Patiently

It's nearing the end of the academic calendar. Your friend Herbert has been at it for 30 years. Teaching is his life. But each year, he asks himself if he should teach another year. One morning, on the way to school, he relates, "Things didn't use to be this way. I didn't use to feel this way. Kids didn't use to act this way. The pressure to perform was not so high. The expectations were more realistic. Parents were more supportive. I was respected in the community. Things have changed." He wonders aloud if they will ever be good again.

You are new to the profession. Herb has greatly helped you get your feet on the ground. You wonder if the years have made him cynical, if you will feel the way he feels after 30 years, or if things really are different. You put yourself in his position. You hate to think about having to retrain for another profession in your golden years, especially because you only recently completed your education. You wonder, "Is my profession going sour? Can I even last 10 years? Will things be even worse then?"

You carpool with Herb, so the next morning, you decide you will probe him about how he has kept at it for 30 years. He says, "Well, after the newness is gone, teachers begin looking at each school year as a single unit. Personally, I refuse to examine my desire to teach until contract time. Another thing, I never question my commitment in the middle of a crisis. I continually evaluate my performance but never my commitment. We know there will be ups and downs during the year, and we know that when the difficult times come, there is a tendency to paint everything with a black brush. So I have learned never to reconsider my commitment until after the school year."

You say, "Herb, you've seen just about every kind of school year there is to see. Why reconsider now?" He says, "That's true, but the kids have changed. Loud and proud kids set me off now. I guess I'm really asking myself if I can learn to be gentle when most of my students have bad attitudes. Before, it would have been one or two a class at most. Now it seems like entire classes are bad. I'm okay if I can control my environment. What I need to learn is to control myself when my environment is out of control. The older I get, the more I question if I am able to adjust—and if I really want to."

As you ponder with Herb the turn that teaching has taken, you wonder if you can contrive an approach that will give you the longevity in the profession that Herb has. You have learned from Herb that refusing to question his commitment to teach during the year has kept him from bailing out. You wonder if approaching your career the same way Herb approaches the school year would work for your career the way it works for Herb. You think to yourself, Herb's idea is a good one. Never question your commitment in the middle of a crisis. But to refuse to ever question your desire to teach, no matter how bad things get, seems strange.

You realize that to make such a commitment means that it's not something with which you can experiment, and if it doesn't work, forget about it. As long as the option of quitting remains open, it destroys the effect of closing out the option. You fully appreciate the fact that if the option of quitting is abandoned, it has a profound affect on your attitude. You decide to get Herb's reaction to this wild idea. Herb is lost in thought for a few unsettling moments. Then he says, "What you suggest is not something new. Old-timers used to do this with a lot of things: Marriage, business deals sealed with a promise, friendships formed with a handshake. It just seems different today."

You decide to make a life commitment to teaching. As the years pass, you find that your crazy commitment has not only kept you steadfast through difficult times, it has developed a fixed attitude inside of you. Your profession has become who you are, not just what you do. You realize that many are doing the work of teaching but are not really teachers inside. They are keeping their options open so that the affections and loyalties of their hearts remain divided among many possibilities. You now realize the profound effect this has on their personalities and their performances. The principle of patient persistence pays its dividends.

Those of you who have thought about it already realize that these eight principles for instilling virtue are all virtues: diligence, generosity, forgiveness, graciousness, selflessness, justice, endurance, and steadfastness. This should not be surprising. Another way of saying all of this is that practicing the virtues enhances virtue. In other words, there is a circular interaction that takes place when this occurs. One feeds the other, which continues to feed the other and so on. It's almost perpetual motion.

> Wholehearted commitment makes teaching more than just what you do. It makes you a teacher.

The Ultimate Question

We've answered the question of how to deepen dutiful desire when it's not all you want it to be. Now the only question that remains is, How do you instill the desire to do what should be done, when the desire is not there at all, as is the case with some of your most difficult students? First, understand that such dutiful desire has to be squandered before they reach that condition. In other words, everyone's born with it to one degree or another, but it can be frittered away surprisingly early in life, long before students reach high school.

Next, it is no answer to say to students, "Just do it," because that begs the question: How do they want to, when they don't want to? If they don't want to, at least to a small degree, they never will. In other words, it takes a certain amount of desire to go ahead and do what they don't want to do. Such desire only comes with a change of heart. Then, what we're really asking is, How does the heart get changed?

Well, it usually comes only through tragic failure or utter defeat. When the heart is left bitter and broken, when the person feels completely helpless and without hope, the events that bring such inner brokenness can also restructure the desires of the heart. But it's not automatic. Here's how it works.

A lack of virtue leads to consequences that shatter lives. The greater the brokenness, the more intense the desire to turn away from whatever led to that brokenness. But many die before their will is ever broken. Yet if people survive the consequences of their lack of virtue, the brokenness that comes from experiencing these consequences changes their desires toward doing what they should. The pain that accompanies defeat and failure teaches them to say "No" to the things that bring the pain and to choose those things that do not. This is nothing more than learning from the school of hard knocks. Until the pain from brokenness restructures their inner desires, they don't change.

However, the connection between learning from pain and becoming virtuous is not automatic. Just because people experience the consequences of an unvirtuous life does not mean they will change and become virtuous. They may die embittered, refusing to respond to the pain that prompts them to change. There is a critical ingredient that must be added to this formula. It must be added at the right moment, and it must be genuine: no synthetics. This ingredient is tender-hearted, loving-kindness. When people show loving-kindness to others who have just been broken and those who are broken receive their love and kindness, that inner change of heart takes place, and a miraculous transfusion of virtue occurs. People suddenly begin wanting to do what they have known all along they should be doing.

It is tragic to see how broken our teenagers are today. Their brokenness surely means more work for you, greater inner frustration, less immediate gratification. But that brokenness also provides you an opportunity to show loving-kindness, if you want to. You can give them a transfusion of virtue by being tender, and loving, and kind. But to give a transfusion of virtue you must have enough and to spare, and you must be willing to sacrifice. Do you really want to see a change in those awful attitudes? Then vindicate virtue in education, and do it personally and individually with your students; and begin with students who are broken. My friend, the vice principal, Mr. Priester, did so over 30 years ago. It made quite a difference in my life!

When Virtue Is Learned

> Virtue is learned
> When the life is broken—
> > When it reaches for love,
> > When it returns contempt,
> > When it desires independence,
> > When it deserves regulation,
> > When it is helpless to change,
> > When it seems hopeless to try,
> > When there is no compelling reason
> > > for anyone else
> > > to show compassion and kindness,
> > > but someone does—
> That's when virtue is really learned!

Things to Review and Remember From Chapter 10

There are eight principles for instilling virtue in those who want to deepen their desire to do what they know they should do.

1. The principle of *exceeding expectations:* Doing more than is required invigorates the desire to do what must be done, diminishes the weight of the work, and cancels a begrudging spirit.

2. The principle of *giving generously:* Generous giving has a heart-opening effect for both giver and receiver. It deepens the sense of responsibility of the giver and prompts an inner responsiveness in the receiver. It bonds students to teachers.

3. The principle of *forgiving freely:* Freely forgiving (without someone asking) releases those offended from self-pity, bitterness, and vengefully overreacting to minor matters. Forgiving when asked (without expectations) also frees offenders from guilt for wrongdoing and thereby enables them to make restitution, which frees them from obligation for their offenses.

4. The principle of *empowering enemies:* Positive encouragement and genuine praise, accompanied by a refusal to react to opposition, disarm adversaries and elicit their support for what they once opposed.

5. The principle of *serving secretly:* Serving others secretly is internally gratifying and surprisingly motivating. It relieves the pressure of working under close and constant scrutiny and neutralizes personality conflicts.

6. The principle of *judging justly:* Equitably handling discipline problems silences and satisfies opposition and prevents frustrating distractions from diminishing the desire to fulfill responsibilities.

7. The principle of *suffering silently:* Silent suffering renews inner strength and heals the wounds of unjust adversity. Complaining depletes strength, wearies friends—who then withhold support—and fuels the fires of criticism.

8. The principle of *persisting patiently:* Patient persistence through crises turns what you are doing into who you are becoming. Refusing to question your commitment to your profession in the middle of a crisis is what makes the difference between a teacher and one who merely teaches.

Those who have absolutely no desire to do what they know they should do can still be reached, but only once they are broken and then, only through lovingkindness.

Resources

Resource A: The LVAQ

The Loehrer Virtue Assessment Questionnaire

Please fill in the following blanks: Name: (print clearly) _____

Gender: Male ___ Female ___   Race: (specify) _____

Age: 13 ___ 14 ___ 15 ___ 16 ___ 17 ___ 18 ___ 19 ___ Other (specify) _____

Grade: 7 ___ 8 ___ 9 ___ 10 ___ 11 ___ 12 ___ Other(specify) _____

Instructions: Your responses should honestly describe your personal experience. You are not expected to spend a great deal of time responding to these statements. Your first response is best. Please circle the letters that best indicate the extent of your agreement or disagreement with each of the following statements.

SD = Strongly Disagree; D = Disagree; ? = Uncertain; A = Agree; SA = Strongly Agree

1.	I can remember "playing sick" to get out of something.	SD D ? A SA
2.	I maintain my priorities so that I can do what is best.	SD D ? A SA
3.	I often refuse to do what I know is right.	SD D ? A SA
4.	I do what I should, even if friends reject me for it.	SD D ? A SA
5.	I frequently insist on my own way, even if I sense I might be wrong.	SD D ? A SA
6.	I have never intensely disliked anyone.	SD D ? A SA
7.	I am fully committed to change whatever keeps me from doing what I should.	SD D ? A SA
8.	I find it hard to really enjoy myself when doing daily chores.	SD D ? A SA
9.	I am an example of wholehearted dedication to duty.	SD D ? A SA
10.	I feel uneasy because I won't help when I know I should.	SD D ? A SA
11.	I sometimes try to get even rather than forgive and forget.	SD D ? A SA
12.	I am consistently true to what is best.	SD D ? A SA
13.	I resist establishing values in my life so I can be free to be who I am.	SD D ? A SA
14.	I gladly respond without hesitation when something is required of me.	SD D ? A SA
15.	I am tired of those in charge trying to show me a better way.	SD D ? A SA
16.	I never resent being asked to return a favor.	SD D ? A SA
17.	I am fully committed to do what I know I should.	SD D ? A SA
18.	I have trouble telling right from wrong.	SD D ? A SA
19.	I can easily distinguish between good, better, and best.	SD D ? A SA
20.	I get angry when those in authority insist I do things their way.	SD D ? A SA
21.	I sometimes feel resentful when I don't get my way.	SD D ? A SA
22.	I openly defend what is right.	SD D ? A SA
23.	I rebel when someone talks to me about doing what I should.	SD D ? A SA
24.	I immediately confess and make it right whenever I do something wrong.	SD D ? A SA
25.	I am afraid of what others might think if I do as I ought.	SD D ? A SA
26.	I have almost never felt the urge to tell someone off.	SD D ? A SA

Resource B: LVAQ Administration Instructions

To the teacher: Please carefully follow these steps to ensure uniformity of testing conditions.

Step 1: Read the following instructions aloud to your class:

> *This is a questionnaire about why we do what we do. It helps us to understand ourselves better. First, fill out the information that describes you as a person, then take the questionnaire.*

Step 2: Pass out the questionnaire to your students and read the following instructions when you have finished:

> *You are not expected to spend a great deal of time responding to these statements. Your first response is best. Answer the questions by circling the letters. If you strongly agree, you circle SA. If you strongly disagree, you circle SD. If you just agree, you circle A. If you just disagree, you circle D. If you do not understand a question or if you do not really know how you feel about it, circle the question mark (?). There is no time limit, but it should not take more than a few minutes. When you have finished, raise your hand, and I will pick up your questionnaire.*

Step 3: Observe your students to make sure they are progressing through the questionnaire. If students have questions of clarification, answer them as best you can. Please do not influence their answers. Collect the questionnaires as soon as students complete them. Make sure you have received back as many as you passed out.

To the teacher: Thank you for taking time from your busy schedule to administer this questionnaire.

Resource C: The LVAQ Scoring Form

Name: School: Grade:

Race: Gender: Age:

No.	Misrepresentation Items	SD	D	?	A	SA
1.	I can remember "playing sick" to get out of something.	5 M-	4 M	3	2 R	1 R+
6.	I have never intensely disliked anyone.	1 R+	2 R	3	4 M	5 M-
11.	I sometimes try to get even, rather than forgive and forget.	5 M-	4 M	3	2 R	1 R+
16.	I never resent being asked to return a favor.	1 R+	2 R	3	4 M	5 M-
21.	I sometimes feel resentful when I don't get my way.	5 M-	4 M	3	2 R	1 R+
26.	I have almost never felt the urge to tell someone off.	1 R+	2 R	3	4 M	5 M-

No.	Virtue Items	SD	D	?	A	SA
23.	I rebel when someone talks to me about doing what I should.	5 V+	4 V	3	2 U	1 U-
15.	I am tired of those in charge trying to show me a better way.	5 V+	4 V	3	2 U	1 U-
20.	I get angry when those in authority insist I do things their way.	5 V+	4 V	3	2 U	1 U-
18.	I have trouble telling right from wrong.	5 V+	4 V	3	2 U	1 U-
3.	I often refuse to do what I know is right.	5 V+	4 V	3	2 U	1 U-
10.	I feel unwilling to help even when I know I should.	5 V+	4 V	3	2 U	1 U-
5.	I frequently insist on my own way even if I sense I might be wrong.	5 V+	4 V	3	2 U	1 U-
8.	I find it hard to really enjoy myself when doing daily chores.	5 V+	4 V	3	2 U	1 U-
13.	I resist establishing values in my life so I can be free to be who I am.	5 V+	4 V	3	2 U	1 U-
25.	I am afraid of what others might think if I do as I ought.	5 V+	4 V	3	2 U	1 U-
4.	I do what I should, even if friends reject me for it.	1 U-	2 U	3	4 V	5 V+
17.	I am fully committed to do what I know I should.	1 U-	2 U	3	4 V	5 V+
22.	I openly defend what is right.	1 U-	2 U	3	4 V	5 V+
19.	I can easily distinguish between good, better and best.	1 U-	2 U	3	4 V	5 V+
2.	I maintain my priorities so that I can do what is best.	1 U-	2 U	3	4 V	5 V+
12.	I consistently remain true to what is best.	1 U-	2 U	3	4 V	5 V+
14.	I gladly respond without hesitation when something is required of me.	1 U-	2 U	3	4 V	5 V+
9.	I am an example of whole-hearted dedication to duty.	1 U-	2 U	3	4 V	5 V+
24.	I immediately confess and make it right whenever I do something wrong.	1 U-	2 U	3	4 V	5 V+
7.	I am fully committed to change whatever keeps me from doing what I should.	1 U-	2 U	3	4 V	5 V+

	SD	D	?	A	SA
Norm Response Totals	3	7	3	9	4
Individual Response Totals	( )	( )	( )	( )	( )

	Misrepresentation	Virtue
Uncertainty Count	( ) of 6	( ) of 20
Certainty Count	( ) of 6	( ) of 20
Raw Score	( ) of 30	( ) of 100
Norm Rank	( )	( )

Misrepresentation		Virtue	
Ranking Description	Raw Score	Ranking Description	Raw Score
Extremely Unlikely	6 to 10	Very Low	20 to 50
Very Unlikely	11 to 13	Low	51 to 55
Unlikely	14 to 16	Moderately Low	56 to 60
Possible	17 to 19	Average	61 to 70
Likely	20 to 22	Moderately High	71 to 75
Very Likely	23 to 25	High	76 to 80
Extremely Likely	26 to 30	Very High	81 to 100

Virtue Response Analysis

Item Number	23	15	20	18	3	10	5	8	13	25	4	17	22	19	2	12	14	9	24	7
Item Rank	1	2	3	4	5	6	7	8	9	10	11	12	13	14	15	16	17	18	19	20
Item Direction	-	-	-	-	-	-	-	-	-	-	+	+	+	+	+	+	+	+	+	+
Item Basis	D	B	D	B	D	B	D	B	D	B	D	B	D	B	D	B	D	B	D	B
Character																				
Conduct																				
Virtue Levels	Examining		Experimenting		Establishing			Evaluating			Embodying									

Virtue Balance	Character (Inner Being)	Conduct (Outward Doing)
Virtue Item Count	( ) of 10	( ) of 10

Resource D: LVAQ Scoring Guidelines

LVAQ Scoring Guidelines

These guidelines provide a simple format for scoring the Loehrer Virtue Assessment Questionnaire. Carefully follow the steps below, and then consider the implications of your findings.

For scoring purposes, "M" indicates misrepresentation, whereas "R" indicates representation. "V" indicates a virtuous response, whereas "U" indicates an unvirtuous response. Plus (+) or minus (-) signs indicate an emphatic response (SD or SA). Numbers (1 2 3 4 5) indicate the raw score for that item.

Begin scoring by placing the Questionnaire and the Scoring Form side by side and then read *Step One*.

No.	Misrepresentation Items	SD	D	?	A	SA
1.	I can remember "playing sick" to get out of something.	5 M-	4 M	3	2 R	1 R+
6.	I have never intensely disliked anyone.	1 R+	2 R	3	4 M	5 M-
11.	I sometimes try to get even, rather than forgive and forget.	5 M-	4 M	3	2 R	1 R+
16.	I never resent being asked to return a favor.	1 R+	2 R	3	4 M	5 M-
21.	I sometimes feel resentful when I don't get my way.	5 M-	4 M	3	2 R	1 R+
26.	I have almost never felt the urge to tell someone off.	1 R+	2 R	3	4 M	5 M-
No.	Virtue Items	SD	D	?	A	SA
23.	I rebel when someone talks to me about doing what I should.	5V+	4 V	3	2 U	1 U-
15.	I am tired of those in charge trying to show me a better way.	5V+	4 V	3	2 U	1 U-
20.	I get angry when those in authority insist I do things their way.	5V+	4 V	3	2 U	1 U-
18.	I have trouble telling right from wrong.	5V+	4 V	3	2 U	1 U-
3.	I often refuse to do what I know is right.	5V+	4 V	3	2 U	1 U-
10.	I feel unwilling to help even when I know I should.	5V+	4 V	3	2 U	1 U-
5.	I frequently insist on my own way even if I sense I might be wrong.	5V+	4 V	3	2 U	1 U-
8.	I find it hard to really enjoy myself when doing daily chores.	5V+	4 V	3	2 U	1 U-
13.	I resist establishing values in my life so I can be free to be who I am.	5V+	4 V	3	2 U	1 U-
25.	I am afraid of what others might think if I do as I ought.	5V+	4 V	3	2 U	1 U-
4.	I do what I should, even if friends reject me for it.	1 U-	2 U	3	4 V	5 V+
17.	I am fully committed to do what I know I should.	1 U-	2 U	3	4 V	5 V+
22.	I openly defend what is right.	1 U-	2 U	3	4 V	5 V+
19.	I can easily distinguish between good, better, and best.	1 U-	2 U	3	4 V	5 V+
2.	I maintain my priorities so that I can do what is best.	1 U-	2 U	3	4 V	5 V+
12.	I consistently remain true to what is best.	1 U-	2 U	3	4 V	5 V+
14.	I gladly respond without hesitation when something is required of me.	1 U-	2 U	3	4 V	5 V+
9.	I am an example of wholehearted dedication to duty.	1 U-	2 U	3	4 V	5 V+
24.	I immediately confess and make it right whenever I do something wrong.	1 U-	2 U	3	4 V	5 V+
7.	I am fully committed to change whatever keeps me from doing what I should.	1 U-	2 U	3	4 V	5 V+

Step One: The first step is to *transfer the responses* circled on the questionnaire (**SD D ? A SA**) to the *LVAQ Scoring Form*. Begin with the box labeled **Misrepresentation Items** at the top of the Scoring Form like that shown above. The numbers in the **No.** column on the left side of the *Scoring Form* correspond to the item numbers on the *Questionnaire*.

Highlight or circle the *box* under the appropriate response column on the Scoring Form that matches the response circled by the student on the *Questionnaire*. For example, if "SD" was circled for item No. 1 on the Questionnaire, then find item No. 1 on the left side of the *Scoring Form* and highlight or circle the box under the column labeled "SD" containing "5M-" on that same line.

Once you transfer all 26 responses (both misrepresentation and virtue items) from the Questionnaire to the Scoring Form, you may set the Questionnaire aside. The rest of the work will be done on the Scoring Form itself.

	SD	D	?	A	SA
Norm Response Totals	3	7	3	9	4
Individual Response Totals	( )	( )	( )	( )	( )

Step Two: Beginning at the top of the *Scoring Form*, glance down the columns and count the number of each kind of response (SD D ? A SA) for all 26 items (including both misrepresentation and virtue items) and put the *totals* on the line that says *Individual Response Totals* like that shown above.

	Misrepresentation	Virtue
Uncertainty Count	( ) of 6	( ) of 20
Certainty Count	( ) of 6	( ) of 20
Raw Score	( ) of 30	( ) of 100
Norm Rank	( )	( )

Step Three: Go back to the top of the Scoring Form and count the number of *Misrepresentation Items* answered with a question mark (?) and enter the number in the *Uncertainty Count* box under the *Misrepresentation* column like that shown above. Do the same for the *Virtue Items.*

Next count the number of *Misrepresentation Items* which have an "M" or "M-" and enter the total in the *Certainty Count* box of the *Misrepresentation* column. Then count the *Virtue Items* which have a "V" or "V+" and write the total in the *Virtue* column of the *Certainty Count* box.

After doing so, add the numbers (1 2 3 4 5) in the boxes of all six misrepresentation items and place the total in the *Raw Score* box like that shown in the *Misrepresentation* column. Do the same for all 20 virtue items. A calculator helps ensure accuracy for this part.

Finally, find the *Ranking Descriptions* in the table, like the one shown below, that match the *Raw Scores,* and enter them in the *Norm Rank* boxes like those shown directly above.

Misrepresentation		Virtue	
Ranking Description	Raw Score	Ranking Description	Raw Score
Extremely Unlikely	6 to 10	Very Low	20 to 50
Very Unlikely	11 to 13	Low	51 to 55
Unlikely	14 to 16	Moderately Low	56 to 60
Possible	17 to 19	Average	61 to 70
Likely	20 to 22	Moderately High	71 to 75
Very Likely	23 to 25	High	76 to 80
Extremely Likely	26 to 30	Very High	81 to 100

Step Four: Return to the top of the page on the *Scoring Form* to the *Virtue Items* portion and transfer the *response indicators* (U- U ? V V+), one by one, to the empty boxes on the *Virtue Response Analysis* table like the one shown below.

Virtue Response Analysis

Item Number	23	15	20	18	3	10	5	8	13	25	4	17	22	19	2	12	14	9	24	7
Item Rank	1	2	3	4	5	6	7	8	9	10	11	12	13	14	15	16	17	18	19	20
Item Direction	-	-	-	-	-	-	-	-	-	-	+	+	+	+	+	+	+	+	+	+
Item Basis	D	B	D	B	D	B	D	B	D	B	D	B	D	B	D	B	D	B	D	B
Character																				
Conduct																				
Virtue Levels	Examining				Experimenting				Establishing				Evaluating				Embodying			

For example, item 23 is a *Conduct* item. You can detect this because the *Character* box is shaded in to prevent you from putting anything in it, and because the *Item Basis* for this item is a "D" for *Doing.* (Conduct is *Doing.* Character is *Being.*) So, in this case, you would put the appropriate indicator (U- U ? V V+) in the empty box below 23. And you can readily see that the next item, number 15, is a *Character* item, because the *Conduct* box is shaded.

Step Five: Last, count the number of virtuous *Character* responses from the *Virtue Response Analysis* table like the one shown above, and enter the total in the *Virtue Item Count* box like that found below. Do the same for the *Conduct* responses. Count only the responses that indicate virtue ("V" or "V+"). Do not include those responses indicated by "U-", "U", or "?".

Virtue Balance	Character (Inner Being)	Conduct (Outward Doing)
Virtue Item Count	( ) of 10	( ) of 10

The *Virtue Balance* portion of the Scoring Form (above) is for the purpose of comparing the internal and external (character and conduct) expressions of virtue. The two should correspond closely. It is insignificant if they vary by one, either higher or lower, from the other.

Resource E:　LVAQ Follow-Up Form

LVAQ Follow-Up _____

Student's Name: _____

Teacher's Name: _____

Class or Period:_____

Please briefly describe the student's attitude in general: _____

_____

_____

_____

_____

_____

Please briefly describe the student's behavior in class: _____

_____

_____

_____

_____

_____

Please briefly describe the student's academic performance: _____

_____

_____

_____

_____

_____

Resource F: Uncertain Response Frequency Distribution and LVAQ Items

Uncertain Response Frequency Distribution and LVAQ Items	
LVAQ Item	Uncertain Count
2	22
3	13
4	19
5	9
7	13
8	15
9	41
10	6
12	33
13	24
14	20
15	7
17	20
18	45
19	12
20	14
22	18
23	20
24	25
25	14

Resource G: How to Contact the Author

For materials or additional information, please contact

Michael C. Loehrer, EdD
Educational Diagnostics
3717 NW Country Road 4300
Frost, TX 76641
254/678-3393
Fax: 254/678-3786
E-mail: eddiag@gte.net
Homepage: http://home1.gte.net/eddiag/

For seminar bookings or speaking engagements, please contact

Ms. Tina Jacobson, Agent
The B&B Media Group
806 W. 7th Avenue
Corsicana, TX 75110
800/927-0517
Fax: 903/872-0518
E-mail: tbbmedia@mail.airmail.net

References

Barton, D. (1993, Summer). *The wallbuilder report.* Aledo, TX: WallBuilders.

Bennett, W. J. (1993). *The book of virtues.* New York: Simon & Schuster.

Bloom, A. (1987). *The closing of the American mind.* New York: Simon & Schuster.

Bloom, B. S. (1956). *Taxonomy of educational objectives: Handbook I, The cognitive domain.* New York: David McKay.

Crowne, D. P., & Marlowe, D. (1980). *The approval motive.* Westport, CT: Greenwood. (Original work published 1964)

Donlon, T. F. (1974). *Testing in the affective domain* (ERIC/TM Report No. 41; DHEW Report No. BBB10279). Washington, DC: National Institute of Education, Office of Dissemination and Resources. (ERIC Document Reproduction Service No. ED 103 493)

Gress, J. R., & Purpel, D. E. (1988). *Curriculum: An introduction to the field.* Berkeley, CA: McCutchan.

Hall, V. M. (1976). *The Christian history of the American Revolution.* San Francisco: Foundation for Christian Education.

Kilpatrick, W. (1992*). Why Johnny can't tell right from wrong.* New York: Simon & Schuster.

Krathwohl, D. R., Bloom, B. S., & Masia, B. B. (1964). *Taxonomy of educational objectives: Handbook II, The affective domain.* New York: David McKay.

Loehrer, M. C. (1991). Measurement of virtue in Christian education (Doctoral dissertation, Biola University, 1990). *Dissertation Abstracts International, 51,* 2334A.

McDowell, S. K. (1988). *America's providential history.* Charlottesville, VA: Providence.

McGuffey, W. H. (1982). *The eclectic second reader.* Milford, MI: Mott Media. (Original work published 1836)

Meilaender, G. (1984). *The theory and practice of virtue.* Notre Dame, IN: University of Notre Dame.

Microsoft Excel Version 3.0. (1991). Seattle, WA: Microsoft Corporation.

Mikulecky, L. J. (1976). The developing, field testing, and initial norming of a secondary/adult level reading attitude measure that is behaviorally oriented and based on Krathwohl's Taxonomy of the Affective Domain (Doctoral dissertation, University of Wisconsin-Madison, 1976). *Dissertation Abstracts International, 37,* 5767A.

Millard, C. (1991). *The rewriting of America's history.* Camp Hill, PA: Horizon House.

Mueller, D. J. (1986). *Measuring social attitudes.* New York: Teachers College Press.

Muirhead, J. H. (1969). *Rule and end in morals.* Freeport, NY: Books For Libraries.

Plato. (1901). *The meno of Plato* (E. Thompson, Ed.). London: Macmillan.

Plato. (1946). *The republic.* (B. Jowett, Trans.). Cleveland, OH: World.

Purcell, J. L. (1968). Developing an attitude scale using the taxonomy of educational objectives—affective domain. (Doctoral dissertation, Washington State University, 1968). *Dissertation Abstracts, 29,* 519A.

Rackham, H. (Trans.). (1945). *Aristotle: The Nicomachean ethics.* Cambridge, MA: Harvard University Press.

Rée, P. (1973). Determinism and the illusion of moral responsibility. In P. Edwards & A. Pap (Eds.), *A modern introduction to philosophy* (3rd ed., pp. 10-27). New York: Free Press.

Sproule, J. M. (1987). Whose ethics in the classroom? An historical survey. *Communication Education, 36,* 317-326.

Statview SE+Graphics. (1988). Calabasas, CA: Abacus Concepts.

Studdiford, W. B. (1967). Willing in androids. In J. N. Lapsley (Ed.), *The concept of willing* (pp. 116-176). Nashville, TN: Abingdon.

Summers, E. G. (1976). *A review of research and bibliography on published attitudinal instruments in reading.* Paper presented at the Annual Meeting of the International Reading Association, Anaheim, CA. (ERIC Document Reproduction Service No. ED 123 558)

Winn, D. K. (1993). Loehrer's concept of virtue as a force influencing participation in adult education (Doctoral dissertation, East Texas State University, 1973). *Dissertation Abstracts International, 54,* 782A.

CORWIN PRESS

The Corwin Press logo—a raven striding across an open book—represents the happy union of courage and learning. We are a professional-level publisher of books and journals for K–12 educators, and we are committed to creating and providing resources that embody these qualities. Corwin's motto is "Success for All Learners."